The Sociology of Loyalty

The Sociology of Loyalty

James Connor
School of Social Sciences, Australian National University, Canberra, Australia.

James Connor
School of Social Sciences
Australian National University, Canberra,
ACT, Australia
Canberra 0200

Library of Congress Control Number: 2007929502

ISBN-13: 978–0–387–71367–0   e-ISBN-13: 978–0–387–71368–7

Printed on acid-free paper.

© 2007 Springer Science+Business Media, LLC
All rights reserved. This work may not be translated or copied in whole or in part without the written permission of the publisher (Springer Science+Business Media, LLC, 233 Spring Street, New York, NY 10013, USA), except for brief excerpts in connection with reviews or scholarly analysis. Use in connection with any form of information storage and retrieval, electronic adaptation, computer software, or by similar or dissimilar methodology now known or hereafter developed is forbidden.
The use in this publication of trade names, trademarks, service marks, and similar terms, even if they are not identified as such, is not to be taken as an expression of opinion as to whether or not they are subject to proprietary rights.

9 8 7 6 5 4 3 2 1

springer.com

'Loyalty, which asserts the continuity of past and future, binding time into a whole, is the root of human strength; there is no good to be done without it.'

Ursula Le Guin, *The Dispossessed*

Preface and Acknowledgements

Loyalty is one of those concepts that infuses our cultural existence. So much of our foundational social mythology uses loyalty or the conflict that a clash of loyalty creates. The great writers relied on the feeling, with Shakespeare being particularly adept—consider his tragedies *without* a clash of loyalties to help so many characters to their denouements. Loyalty, perhaps regrettably, is not limited to the demise of so many literary characters—the death and destruction that has danced with loyalty is incalculable. The need for our loyalties to be defined against another inevitably leads to *my* loyalty being better than *yours*. It is the passion that accompanies loyalties that encapsulates how motivating the concept can be—loyalty has justified countless activities, feelings and thoughts. It is not surprising then that I have been fascinated by loyalty since first exploring the literature for my honours thesis in 2000.

It was therefore with some shock that I discovered so little academic engagement with the concept. The most in depth analysis was almost 100 years old (Royce 1908) and I could not help but think that perhaps after so long, and such social change, the concept needed to be revisited. My honours thesis illustrated how under-theorised the concept is, particularly in consumer capitalism, where the term has acquired even more sites of manifestation, such as frequent flyer 'loyalty' programs. I discovered that the marketing literature was heavy with the term loyalty, but lacked an appreciation of what I considered far more important—the *emotion* of loyalty. With my intellectual curiosity still unsatisfied, I embarked on a PhD at the Australian National University with the aim of placing loyalty into sociology.

Consequently, I was drawn to the emotions literature and theory because it appeared to be the only approach that could explain the passion of loyalty and the way it is invoked across such diverse social sites. Unfortunately, the specific literature on emotions had generally ignored loyalty or subsumed it within another, such as trust (e.g., Barbalet 1998). My PhD thesis sought to remedy this and this book is substantially based upon my thesis.

When embarking on such a journey there are always many helping hands and minds. Below are the people I feel the need to single out for their help and support. Suffice to say, thank-you to everyone who as helped me reach this point. My supervisory panel at the Australian National University; Alastair Greig for his intellectual rigour and beer at the pub and Valerie Braithwaite, for excellent feedback—I hope this book does justice to your advice. My colleagues for distracting, helping and encouraging in equal measure. Judy, Fiona and Paul all deserve special mention—thanks for the coffee, chats and friendship. Many people have made time to chat with the person doing strange things with loyalty—thank you for your collegiality. Particularly; Jack Barbalet, John Braithwaite, John Brewer, Carl Pletsch, Larry Saha, Stephen Mugford, Anni Dugdale and Lauren Langman. I hope that this book does our conversations justice. I must also acknowledge the anonymous journal, conference and book proposal reviewers—you have strengthened my argument and I am grateful for that. I also wish to acknowledge a grant from the Australian Society for Sport History (ASSH) as part of the Tom Brock bequest that they administer. This assisted with the research for parts of Chapter Six, specifically on the South Sydney Rabbitohs. Colleen, for editing the draft and accepting that the *actor* can have *their* emotions. Mum, whose love and support is always there. My Ladz, for grounding my existence and reminding me of my purpose; Sebastian for opening a new world, Jude for being a rascal and Zac for giggles.

And most importantly, Melissa. Without you I would never have embarked on this journey; your love, support and tolerance are remarkable. I have gained immensely from your intellectual brilliance. Lissa, your loyalty sustains me—thank-you. This book is dedicated to *you*.

Contents

1. **Introduction** 1

2. **Loyalty and Theories of Emotion** 9
   Introduction 9
   What is Loyalty? 10
   The Theorising of Emotion 16
   Biological Approaches to Emotions Theory 17
   Biocultural Approaches to Emotions Theory 18
   The Sociological Theories of Emotion 25
   The Existentialist Theory of Emotions 30
   The Implications of Loyalty as an Emotion 33
   Conclusion 34

3. **Elements of Loyalty** 35
   Introduction 35
   Notes on Methodology 36
   The Language of Loyalty 38
   Emotion(al) Discourse—Gender, Power and Control 41
   Seeing Loyalty 45
   Loyalty Layers: An Individual's Multiple, Competing Loyalties 47
   Identity and Loyalty 49
   Motivation to Action 51
   Is It Just a Behaviour? 53
   Conclusions 55

4. **Family Loyalty** 57
   Introduction 57
   Family Loyalty—a Primordial Relationship? 58
   Blood Is Thicker than Water 63
   Family-Like Loyalty 69
   Gang Loyalty – A 'Brotherhood' 70
   A Soldier's Loyalty 71
   Family the Quintessential Loyalty? 74

Contents

5. National Loyalty 77

    Introduction 77
    A Loyal Nation? 78
    Nation, Identity and Loyalty 79
    The War(s) Around Loyalties 82
    Conscripting Loyalty 85
    Dual Loyalties – The Immigrant's Conflict 89
    No, Where Do You *Really* Come From? 91
    McCarthyism—Rampant National Loyalty 97
    Conclusion 99

6. Sport and Loyalty 101

    Introduction 101
    Product, Spectacle and Marketing 102
    South Sydney Rabbitohs 105
    The Canterbury Bulldogs' Crises 111
    Conclusion 116

7. Cultural Loyalty 117

    Introduction 117
    Loyalty and Buffy the Vampire Slayer 117
    Buffyverse Loyalty 119
    Loyalty Is Socially Constructed 120
    Loyalty as Motivation 121
    Loyalty and Identity 122
    Loyalty Operates at a Number of Layers 123
    Loyalty Is Contested 124
    Television, Loyalty and the Buffyverse 126
    Mediated Loyalties—Conclusions 126

8. Conclusion 129

    Layered Loyalty 130
    Loyalty and Identity 132
    Loyalty and Action 133
    Definitions of Emotion 134

Epilogue 143

Bibliography 145

Episodes of BtVS 155

Index 157

Chapter One
Introduction

> A well-developed appreciation of emotions is absolutely essential for sociology because no action can occur in a society without emotional involvement.
>
> Jack Barbalet (2002:2)

Why we engage in what we do is a consuming passion of our existence. Motivations are searched for, discussed, lamented and sometimes even wished away. A range of labels, descriptors, markers, terms, signs and symbols are invoked to explicate the *why*. This is particularly the case with the cluster of emotion terms that are employed to explain our passions. Riven with anger, driven insane by jealousy, wracked with guilt, leaden with sorrow, twitching with anxiety, tormented by angst—these all speak to the way passion and action are linked or, in other words, how our emotions sign post the world. It is intriguing that we have such a range of emotional states, feelings and passions, that have, to a large extent, gone un-theorised. This is especially the case with specific, individual emotions and their role in social life.

While some of the emotions or passions have been the subject of academic inquiry and debate, such as shame (Braithwaite, 1989), love (Cancian, 1987) or trust (Misztal, 1996), one, in particular, has a curious absence: loyalty.

If, as Barbalet (2002:2) posits, emotions are central to social action, then the emotions offer a window into the why and how of social interaction. Thus, they are not only a useful means of exploring the social world, but an essential avenue of research. Emotions are also part of the explanation that is offered by social actors for their own behaviours, thoughts and feelings. The use of loyalty is one of those explanations that actors offer, and it encompasses a wide variety of situations, relationships and events. Explicating loyalty builds upon the work already done in establishing the emotions as a *prima facie* site of social research and investigation. Loyalty is a phenomenon that crosses social time and space and it occurs (or is identified by actors) within micro and macro sociological interactions. This makes it both rewarding and difficult to study. The very diversity of loyalty interactions is demonstrated by the material I use in exploring the emotion, to which the following examples are but a snapshot.

An avid sports fan, distraught that his team has lost its battle to keep playing in the national competition, moves his family to another State. When the family's team earns a reprieve at the eleventh hour they return, $20 000 worse off for the moves. Yet they are joyous—the object of their loyalties survives.

A six year old girl, discussing her two families, confides to a therapist that she feels the need to be 'a little mean' about the other family when she switches houses. The therapist couches her actions and feelings as conflicted loyalties, and sees the girl as torn between the social requirement of an unwavering commitment to one family and the girl's reality of two families.

The brother of the infamous Unabomber, David Kaczynski, was torn between loyalty to his brother and a duty to do what was considered morally right. Another family ostracises one of their own because she opposes the death penalty for the murderer of her brother; the family cannot understand her disloyalty. A sister is defended in court for obstructing police out of misguided family loyalty.

A soldier laments that loyalty to his unit is all that you have—you have to support your 'band of brothers' to survive. Another soldier bemoans that his loyalty to country is questioned, not because he was born in another place, but because his parents were. A migrant asks why he gets questioned on where he came from when he has been 'here' 40 years and even fought for the country—yet his loyalty is queried.

Average Americans are hauled before a congressional committee to have their loyalty tested, a Presidential proclamation is made and May 1st is christened 'Loyalty Day' in the USA. The campaigns for and against conscription of Australians for the First World War were fought through the discourse of loyalties; to mates, family, church, nation, and empire.

These vignettes illustrate the varied understanding and use of loyalty in Western, English-speaking countries. As they all show, the idea of loyalty is applied to a myriad of relationships, from the intensely personal and familial, to the nation-state. It is invoked for family, friends, sports, politics, religion, race, ethnicity, class, locality, interest groups and nations to offer a list spanning a wide variety of social interactions. Why is loyalty invoked across such a diverse set of relationships? Is it merely a heuristic that we have been too lazy to delineate across different social organisations? Or does it capture an aspect that is common to all these relationships—the invisible pull of a particular connection?

Loyalty is invoked consistently and repeatedly in popular discourse, from newspapers to television drama to parliamentary speeches. The concept is employed to denote such a range of diverse connections and relationships that it appears to be almost too broad a term to have a definitive meaning. Perhaps this encompassing aspect of the concept is why there is such a paucity of analysis and discussion of loyalty.

The work that has been written specifically on this concept of loyalty is often very narrow and focuses on particular manifestations of loyalty. Hirschman's (1970) book, *Exit, Voice and Loyalty,* deals with loyalty in the sphere of economic exchange. Several works deal with the negative side of loyalty, or, more specifically, disloyalty and treason; such as Shain's (1989) *The Frontier of*

Loyalty: Political Exiles in the Age of the Nation-State and Grodzin's (1956) *The Loyal and the Disloyal: Social Boundaries of Patriotism and Treason*.

The individual and loyalty has been dealt with in a number of older works. Bloch's (1934) *The Concept of our Changing Loyalties* and Royce's (1908) *The Philosophy of Loyalty* offer theoretical explanations of loyalty from the perspective of the individual. Wolff's (1968) *The Poverty of Liberalism* offers an explanation of loyalty along two axes, the natural and the contractual. Fletcher (1993) offers a thesis that loyalty is a membership—not a relationship—based entity in his *Loyalty: An Essay on the Morality of Relationships*. Some work has also been done on how the concept of loyalty can be abused by those in power. In *Loyalty in a Democratic State* (1952), edited by Wahlk, the contributors discuss how the US government used loyalty oaths to weed out communist and left-leaning academics and public servants as part of the McCarthy era.

While concerned with aspects of loyalty, these works fail to integrate the multitude of differing social sites that have loyalty attached to their interactions. And, to preface the first half of Chapter Two where I deal with what others have argued loyalty is, their approaches do not question the assumptions that suffuse the use of loyalty in popular discourse and, tellingly, academic discourse. My research into understandings of loyalty has been, at times, consumed with fruitless articles and books that take the concept at face value, and all of the underlying responsibilities, reciprocities and relationships as a given. This, in itself, is illuminating as it indicates that loyalty needs deeper analysis. Thus, the concept itself is worthy of a sociological unpacking and, to borrow from C. Wright Mills (1959), a questioning of the common sense understanding and use of the term.

Thus, the central question that has driven my research is: *what is loyalty?*

In my explorations of the concept I was drawn to the sociology of emotions literature. Not because it had already engaged the concept, it had not, but it did offer the potential of a way to unpack loyalty. The most encouraging aspect of the literature is that I felt it could provide me with a theoretical framework with which to explore loyalty. There have even been calls within the literature to move away from grand theories of emotion and to instead focus on specific emotions. Barbalet (1998: 2, see also Scheff, 2003 below), for example, has argued that what 'is needed in sociology is not another general theory of emotion but a deeper understanding of particular emotions'. My work here is an attempt to answer that call.

The journey begins with a defence of my view of loyalty against a particular, and oft repeated, question. It is a comment that I have encountered repeatedly at conferences, in discussions with academics, lay people and from journal reviewers. It follows this general pattern: but loyalty is not even an emotion?! To which I respond: then what is it? A few do offer an alternate explanation; that it is merely a contractual relationship, or just a behaviour, or merely a cognition, or that it is an aspect of other emotions like trust or love but that it, in itself, is not an emotion. Another, perhaps more challenging, contention is that loyalty is merely a signifier of specific inter-relationship feelings, obligations and reciprocities, a cognitive shortcut or heuristic that allows the actor to understand a relationship quickly. The increasing use of the term loyalty in marketing contexts further obscures its meaning, as there is an explicit contractual basis to loyalty in this sphere.

Thus leads to the key problem of this book: is loyalty an emotion? The initial response is: but it depends upon what you think loyalty is, and then, what an emotion is. The way I approach this issue is to take a range of definitions of loyalty from others. This serves to both review what has been argued in relation to a definition of loyalty as well as helping to set up the argument for loyalty as an emotion. This evaluation of loyalty in the first part of Chapter Two develops a typology of loyalty that points to it being an emotion. Or, at the very least, the synthesis of the views indicates that loyalty shares many of the same aspects of other conventionally accepted emotions like love, shame and trust.

This tentative assertion, that loyalty is an emotion, is well supported by my review of others' opinions. The idea that it may be an emotion inevitably leads to the issue of just what is an emotion? The second section of Chapter Two therefore deals with a range of theories of emotion, specifically biological, bio-cultural, sociological and existentialist models. These theories can be classed as various epistemological approaches to the generic question of what emotions are and from where they originate.

This review of the theories, using the provisional definition of loyalty that I have already discussed, serves to limit the scope of this book. By discussing the approach of each and testing it against my provisional loyalty definition I can establish which perspective best fits loyalty. This is critical for my argument as the perspective(s) chosen inform the methodologies employed and the epistemological approach that I subsequently take. I conclude Chapter Two with the contention that a sociological view of the emotions appears to be the best theoretical perspective to take in explaining loyalty. In short, this perspective argues that emotions are constructed through and by an actor's interactions within the social world. This is tempered with an acknowledgment of the existentialist position on emotions, specifically that emotions are 'magical' world-transforming phenomena of belief. Or, in slightly more grounded terms, emotions are about the beliefs and perceptions of the actor.

By this point, I have defended the sociological view of emotions, reviewed the concept of loyalty and developed a provisional definition of the concept and argued for its (interim) inclusion in the typology of an emotion. I then turn to an issue that is key to the nature of the evidence that I use. This is the question of how to find and identify instances of loyalty. When can a researcher and an actor know that loyalty is involved in a social interaction? I begin to address these questions in Chapter Three. In an attempt to address this difficulty in 'knowing', I argue that the behaviours, actions and thoughts that are described as loyalty must fit a certain pattern. This pattern, to summarise, is that the term loyalty must occur and that the occurrence then be tested against the aspects of loyalty that I construct in the remainder of the chapter. In this lengthy discussion I also offer a defence of the sources of evidence I use to explore loyalty. These sources are popular culture resources that employ the terminology of loyalty. By popular culture I mean the broadest interpretation of the term and I use historical sources, newspapers, television programs, radio interviews, web sites, web logs (blogs) and books. I argue that using these sources provides the researcher an unparalleled insight into an emotion that occurs across a very diverse range of social sites. Secondly, these sources are the only reliable means of exploring the manifestations of loyalty historically, as secondary sources are the only means of accessing how the actor felt. Lastly, I am arguing for a holistic understanding of loyalty. Had I attempted to interview, question or focus group a range of subjects I would be left with a very narrow exploration of loyalty that was not generalisable, either across society or historically. Thus, despite the potential flaws within the material I use, I contend that it is the best means to explore the questions around loyalty that flow from the premise that it is an emotion.

Devoting two entire chapters to theoretical explorations of emotions and loyalty may seem excessive. It is not; Chapters Two and Three are critical in laying the methodological groundwork for the remainder of the book. Secondly, I extend the current literature on emotions by placing loyalty within the field and I show that a sociological approach is the most valuable when dealing with a phenomenon like loyalty. This definitional debate has been acknowledged as critically important in furthering the sociology of emotions field. For example, Scheff (2003:1) argues that

advances in our understanding of emotions will continue to be minimal until we have developed unambiguous definitions for particular emotions, rather than rely on current usage. The vernacular language for emotions in most languages is confused and confusing, especially English.

This book will, I hope, answer this call of Scheff's and generate a definition of loyalty informed by a sociology of emotions.

The next issue considered is: what function does loyalty perform? What are the effects of loyalty in relationships and how do we perceive the emotion? The second section of Chapter Three establishes the particular and unusual aspects of loyalty that I will explore with a view to explaining the concept. The first is that loyalty is a layered emotion, by which I mean that it operates at a number of levels within social interaction, from loyalty to family, to friends, church and nation. This peculiar aspect of the emotion makes it quite different from other emotions which have a smaller social footprint. The second is that loyalty is key in furnishing identity, primarily because it denotes membership and belonging. The third is that loyalty motivates action, or to put it into terms in which it can be researched, it is a justification for action, behaviour and cognition. These claims help build an overall picture of what loyalty is and how it functions. I hope that this in depth exploration of loyalty, using an emotions framework informed by popular culture, will further the sociological literature on emotions.

My establishing chapters are completed by addressing one final issue: is loyalty merely a behaviour? I argue that it is not, particularly in light of the preceding discussions of emotion and loyalty which do indicate the strong likelihood that loyalty can indeed be an emotion.

There is one last caveat that must be added: the idea that loyalty 'does' things is an ontological illusion. We can see the effects of loyalty relationships. We can hear, read and see loyalty invoked as a justification both before and after an event. However, the emotion of loyalty does not 'do' anything. Loyalty denotes relationships, reciprocities and expectations that link the actor within a myriad of social connections. Thus, when I write of loyalty 'doing' something I mean it in the context of a complex social interaction that acknowledges the often combined and mixed forms of emotion and existence.

In the following chapters I begin the explorations of specific loyalties with the case study chapters (Four through Seven). A note of caution is warranted in regards to the case studies. I am using the examples to explore loyalty, not the underlying social force that those loyalties occur within. Consequently, I will not be exhaustively reviewing or discussing the specific literatures that apply in each of the case study chapters. I will make use of some of the theory of the area in each chapter, but only as a grounding. The purpose of the case studies is to explore *loyalty*. My evidence relies heavily on Australian source material, with sufficient British, Canadian and American examples to justify my claim that loyalty is similar across English, Judeo-Christian heritage countries.

The first case study is the family in Chapter Four. I start by questioning the common sense notion that family is the prime or original site of loyalty. This leads to the examples and illustrations of family loyalty where I look for evidence of the influence of loyalty and its effects. In one sense family is a strictly defined relationship of blood or marriage (and its equivalents) connection between actors. However, familial nomenclature has also crept into other relationships, including in the military, religion and crime gangs. I explore these relationships for both loyalty and family as a way of exploring if familial loyalty does perform as the prototypical or base form of loyalty. I conclude Chapter Four by discussing the implications of the finding that family loyalty is the quintessential loyalty social site.

Instead of building a picture of loyalty that starts with the micro-loyalties of the family and moves up the scale of social interactions, in the following chapter, Chapter Five, I move to national loyalties. This serves as a useful counter-point to familial loyalty as it is at the opposite end of social relationships for scale, yet has remarkable similarities to familial loyalty. The first section looks at the conscription debates in Australia during the World Wars and Vietnam conflict and how loyalty was invoked by both sides of the debate. I then turn to the treatment of migrants in Australia, again to explore how loyalty in this setting is constructed to sometimes exclude the migrant. I then look at how loyalty was used during the McCarthy period in the USA. This allows me to explore how, and for what purpose, national loyalties operate.

The cases considered thus far have, at their core, the assumption that loyalty is an automatic connection as a result of birth, be that to family or by virtue of birth location, nation. Chapter Six (Sporting loyalty) looks at a site of loyalty that involves a lot more choice (although the true extent of that will be assessed). I begin with a short review of the nature of sport in a globalised, professionalised setting as this is key in understanding the events around the first case study.

This case focuses on the South Sydney Rabbitohs, a Rugby League club that was excluded from the Australasian competition in 1999. The responses of the fans and the way they express loyalties are very illuminating for this book as it points strongly to the identity forming and motivation for action aspects of loyalty. The second study focuses on another Rugby League club, the Canterbury Bulldogs. This club faced a series of crises from 2002 to 2004—the first was so serious that Canterbury lost all of its competition points and moved from being at the top of the ladder, and certain finals contenders, to bottom. The intriguing factor at play in these crises is that the Club itself has to take most of the responsibility for the problems. This sets up a dilemma for fans: on the one hand they express their loyalty to Canterbury, yet on the other it is the Club itself that is causing the problems. This furthers my analysis of loyalty by showing how loyalty requires an 'other'. I also demonstrate that those within a loyalty relationship will often look to blame those outside the relationship for adverse occurrences. While the examples I draw on are specific to Australia, very similar events have occurred across countries and codes—I leave it to the reader to consider how my theoretical exploration applies to sport that they are familiar with.

To round out my exploration of loyalty I turn to cultural representations of the emotion in Chapter Seven (Cultural loyalty). This case study is an exploration of how loyalty is played out in a long running, critically acclaimed and academically studied television drama, *Buffy the Vampire Slayer*. This serves to test if this highly popular medium reflects a view of loyalty that accords with the case studies already presented. The use of a popular culture case study will help to demonstrate how principles of loyalty are transmitted in cultural discourse. The case study will show that the conclusions I have come to regarding loyalty at specific layers (nation, family) is replicated in dramatic representations.

In the concluding chapter, I explicitly test the concept of loyalty, that I have built through the explorations in this book against a range of definitions of emotion. This will test if loyalty can be considered an emotion—but I will leave the proof to that chapter.

Astute readers will note the absence of an in depth discussion of employment based loyalty and marketing loyalty. I have consciously decided to exclude these two layers of loyalty as the influence of financial rewards tends to obscure the emotion that can occur. Further, the literature of both fields that purports to deal with loyalty very rarely does. The tendency is to simplistically define loyalty as merely repeat purchase (the marketing literature) or employment longevity (the human resources literature). This explicitly contractual, return based loyalty makes dis-entangling the emotion from the contract exceedingly difficult. I have no doubt that in some instances customers and employees experience the emotion of loyalty as I describe it in the following work. However, I am also convinced that often the term loyalty is used in these instances as a bastardised short-hand for the passion that I seek to explore. Lastly, my argument does not need to incorporate these layers as the range of loyalties I investigate covers a wealth of human interaction. I will leave the application of my theoretical position to employment and marketed loyalty to the next book.

In short, I make a number of arguments within this work. Firstly, I am positing that loyalty is indeed an emotion, and can be classed with other emotions such as shame, trust, pride and love. This, in itself, is an addition to the scholarship on loyalty and fulfils the call that several leading scholars of emotion have made in regards to definitional arguments around emotions. I then attempt to apply a range of emotion theories to a provisional definition of loyalty to test if any of these theories are applicable to an exploration of loyalty. My assertion that a sociological viewpoint is the best model to apply to loyalty is an extension of the current emotions theories and, as I show, an indication that this perspective is a better model with which to explore emotions. Not content with establishing that loyalty is an emotion that can be explained within the sociological fold, I posit that loyalty across the layers of its expression exhibits certain common, fundamental attributes and performs certain tasks within social relationships. These include regulating social intercourse, defining roles, informing identity and giving reason for action. I then take these hypotheses regarding loyalty and apply them to a range of case studies. These cases all feature loyalty as a key emotional component, yet range from the family, to sports, organisations and nation states.

The methodological approach to the case studies is textual analysis of popular culture sources where loyalty occurs. This particular approach to emotions is also different from many other studies in that I do not undertake any focus group, observation or questionnaire work. In chapter three I offer a strident defence of my sources and they way I use them, which adds to the current methodological literature on sociologically-inspired investigations into emotion. This approach gives a unique insight into loyalty because I can investigate it in multiple social spaces and across history. I can then make the claim that the social relationships, reciprocities and connections that are labelled loyalty are indeed an emotion and that when loyalty is invoked, it refers to a specific social interaction that has, at its core, a commonality across social spaces and serves a set of specific purposes.

To establish the validity of the claims I have just made it is necessary to start investigating what others have claimed for loyalty. That is where Chapter Two begins.

Chapter Two
Loyalty and Theories of Emotion

If vitality gives a man's perspectives color, if community bonds give them breadth, if awareness of the land makes them realistic, a deep sense of loyalty gives them personal meaning and integrity.

Harry Huntt Ransom

Introduction

Combining loyalty and emotion appears at first glance a given. Loyalty, as I will explore, is often tied with emotional, passionate and feeling events in an actor's existence. The common sense understanding of the concept is that it has a role in emotional life. This has not been reflected in the academic work devoted either to the concept or to the more general field of emotions theory. I will be challenging both sets of literature, by arguing that loyalty is an emotion and operates like all other emotions. In establishing this point, this and the following chapter will discuss loyalty, emotion and social theory.

This chapter comprises two sections, the first dealing with various definitions of loyalty and the second discusses a range of theories of emotion. This builds towards the next chapter that deals with the implications that arise from the proposition that loyalty is an emotion. The first section, 'What is loyalty?' is concerned with reviewing and critiquing a range of definitions of loyalty that have been offered over time. This definitional debate allows me to sketch a broad picture of loyalty which I will use to discuss emotions theory. I then step back from the minutiae of loyalty and canvass a range of theories of emotion, ranging across biological, bio-cultural, sociological and existentialist. The preceding discussion of loyalty then allows me to postulate how loyalty might fit within each perspective.

This logic is primarily based upon the principle that loyalty is sometimes considered an emotion. I will tour a range of explanations of what loyalty is first as this helps to create a definition of loyalty. This definition, while provisional, will allow me to question the theories and definitions of emotion as they may apply to the concept of loyalty. The second purpose of dealing with other theorists' definitions of loyalty is that it serves as a review of how loyalty has been conceived of in the past, and consequently points to how I can build upon the approaches offered.

This exploration of loyalty provides two significant outcomes: the first is a definition, and the second is the proposition that loyalty can be considered an emotion. I need to establish the plausibility of loyalty as an emotion before moving into the discussion of emotions theory—otherwise I do not have a logical basis with which to begin the discussion. Or, in other words, why talk about emotion before I have even established the *possibility* of loyalty being an emotion? This discussion is necessary because there is no agreed view of what loyalty is. Once I have established this possibility I examine generic theories of emotion. These theories can be classed as various epistemological approaches to the question of what emotions are and where they originate from.

My discussion of the generic theories (biological, biocultural, sociological and existentialist) is undertaken with a view to establishing which is most likely to provide the theoretical perspective and methodology best suited to understanding loyalty. Specifically, which theory or theories provides a means to contextualise, explore, explain and argue for loyalty as a social force. Establishing my theoretical approach first then allows me to test the idea of loyalty as an emotion against the definitions of emotion within the general theories of emotions—something that would be a Herculean task if I had not already discounted some epistemological approaches. In effect, I will be dismissing as many of the competing means of explanation early in this book so that I can move into the sociological exploration of loyalty. To preface the following chapter further, I then explore the problems of emotion research and consider the implications of the proposition that loyalty is indeed an emotion. To get to that point however, I need to first investigate the various explanations of what *loyalty* is.

What is Loyalty?

Harry Huntt Ransom echoes many writers, philosophers and thinkers when he describes loyalty as providing 'a deep sense of personal meaning and integrity'. The real question that must be asked, however, is: what is this thing called loyalty? Is it a behaviour, an emotion, a cognition, a contractual arrangement or a metaphor for interconnectedness? Guido-DiBrito (1995: 223) acknowledges the difficulties of defining loyalty by pointing out that '[a]lthough scholars and lay persons alike attach a highly charged, unbending emotion to loyalty, a consistent definition has not evolved. It appears to mean different things to different people'. Guido-DiBrito identifies two key themes within the discourses of loyalty: the highly charged nature of loyalty and that it means different things. These issues within the definition run through many of the following discussions and point to why it is so difficult to agree on a definition of loyalty.

One of the reasons that loyalty may vary from person to person is that the concept has changed over time. These shifts in emotion and emotional expression are not limited to loyalty. For example, Stearns and Stearns (1986) argue that anger has undergone a similar transformation as a response to the needs of capitalism. Elias in *The Civilizing Process* (1994) makes a similar case for the importance of manners and how they have changed with the rise of the modern state. Stearns and Stearns (1985) have also argued that studying emotions and expression across time-frames offer an important contribution to understanding both history and the present. They argue that 'historians can now point to major emotional shifts over time . . . henceforth, emotional changes must be considered, along with other shifts in mentality and behaviour' (Stearns & Stearns, 1985: 820). It is this viewpoint that pushes me to not only look at current loyalty relationships but also to identify any historical shifts in the narrative of loyalty. This will illuminate not only the history of loyalty but also the unique attributes of current conceptions of loyalty.

Newton makes a similar call to study history in understanding emotions, particularly from the social constructivist perspective (I discuss this perspective later in the chapter). He argues (1998: 60) that when

one acknowledges that emotion is socially constructed one is implicitly drawing attention to the historical, based on the simple argument that the social and cultural are historically formed . . . How can we aim to understand contemporary issues in emotion without exploring the historical context in which they have evolved?

This provides the rationale for this book to range widely across loyalty in both the historical and situational senses. Thus, my review of loyalty is an historical review, explicating the origins of the term as well as the current understandings. This exploration of how a range of theorists, thinkers and commentators have conceived of loyalty is designed to answer whether loyalty can be envisaged as a class of social and personal feelings and actions that constitutes an emotion.

We know 'loyalty' has been discussed in Western civilisation since the time written records were kept. If the word itself was not used, then the translators inferred it. Aristotle discusses how those who aspire to governing positions must have loyalty to the established constitution (Aristotle, Politics V: IX). The Bible speaks of loyalty throughout, from family loyalty (RU 3:10) to friendship loyalty (2 Samuel 16:17) and religious loyalty (Jos. 24:23). The concept of loyalty was also used in what is now Mexico by the Olmecs, in 650 BC. This very early writing was used to indicate pledges of loyalty to a King (Hecht, 2002: 21). This indicates the cross-cultural universality of loyalty commitments as well as the temporal universality of the concept. Loyalty was articulated in the Middle Ages; for example, it is mentioned in *Beowulf* and in *Sir Gawain and the Green Knight*. The rise of the nation state witnessed a further extension of the use of the term loyalty. The conscription debate in Australia during the First World War illustrates the importance of loyalty and the nation state and I explore these events in Chapter Six. Interestingly, this debate was the first place a mass marketing 'loyalty' campaign was carried out in Australia and loyalty was used both for and against conscription (Withers, 1972: 4–9).

The word loyalty stems from the Latin *lex* and the French *loi* (Byron, 1972: 25), root words for 'law'. This suggests that loyalty, like law, is dichotomous—one can only be lawful or unlawful—there is no median position. Similarly, many argue that the actor can only be loyal or disloyal—one is either a patriot or a traitor, one can never be partly loyal (Fletcher, 1993: 62). The grey area of 'partly' loyal is one of the focuses of this book and will be discussed in greater detail later. Suffice to say that for now, loyalty, while often conceived of from a dichotomous either/or mentality is certainly not unambiguous, as the case studies will reveal. There appear to be differing levels and applications of loyalty which point to its negotiated and interpreted expression in society. The existence of conflict over loyalty points to its ambiguous nature.

The first known use of 'loyal' in written history is from the Fifteenth Century, and refers to the noble 'labouring to sustain loyalty', presumably to the sovereign (Oxford English Dictionary, 1933). While this is the first use of the actual term in English, 'loyalty' clearly existed before this point in various forms and with different names. As the examples of the Bible and Aristotle indicate, it has a long history as a concept. The specific word that we now use arose at a particular time to denote a specific relationship. Loyalty developed from the need to distinguish those committed to a cause from those who were not. It came from feudal power-relations between nobles, defining who was committed to whom and denoted where loyalties lay in intricate power structures (Carpenter, 2000). The term later expanded to the family, church and other organisations, representing an individual's commitment.

Loyalty has been identified as a key component of the social relationship known as 'renaissance patronage', indicating a continuation of the social structure present in feudal systems. Cooper (1996: 24) argues that:

systems of patronage functioned *informally* within the political system as networks based on kinship ties, family allegiances, and regional. The relationship between patron and client was predicated on the distribution of privileges and position in exchange for loyalty and service. (emphasis in original)

This invisible connection tied actors together and served to distribute power and favour. This form of political relationship became less important as the increasingly bureaucratised nation states gained power and the ability to distribute wealth and support in a 'fair' manner.

With the heightened political importance of the centralised nation states and national governments in Europe during the Eighteenth Century, a new focus for loyalty was created (Anderson, 1991: 11). With the newly arising centralised forms of government, nationalism and patriotism grew. This change in governance represented a major shift in context for loyalty and the creation of a new layer of loyalty. Now the nation state and sovereign government could be an object of loyalty for the individual. No longer was the actor bound solely to their master or lord (Shain, 1989: 3). The power of the lords was being broken by the strong centralised monarchies and emerging governments. This in turn changed the feudal concept of loyalty; the liege was no longer an object of loyalty (Silver, 1985, 53–55). Mass loyalties began to arise as a result of continuing revolutions within society, especially the industrial revolution with its increasing division of labour, advances in communication, mass production and the creation of mass armies (Grodzins, 1956: 10–11).

The nation-state is a central component of the change in loyalty. Loyalty to one's country is a pervasive ideal in modern society (Anderson, 1991: 7). The nation helps shape identity; it controls the structures and institutions that raise, educate and sustain individuals within society. As Grodzins (1956: 20) argues: '[t]he whole social structure tends to promote the relationship, binding human satisfaction to national welfare'. Loyalty to one's nation can inspire patriotism and self sacrifice for the greater good of that nation (Anderson, 1991: 144). I will explore this proposition in relation to the idea of family loyalty being the quintessential type in Chapters Four and Five. However, what the shift in usage of the term loyalty over time illustrates is that loyalty is a socially negotiated, contested, contingent and re-enforced emotion.

A psychologically inspired definition of loyalty is offered by Boszormenyi-Nagy and Spark (1984: xix) who argue that:

> loyalty has turned out to be one of the key concepts which refers to both systematic (social) and individual (psychological) levels of understanding. Loyalty is composed of the social unit which depends on and expects loyalty from its members and of the thinking, feelings and motivations of each member as a person.

From this perspective, loyalty refers to an individual's feelings and motivations wrapped up in the web of social interaction. This definition can be expanded upon by the inclusion of an acknowledgement that loyalty operates within a web of power structures, as the previous two historical definitions pointed to. Further, the combining of cognition (thinking) with emotion (feelings) can confuse the issues, particularly when motivation for action is included. This confusion hints at the continued dichotomy within western thought between reason and emotion, or logic and feeling. A further value in this definition is that it points to loyalty existing as a concept that applies to individuals and to social structures. I will explore the interaction of the social and actor at length in the case studies.

Starting from a political science perspective, Shklar (1993) explores loyalty and its connection to obligation. Shklar (1993: 182) laments that the two discourses of loyalty and obligation are often interwoven, yet these two 'have had little to do with one another'. This mixing of terminology confuses the effects each has on social relationships, and as Shklar (1993: 183) points out we need to 'make clear the distinctions between obligation, commitment, loyalty, allegiance, and fidelity'. Shklar's (1993: 184) complex and nuanced definition of loyalty is worth quoting at length:

> What distinguishes loyalty is that it is deeply affective and not primarily rational. For the sake of clarity we should take loyalty to be an attachment to a social group. Membership may or may not be chosen. Belonging to an ascriptive group to which one has been brought up in, and taught to feel loyal to, since one's earliest infancy is scarcely a matter of choice. And when it comes to race, ethnicity, caste, and class, choice is not obvious. The emotional character of loyalty also sets it apart from obligation. If obligation is rule driven, loyalty is motivated by the entire personality of an agent . . . When it is a result of choice, loyalty

commitment that is affective in character and generated by a great deal more of our personality than calculation or moral reasoning. It is all of one that tends to be loyal.

There are several propositions that come out of this definition of loyalty that are worth discussing at this point. The first point that Shklar makes is that loyalty is an emotion and not a cognition, and thus she confirms the view that loyalty is indeed an emotion. This consequently lends weight to the use of emotions theory as the explanatory tool to discuss the phenomenon of loyalty. Shklar also argues that loyalty is part of an attachment to a social group. This raises a number of avenues of exploration in the later case studies, such as the question of whether loyalty can manifest itself outside a social relationship. Or, to preface the following chapters, is it an emotion of the social world and hence a social construction (as opposed to biologically based)? Choice of the actor is another issue raised by Shklar, and something that I deal with in national and family loyalty, two realms where potentially the actor is not given a choice about loyalty but has it ascribed at birth. To phrase it as a question: does the actor have choice over ascribed loyalties and how does this choice, or lack thereof, affect the actor? The last point that Shklar makes is perhaps the most challenging and intriguing: the idea that loyalty is a whole-person commitment. If there are instances of loyalty that require the commitment of the entire actor to a cause to the exclusion of all others, then her proposition will stand.

An important consideration with loyalty is that an explicit overt agreement of a connection is not necessarily needed. In the case of loyalty to a country, the citizen does not need to ever profess their loyalty—it is an assumed cultural artifact of their existence within a country. Loyalty, according to Wolff (1968: 60–61), differs in its origin on two axes, that of contractual loyalty and that of natural loyalty. Natural loyalty arises out of human relationships, such as the parent-child bond or friendship ties. Contractual loyalty originates from an explicit act of commitment, a pledge of fealty or membership ceremony. I will argue that a loyalty that does not need a pledge, such as nationalistic loyalties of those born within a country (as opposed to immigrants and naturalisation ceremonies which, by being called 'naturalisation ceremonies' betray the innate, normal and accepted status of loyalty to one's country) should be considered natural in Wolff's typology as well. As Oatley and Johnson-Laird (1987: 46) point out: 'mutual relations are established without explicit promises or acknowledgments. They arise implicitly by precedent and custom, in families, friendships, in larger communities, and even in nations'. The question this view raises is; can there be a loyalty relationship without the actor's acknowledgement? Further, how and when does this loyalty connection motivate the actor? The answers to these questions will help explain the origins of loyalty for the actor.

The primary site of loyalty is also a matter of contention in the literature. Boszormenyi-Nagy and Spark (1984) argue for the family as the primary or natural loyalty, an idea I critique at length in Chapter Five. Shklar (1993: 186) takes an alternative view and argues that 'the age of ideology has left us with only one survivor able to make claims upon primary loyalties: nationalism. It is all the more powerful because it has no serious rivals'. This is a strong claim worth serious investigation in my analysis of national loyalty. Shklar is arguing that national loyalty dominates the discourse of loyalty as it is a prime site of modern conflict. In discussing political parties, Shklar (1993: 186) argues that these groups 'are the sites of most political action [and] they are also the loci of conflict, and part of their language of combat is about loyalty'. If this is the case then the sociological implications of having the family and or the nation as a prime loyalty are profound—given that conflict is central. Further, to presage my later discussion, what purpose does having national and family loyalty as such strong loyalties serve for society?

Another discourse surrounding loyalty is the argument that human connections are being 'lost' in modern society. Numerous contemporary commentators decry this loss and loyalty is supposedly one of those human connections that is vanishing. Sennett (1997: 171) argues that the current workplace cannot foster a sense of loyalty because the new political economy cannot accommodate it as workers can no longer rely on a job for life. Clark, conversely, believes this loss (1997: 139–140) results from an inability to ascribe to blind loyalties, such as in the workplace. Rosenspan (1998: 24) claims that 'loyalty itself is becoming a rare commodity in virtually every human situation'. The issue of 'decline' and change in loyalty is one of the aspects of this book, describing from a sociological base the reasons why and how our loyalties have changed over time. The evidence does not point to a 'decline' at all but a shift in understanding and use, akin to the change in 'loyalty' that has occurred with modernity.

What this theoretical discussion has shown is that in many cases loyalty is considered an emotion. However, as C. Wright Mills (1959) reminds us, this is not really questioning taken for granted assumptions, nor particularly enlightening. A sociological account requires the explanation of the individual experience in light of the social and historical forces at play. If loyalty is an emotion, one is immediately inclined to ask what is an emotion? What are the current theories regarding emotion? Do any of them fit with what loyalty seems to be? Which of these theories, or combination of theories, could provide an adequate theoretical grounding with which to explore the various dimensions of loyalty? Or, in other words, what theories generate methodologies and research questions applicable in exploring and ultimately elucidating loyalty? The choice of theoretical school will dictate the definition of emotion that I use.

As a consequence, I will now turn to an exploration of the various theories of emotion to consider which, if any, seem to be applicable in understanding loyalty. I ask for the indulgence of the reader on two points. The first is that the proposition that loyalty is an emotion be accepted at face value for the time being, but with a promise to return to this issue in the conclusion. And second, that a certain amount of latitude be granted in my descriptions of loyalty and its possible 'fit' with certain theories until I begin the exploration of loyalty through the case studies in Chapters Four through Eight. I ask for these indulgences as I cannot assess the validity and usefulness of the emotions theory unless it is provisionally accepted that loyalty *could* be an emotion. As I pointed out in the introduction to this chapter, my discussion has a certain circularity in its logic. I need to establish what loyalty is, if it can be an emotion and how the various theories of emotion might explain loyalty. It is the starting point in the elucidation of these three issues that requires the indulgence of the reader as I have chosen to start with the question of what loyalty is.

The Theorising of Emotion

Emotions are a constant and necessary aspect of human existence. They infuse the actions, behaviours, thoughts, feelings and decisions made by actors. Emotional feeling crosses cultures and epochs, though curiously some emotional expressions are culturally specific while others are universal. This section explores a selection of grand theories of emotion, ranging from biological approaches, to bio-cultural, sociological and existentialist. To adequately discuss definitional and categorisation issues, I need to explore these generic theories and postulate whether loyalty has a place within them. This is important methodologically, as how one defines emotion derives from the theoretical perspective one takes. It is also necessary to discount competing explanatory methods before delving into loyalty proper.

The origin of human emotions is a long, enduring debate. Are they socially and culturally created or is there a biological basis to emotions? While a definitive answer is unlikely to ever be agreed upon, it is important to identify the underpinnings of the various emotions theories to catergorise their position within this debate. In fact, many of the theories can be placed along a continuum, with biological determinism at one end and social determinism at the other. The broad theories of emotion can be categorised into certain groupings as a result of their approach to the base of human emotions. Thus, this section discusses the major theories of emotion by placing them within the categories mentioned above. These categories conform to many of the theorists' own perceptions of their position as well as conforming to generally accepted theoretical and disciplinary boundaries. I acknowledge that this division continues to perpetuate the separation of these theories and serves to maintain an opposition between them by definition. However, it is a useful heuristic mechanism with which to discuss the theories as the theorists themselves often place their work into specific camps.

While the emotions have been a sporadic topic of study over the last 300 years, only in the last thirty years have in-depth scholarly enquiries commenced in the area (Williams, 2001: 1–3). Much of the scholarly material being generated is still in a theoretical vein, with academics arguing about generic theories of emotions or focusing on a limited number of specific emotions such as shame (Braithwaite, 1989), love (Cancian, 1987) or trust (Misztal, 1996). The continuing arguments around generic theory, which often descend into a debate about what the basic emotions are and how more complex emotions fit in has been attacked by some theorists, such as Barbalet (1998: 2) as being unhelpful to a further elucidation of emotion.

This study of a particular emotion, loyalty, is intended to fill a gap in scholarly work on specific emotions, while extending the broad theories of emotion. Notwithstanding the criticisms of generic theory (as being too broad to actually explain specific emotions), I will now turn to those theories and deal with them on two levels. First, I provide a general description and critique of each theory and its philosophising of emotions, and second, I examine whether loyalty, as I have provisionally explored it with the definitions of in the previous section, can be understood from within the perspectives.

Biological Approaches to Emotions Theory

The issue of the biological basis of emotion began with Darwin's (1872) *The Expression of the Emotions in Man and Animals*. This work pioneered the argument that emotions are biologically based, inherited genetically and that they determine actions and responses (Turner, 2000: 66–67). The basic argument, expanded upon by those who followed in its wake, is that as animals we inherit through our genes certain emotional responses. The most commonly cited emotions are fear, anger, sadness and happiness (Turner, 2000: 67). Ekman (1999: xxiv) argues that despite some continuing disagreement, there is a broad acceptance of Darwin's position on the expression of emotion. This is that some expressions are universal across cultures and therefore must have some form of biological base. Ekman posits that there are a number of basic emotions and that these emotions have evolved 'for their adaptive value in dealing with *fundamental life-tasks*' (1992: 171, emphasis in original). Thus they are evolutionary because they have come into being as responses to (ancestral) life pressures. Fear is often cited as the primary example of an evolutionary emotion. If humanity had no 'fear' response then survival of the species would be very difficult as our ancestors would be constantly wandering over a cliff or investigating a lion close up—neither likely to encourage reproductive success. Ekman (1992: 171) argues that the primary function of emotion

> is to mobilise the organism to deal quickly with important interpersonal encounters, prepared to do so in part, at least, by what types of activity have been adaptive in the past. The past refers in part to what has been adaptive in the past history of our species, and the past refers also to what has been adaptive in our own life history.

Thus, basic emotions for Ekman have two 'learned' aspects; there is species or hereditary learning (the quintessential survival of the fittest argument) and individual learning (or personal experience). Ekman's argument can be developed further through acknowledging another source of learning—social learning or history.

Kemper hints at an explanation for this dynamic—of social learning and history—when he argues that 'emotions have not simply biological, but social survival value' (1984: 373). Thus, in the biological perspective, social survival can be seen to be as important as physical organism survival. To be cast out of one's social milieu or, worse, to be consciously attacked within that milieu, is likely to seriously limit an individual's survival and thus reproductive success. What biologists often underemphasize is that culture and society transmit social learning between the generations. This transmission of emotions in a society is important to the social and cultural continuation of that society.

To expand upon the survival of the fittest argument with respect to emotions, an individual's survival and thus reproductive success will be enhanced if they learn, understand and use emotions successfully. This is true at the micro as well as the macro level—what is good for an individual is often good for the social unit. Some groups or tribes have a particular emotion that serves a purpose in maintaining cohesion within that group. An example is the Gururumba tribe and the activity of 'being a wild pig' (Newman, 1964: 1–19), which allows men in situations of social distress to run amok as a means of signifying their difficulties. This enhances the cohesion and well-being of the group, which can be an evolutionary profitable and successful strategy.

To turn to fear as a way of exploring and critiquing this biologically based theoretical perspective: social learning of fear responses are critical to the individual's response. How do we know that the strange combination of symbols for biohazard or radioactivity are dangerous? There is no ancestral fear response, as could be argued in relation to the lion, if one accepts the biological viewpoint. In our own life history we may have never experienced the hurt that these symbols denote, yet we fear them. As individuals, actors may not have had an 'adaptive in [their] own life history' (Ekman, 1992: 171) experience of how to deal with these symbols of fear. Clearly social learning plays an intrinsic part in directing our fear responses. They must be learned in the overwhelming majority of cases. The emotions, even the basic ones, are to an extent, culturally and socially constructed, the expression and bodily responses attached to them may be biological and hereditary but the target is learned. A purely biological perspective cannot inform this book as it does not allow for social learning and the influence of culture.

However, one useful proposition that can be drawn from this literature is that loyalty may be a good example of a socially transmitted emotion. As I highlight throughout, loyalty is socially constructed and learned. It exists to foster social cohesion (although that does not discount the conflict that it can cause both within and between individuals). This is the contribution the biologically based theories give us in relation to loyalty. As a complex, learned emotion loyalty must have some benefit in the continuation of the culture it is part of—thus to understand loyalty we should look at its strengths in ensuring reproductive success for the individual *and* their society. Thus a historical reading of loyalty and how it has changed depending upon surrounding social relations can provide insight into the emotion as well as social reproduction.

Biocultural Approaches to Emotions Theory

One means of reconciling the nature-versus-nurture debate is to take a biocultural view of the emotions. McNeal (1999: 216) argues that emotions can be viewed as *fluctuating, biocommunicative states that are elicited contextually through ongoing cognitive processes of evaluation and differentially labelled, emphasized, or ignored through the influence of culture and individual experience.* (emphasis in original)

This definition suggests that emotions have a biological basis to them. As a biological entity, humanity has a range of physiological responses and states that can arise. These include states like adrenalin surges to promote fight or flight responses and any of the myriad of other mood and affect altering chemicals that human bodies release. The important extension in the field of emotions study that McNeal offers is that while there is a biological base to emotions, it is the mediation of these fluctuating physical and mental states by culture and society that is particularly relevant in understanding emotion. The core underlying aspect of our existence that must be acknowledged is that we are embodied—we have bodily sensory systems that mediate our perceptions of the world. It is through our physical existence that we understand what occurs around us through any of the six senses. However, it is society and culture that contextualises biology and provides the appropriate behaviours, action or inaction of an emotional response.

A useful heuristic device that McNeal (1999: 228–245) develops is the analogy of the computer as human emotion. The basic hardware is the biological base that all humans have for emotional processing. The various parts of the computer, like the hard-drive or the motherboard, can be compared to various human hardware systems like the limbic system and the brain. This contrasts with the software which is the social and cultural learning of the individual. To maintain the analogy, the software, within the confines of the hardware's capabilities, interprets and understands the world around it. The software informs the hardware as to which tasks to complete. Thus to return to emotions, we have a base of biological responses which are mediated through social and cultural learning.

To continue McNeal's (1999) computer analogy, emotions can be seen as a mainframe or server which provides direction on feelings, actions and thoughts to the individual computer, which the actor then interprets through his or her software and hardware (or social learning) which then provides a response back up the line. This does not exclude aspects of the emotion residing with the actor, in the manner of a server which has similar software to the actor's machine.

Loyalty can be explored within this framework. It could help conceptualise that loyalty is a connection emotion which operates to link actors. Like a server, it links individuals and groups. Alternatively, loyalty could be seen as a particularly complex piece of software which only explicitly activates in certain cultural milieus. This software combines a number of lower order emotions to match a cultural and social need for a certain type of behaviour, thought and action motivation, such as loyalty. The 'linking' nature of loyalty is a question to be explored with the case studies by looking for instances when loyalty connects an actor to their social milieu.

A further argument from the biocultural perspective is that even complex emotions must be hard wired, at least partially. As Turner (2000: 77) points out:

> complex emotions like guilt, shame, grief, delight, regret, depression, dread, and nostalgia are, I suspect, more hard-wired than constructed, or, at the very least, human brains are wired to learn these emotions with very little coaching.

Turner (2000: 76–7) argues that early humanity did not posses the brain capacity for complex socially constructed emotions, and that consequently they must have some hard-wiring within the brain. He (2000: 153) further argues that learning, an essential aspect of any constructivist explanation of emotion, cannot account for human emotions:

> learning is the key to activating humans' innate potential for using and understanding emotional syntax and to invoking the relevant emotionally ordered stocks of knowledge, but learning alone cannot explain humans' incredible facility with emotions.

Thus, according to Turner, it is the interaction between hard wired, hereditary emotional predisposition and society that determines the emotional expression of the actor. He (2000: 152) argues that humans, across all cultures and epochs, seek information on culture, structure and transactional needs from an early age. This, Turner contends, points to a biological base for emotions and means that some social behaviours, like culture, structure and transactional needs, have been hard wired by evolution into our psyche. However, this structural argument leaves little space for human agency. It assumes that human beings are genetically predisposed to seek certain emotional scripts that are connected to the broad categories of culture, structure and transactional needs.

Loyalty could be seen as a very good example illustrating Turner's point regarding how humans seek information on society. Does loyalty give information to the actor regarding social values, norms and reciprocities? Does the feeling and understanding of loyalty for the actor give insight into power and status relationships? Turner (2000: 152) argues that perceiving transactional needs is important to allow an actor to understand their social space, and that these interactions include 'exchange pay-offs, self-confirmation, trust, predictability, and intersubjectivity'. Is loyalty one of the markers/scripts/feelings that indicate to an actor that a transactional need is occurring? If so, then the case studies would need to demonstrate this by showing that actors rely on loyalty to inform them of emotional debts and obligations.

Another analogy within the bio-cultural perspective are the building block models of emotion. Simply, these theories argue that humans have a small number of innate, genetic emotions and that all other emotions are combinations of these. This is often conceptualised as lower order versus higher order or biological versus social emotions.

One of these models is proposed by Ekman (1984, 1992), who argues that a means of conceptualising basic/combination emotions involves 'emotional plots' (1984: 329). Ekman (1992: 194) points out that complex emotions such as grief and jealousy provide a specific contextualisation of what is occurring with a particular emotion. The emotion plot also has much more information than the basic emotions, as Ekman (1992: 194) explains with jealousy:

> It tells us the cast of three, their roles, something about the past history, and the emotions each cast member is likely to feel. Anger may be felt by the spurned one, but sadness and fear may also be felt. We also know something about the feelings of the rival and the object of mutual attention.

Thus, 'emotional plots' are complex as they incorporate a number of basic or lower order emotions, such as fear or anger. The emotion plot also carries with it information regarding the likely origin, manifestation and target of the emotion. Thus, with jealous anger the actor can have some understanding as to the origins of the anger, at least in a general sense. However, with just anger its origin is unknown without further explanation. Thus, an emotional plot carries further information on the social occurrences that have led to a particular emotional state.

Oatley and Johnson-Laird take a similar position on higher order emotional states and call these 'complex emotions' (1987: 46). These complex emotions are based upon the basic emotions of fear, sadness, happiness, anger and disgust (Oatley & Johnson-Laird, 1987: 33) but include 'a propositional evaluation which is social and includes reference to the model of the self' (1987: 46). Thus complex emotions, and Oatley & Johnson-Laird use remorse as an example (1987: 44–6), require some reflexive thought on the part of the actor in relation to the obligations and place within the social world that the actor occupies.

Another means of looking at emotional plots, and one that incorporates the biological and constructivist viewpoints, is to consider the various emotions on a continuum from biological to constructed. As Evans (2001: 21–2) argues:

> rather than thinking of basic and culturally specific emotions as two completely different kinds of thing, we should see them as sitting at opposite ends of a single spectrum. Depending on how many special conditions are required for a given emotion to develop, and on how special they are, the emotion will be located more towards the 'basic' end of the spectrum or more towards the 'culturally specific' end.

Evans' idea can be combined with the concept of complex emotions. Thus we have a spectrum of emotion, with the biological at one end, and culturally specific emotions at the other. An example of culturally specific emotions could be the particular expression of renaissance loyalty through patronage. However, the continuum is more like an inverted pyramid, with the basic emotions at the base, being the point and the complex emotions made from those emotions below.

Turner (1999) has attempted to develop a sociologically informed theory of basic and combination emotions. His argument is that emotional arousal occurs through a given set of stages or processes. This arousal impacts on the sense of self an individual has and then emotions manifest. These emotions are combinations of the basic, biological emotions. Turner argues that emotions are generated by 'congruity or incongruity between (1) what is expected and (2) what is experienced in a situation; and when there is high incongruity, emotional arousal ensues' (1999: 134). This arousal is also mediated by personal history and learning as well as biological mechanisms. Most importantly for Turner's conception is the concept of the 'self', or, the social identity of the actor. He (1999: 138) defines the self as the 'set of images that individuals have about themselves with respect to (1) who they are, (2) what they can do, and (3) how they should be treated'. The self is what comes into conflict with the emotional situation, triggering emotional arousal and/or defensive mechanisms. These defence mechanisms 'seek to protect self from unpleasant emotions, especially those directed at core self' (Turner, 1999: 142).

When there is incongruity between expectations and arousal, emotions result (Turner, 1999: 144). According to Turner (1999: 143–4),

if there is an incongruity below expectations for reinforcing outcomes or associative experiences, then the three primary emotions of assertion-anger, aversion-fear, and disappointment-sadness are activated... An incongruity that exceeds expectation for either positive or negative outcomes, a variant of the primary emotion of satisfaction-happiness is stimulated.

Turner (1999: 147) adds a fifth emotional response to his typology of primary emotions, startlement-surprise, which adds to the intensity of the emotions felt. The arousal one feels is also related to the response of others; this raises the salience of self and thus the emotional response (1999: 147). This concept is very much within a social constructivist fold of emotions (see next section). Not only do emotions need a social anchor, they can be enhanced or suppressed by the actions of others. This arousal relies on the concept of 'self', an inherently social construct which exists within the social world and is created, reinforced and negotiated through interactive engagement in society.

Turner's theoretical model is based on a typology of basic emotions that in various combinations point to the higher order emotions, such as shame and guilt (Turner, 1999: 150). Turner does not refer to loyalty, and the research question that follows is: can loyalty be added to this perspective? Important to Turner's (1999: 149) model is that basic emotions have a range of intensities: 'satisfaction to happiness, aversion to fear, assertion to anger, disappointment to sadness, and startlement to surprise'. It can be argued that humans have low intensity emotions simmering away all the time, with this being the neutral or standard state of affairs. However, Turner (1999: 149) argues that 'humans and other higher mammals have the neurological capacity to elaborate this lower intensity state to a much higher level of amplitude'. Thus, assertion can become anger which can even turn into hatred. Hatred is a very intense form of anger, which is ascribed to human behaviour but rarely would an animal engage in hatred. This is not always the case, as hatred does not need to develop from anger, nor always follow on.

This leads us to Turner's (1999: 149) assertion that 'emotions are combined in first-order combinations revolving around the mixing of two primary emotions in varying proportions or ratios'. In effect, Turner is arguing that there are certain innate emotions that all humanity possess. These innate, basic emotions then form all the higher order emotions. Turner uses the examples of shame and guilt to illustrate the point. With respect to shame he argues that 'the most prominent emotion in shame is disappointment-sadness at self for behaving inadequately in the eyes of others and in one's own self assessments'

(1999: 151). Shame also comprises other basic emotion combinations, including assertion-anger (at one's behaviour) and aversion-fear (possible consequences) (Turner, 1999: 151). Turner's typology also specifies outcome emotions from the combinations of lower order emotions. Thus, guilt is the combination of joy and fear and envy is a combination of sorrow and anger (Turner, 2000: 76).

This model generates a specific picture of what loyalty would look like. If you expect loyalty from a family member in a dispute situation and that person does not support you, you would have an emotional incongruity below expectations. Your emotional responses may be activated and often an anger/disappointment combination of primary emotions will be elicited. You may be disappointed because you expected the family member to support your cause (after all that is what family is for) and you may have supported them in the past. There may well be anger as you are relying on the support the family member may have been able to provide and as a consequence your position is made weaker and more vulnerable in the dispute. Thus, the case studies would need to show this type of complex combinational emotion response.

Turner's (1999) fifth basic emotional response may also come into play in this situation. The actor may very well be surprised, startled or even shocked that she is not receiving the loyalty expected. This occurs as loyalty appears to be a relationship that can build over time through reciprocity and commitment, both emotional and practical. Thus, the shock of disloyalty magnifies the subsequent emotional incongruity and thus impacts on the actor. This could be shown by having examples of an actor's response that shows their increased feeling as a result of the shock.

The idea that there must be some reducible, basic set of natural emotions is by no means new. Thinkers from Descartes, Hobbes and Spinoza to Hume and Adam Smith have all developed typologies of basic emotions (Solomon, 2002: 116–117). However, this idea, and by extension Turner's analysis above, has come under sustained criticism in recent times. Solomon (2002: 118), one of the leading critics of this view, proclaims:

My aim is to combat what I see as a debilitating reductionism in emotion theory and to defend the view that emotions provide a particularly rich field of complex phenomena in which chemical and building-block models are simplistic, inappropriate and utterly misleading.

According to Solomon, the main problem is that the basic emotions theses require a biological essentialism at their core. Yet the emotions are nothing without the social world attached. This does not discount the presence of the body—we mediate all action through bodily sensory systems. Solomon (2002: 133) argues the point thus:

To twist around a question from William James, 'once you subtract the cognition and culture from an emotion, what is left?' The answer is *nothing*, or at any rate not much that would be identifiable as an emotion. (emphasis in original)

In identifying emotion, it is becoming increasingly obvious that a collated set of bodily reactions, whether they be heart rate, blood pressure, skin temperature, sweating or in more difficult to measure changes in hormones and chemicals within the body, are not an emotion in the sense of the term accepted by the vast majority of 'lay' people. Again, as Solomon forcefully argues (2002: 134), 'emotions have a neurological basis but the identity of particular emotions lies elsewhere, in their phenomenological structures'. Thus it is the social context of the emotion that matters.

Solomon identifies a second problem with the basic emotion perspective. It simplifies emotions to bodily responses and takes us back to the belief that emotions are irrational and uncontrollable. As Solomon (2002: 138) puts it, this view 'makes emotions look stupid and reinforces the old stereotypes of emotions as mindless, disruptive reactions that get in the way of human flourishing'. Thus it is unhelpful to the social researcher to again be brought back to the belief that as it is 'basic' to human existence it must be universal and innate and ultimately un-controllable. This leads to the limiting of research and discussion if emotions are considered in that way. If I took that approach in this book I would be compelled to interrogate loyalty as a universal and innate emotion. This would be very challenging as it appears that loyalty is *not* universal and manifests in different time periods as a result of differing antecedents.

The identification of a possible biological base to loyalty does not invalidate a sociological enquiry into the concept. If we accept the proposition that there is some inherited base to the emotions we do not have to accept that the entire expression of the emotions in society is a product of biology. Consequently there is ample scope for the study of the social origins and manifestations of loyalty, particularly as the expression of emotion is governed by social structures and learning. Planalp (1999: 137) argues that 'society is not just a social overlay on a biological foundation; the social nature of emotion seems to be built into our genes'. Thus, while the need for the social could be hard wired, the nature of the social is not.

A further critique of Turner's (1999) position, and the theorists that share his views, is that there is no inherited biological predisposition to certain social phenomena. Culture, structure and transactional needs are such strong social values that it is inevitable that any individual entering the social system will not only actively seek to learn about these, but also unconsciously absorb the meaning. The problem that Turner, and for that matter any other theorist interested in differentiating between the nature-nurture debate, faces is that evidence is extremely difficult to amass. It is not possible to experiment on people to the extent required to begin to answer the nature-versus-nurture debate. It would require experiments of the scale depicted in Peter Weir's (1998) movie *The Truman Show,* where an entire town (hence social world) is constructed and manipulated around one 'experimental' test subject. Even then, the experimenters will be drawing upon and using their own socialisation to construct the very world. Thus we are left with assertions backed up with dubious cross-species evolutionary evidence. This difficulty informs my methodology, as I take popular culture sources, both current and historical, as my evidence in an attempt to circumvent the difficulties of knowing when emotion occurs. I discuss these methodological issues in more detail in Chapter Four.

The biocultural approach to the emotions is a useful way to integrate the competing dichotomies. As Armstrong (1999: 269) points out '[t]he existence of the neurophysiological states of emotions does not preclude a cultural definition of emotions: the neuroanatomic data reviewed . . . predict that both biological and social forces are important'. Both forces, social and biological, are clearly important in the construction and expression of emotion. They do not preclude the existence of the other. We are embodied and we must mediate social interaction and our emotions through our bodies. Hence the role that biology plays. However, our biology cannot be conflated to an explanation for emotion. For, at best, biology shows us how and what we experience as emotion—it does not explain it.

The Sociological Theories of Emotion

If we accept that the term 'sociologically' can have a broad application then there are a number of significant approaches to emotion that fit within the discipline. In this section I review the key sociological offerings on emotion. I begin by discussing the social constructivist position—the first substantive approach to the study of emotions by sociologically informed thinkers (with the exception perhaps of William James). I then move to Randall Collins' interactional theories of emotion which contains critical micro-sociological observations of emotion. Lastly I assess the contribution of Jack Barbalet, who has critiqued and modified the constructivist position.

The social constructivist model of emotions is much more in keeping with most sociological tradition. According to this perspective it is society and culture that determines the emotions, rather than biology. A leading exponent of this perspective, Harré (1986: 3), points out that 'the overwhelming evidence of cultural diversity and cognitive differentiation in the emotions of mankind has become so obvious that a new consensus is developing around the idea of social construction'. Social constructionist accounts of emotion relegate biology to a secondary role in the emotions, at best:

in the case of emotions, the overlay of cultural and linguistic factors on biology is so great that the physiological aspect of some emotional states has had to be relegated to a secondary status, as one among the effects of the more basic sociocultural phenomena. (Harré, 1986: 3–4)

Another leading researcher in this perspective is Kemper (1978: vii), who argues that 'most human emotions result from the outcomes of interaction in social relationships; hence a complete theory must include the social bases of emotion both descriptively and causally'. Kemper also explains why sociology offers the best theoretical tools to analyse and understand the emotions:

Sociological terms allow us to examine the social environment and its effects on the emotion[s] . . . We can move quite directly from social class to emotion, or from power to emotion . . . Indeed the central contribution of a sociological approach to emotions is the specification of a comprehensive model of the social environment. . . . This allows for the formulation of empirically-based hypotheses linking variations in the social environment with varying emotions. (Kemper, 1984: 370)

Kemper's last line offers an intriguing approach to studying emotions, and potentially to the study of loyalty. Do variations in emotional expression change according to the social environment? Or, to phrase it differently, which social environs tend to promote certain emotions? Returning to loyalty, does loyalty occur in certain social environs and can a pattern be discerned?

At the level of the actor, Kemper (1984: 374–6) argues that emotions are guided by three principles: reciprocity; prior structural effects and devolution. Reciprocity implies that if actor A does something for B, then B will return the favour and so on. This notion can be tested through loyalty, as reciprocity appears to be an essential ingredient of a loyalty relationship. Kemper (1984) points out that the principle of reciprocity also works in the negative sense, hatred is likely to be returned, often with increased venom. This is borne out by several examples in the case studies when loyalty is not returned or reciprocated.

The principle of prior structural effects refers to 'the influence on interaction and emotions of the existing social and personality structure' (Kemper, 1984: 375). This is the history, beliefs and understanding that an individual brings to emotional interaction and consequently helps to define a reaction to the new emotional stimuli based upon previous experience. Thus, if an actor's experience of loyalty is one of previous betrayal, they are more likely to take a negative or cautious approach to forming new loyalty relationships.

The principle of devolution (Kemper, 1984: 375–6) refers to the likelihood that emotional interactions that start well will decline in efficacy and positive effect as the interaction continues. Thus, the first time a loyalty relationship is called upon it will function in the expected, positive reciprocal way, but as it is repeatedly called upon, the outcome potentially declines with less likelihood of positive interaction. This notion of devolution is as a negative influence. It does not merely devolve; actions can enhance and re-invigorate relationships. These might include a return on loyalty over and above the actor's expectation or rituals and events that subsume the individual back within a loyalty milieu, such as sporting loyalties being revived by a good team performance. The loyalties of sports fans will be addressed in Chapter Seven where I will test this principle. The principle of devolution needs to be tempered with an acknowledgement that individuals, groups and organisations make conscious attempts to foster and maintain emotional relationships and the processes these involve. In taking Kemper's view on devolution to loyalty, I will be examining instances when loyalty no longer motivates the actor as well as instances of re-invigoration. Emotion is continually fostered and re-enforced through various behaviours. There is not an automatic decline in feeling. Rather, it is the combination of devolution with what we might call evolution in the emotional relationship that determines the longevity and intensity.

To return to the issue of fear as a way of comparing theoretical positions, the social constructionist approach offers another explanation for the emotion of fear.

Kemper (1984: 377) points out that fear results when there is a differential power relationship—either the fearful actor has too little power and is scared of the other actor, or the other has an excess of power, intimidating the fearful actor. The power relationship is determined by social factors and behaviours. Thus it is not just an evolutionary survival mechanism, for example against the lion, or an attempt to expunge the object of fear symbolically, but a reflection of social status and influence through power relationships. This perspective then adds several key sociological insights into fear—that there is status, power and influence involved. These observations are typically sociological and are a useful reminder that even supposedly biological emotions like fear can have their origins in social interactions.

Another way of conceiving of emotion is the 'emotional energy' approach of Collins (1984, 2004). Collins argues that '[e]motional energy not only upholds the social structure, but is produced by it' (1984: 385). Thus it is interaction within the social structure that gives an individual emotional energy and maintains that social structure by the individual returning the energy to the system, maintaining and reinforcing it. According to Collins (1984: 385), these 'interactions have a ritual quality, which reproduce, increase, or decrease the emotional energies of individuals'. For loyalty to have emotional energy, it would need to reproduce, increase or decrease emotional energies depending on the reaction of the target of loyalty. Collins places loyalty into a specific function within his emotion theory. To Collins (1984: 386) social structures require 'continuous monitoring by individuals of each other's group loyalties'. This enables the actor to maintain her knowledge of status, power and authority positions within society, allowing the actor to function more effectively within society as the knowledge imparted increases the actor's ability to successfully interact within the social structure without causing undue offence or overstepping the bounds of her own influence and power (Collins 1984: 386).

At the macro-sociological level, emotional energy can also be changed through the use of ritual, communications technology and culture-producing specialists (Collins, 1984: 395–6). Collins (1984: 396) argues that the use and distribution of these resources are 'crucial factors in the struggle for power in any particular historical society'. He points out that the history of 'shifts among tribal, patrimonial-feudal, and bureaucratic forms of organization are shifts among diverse sources of emotional impression-management' (1984: 396). This is building upon Weber's idea of different authority types, and what particular emotions that they draw upon.

For loyalty to fit the perspective that Collins (1984) argues for, loyalty will have had to play a particular role across these epochs of organisational emotional impression management. Thus, I examine changes in the way loyalty has been used and invoked across history. If there is a difference then weight will be added to Collins' position. Specifically for loyalty, the target, focus, behaviours and expectations of this macro layer of loyalty will need to have shifted with the change in organisational structure. For example, loyalty in the patrimonial-feudal era was built around the notion of loyalty to those above in social station, from the serf to the noble to the King. These loyalty relationships had specific rights and responsibilities attached to them; the serf must provide taxes to the noble and respond when a call to arms was made. Conversely the noble had to protect the serf and provide rulership and leadership. Loyalty was a central part of a coerced system of social discipline and order (Dunn, 1988: 74), designed to maintain a rigid feudal class system (Grodzins, 1956: 10–11). As Collins argues, the conflict around emotion management is a central conflict in the struggle for power, and loyalty represents one of the emotional energy management tools available in this struggle. As this type of loyalty no longer exists in this form in Western democracies, this points to the way emotions are managed.

The sociological approach to emotions has come under attack from a number of perspectives. One of those, not surprisingly, is from those who argue that there is a biological base to the emotions that determines expression in society. Turner (2000: 80) makes a forceful call for sociology to accept more biology:

Too often, we simply view everything as socially constructed; and yet this approach is not adequate for such primal forces as human emotions; just how much and what kind is not so easy to say, but we need to ask the questions because it may well be the rapid advances in neurology may soon be able to provide some answers. And it makes a great deal of difference for understanding the flow of interaction as to whether an emotional elaboration is innate or socially constructed.

Undoubtedly there is biology involved in every emotional expression. Turner's critique is a valid reminder that we are embodied. Human beings are biological entities and as such all of our thoughts and actions could be reduced to biology; everything we do, see, hear and feel is mediated through biological interpretative and expressive mechanisms. However, to claim the supremacy of biology over culture because we are biological entities is unhelpful as it hides the social nature of emotion, specifically the embedded power structures and forces that researchers could miss if they accepted the primacy of biology. As many have argued and, as this book will examine, emotions have a strong socially constructed basis to them.

Barbalet (2003: 1) offers some theoretical extensions to the social constructivist position, by arguing that emotions can be conceptualised as an 'experience of involvement'. The extent of one's involvement is not relevant, nor is the intensity of direction of involvement. Thus, it is an emotional occurrence when a person registers interest in a happening, according to Barbalet (2003: 1):

It is this experience that is emotion, not the subject's thoughts about their experience, or the language of self-explanation arising from the experience, but that immediate contact with the world the self has through involvement.

Barbalet argues that an actor must care about an event for emotion to manifest, but that this care can range from slight to overwhelming. Thus, there cannot be emotion in isolation from the world. Emotion must be connected to something—not necessarily a living thing, but an object within the world. This involvement then registers either in the physical or dispositional bearing of the individual. So the actor can have a physical response such as sweating, shaking or palpitations or a dispositional bearing such as a change in the way the actor views another person or event; for instance respect becomes disdain as a result of an event. This perspective generates a number of hypotheses. To test this position, the case studies will need to show that loyalty can be positive or negative in effect and that it can have a range of influence, from weak to strong, on the actor's existence. Further, I will examine dispositional shifts in the actor's bearing. Or, to phrase it differently; does loyalty change the way an actor perceives, feels and engages with the world?

Barbalet's proposition that emotion is involved when the actor is subsumed within an interaction and not when the actor thinks about or relates verbally to that emotional state is quite challenging. This proposition critiques the large linguistic field of emotions theory (e.g., Wierzbicka, 1995), and suggests that you do not need a verbal expression to experience an emotion. The actor does not need to 'name' the emotion—this is distinct from verbalising it through other terms that describe the feeling. For example, it is entirely possible to feel the Japanese named emotion of 'amae' as a westerner (the feeling of comfortable dependence, Evans 2001), but not have the language to succinctly express that emotion in a single word. In Barbalet's view the emotion occurs because the actor is in the experience of amae—they are comfortably depending upon someone.

Clarke (2003: 156) offers an illuminating definition of the social constructivist perspective arguing that

> from a social constructionist viewpoint we have a number of conditions which affect emotional response. In the broadest sense they are first, the local moral order. Second, the historical context of an emotion in a given culture and in particular the local language. Finally, there is an emphasis on political economy, and in particular the socio-economic position of a person. In other words our emotional feelings are a cognitive response to how we would be expected to feel in a given situation.

This is a useful summary of possible ways to explore loyalty. This requires an analysis of the use of language and most importantly how the use of loyalty has changed over time. I will question whether loyalty also has a central role to play in political economy, both in explaining and directing action and in securing hierarchies of power.

However, Clarke (2003: 156) goes on to critique the constructivist position by asserting that 'the problem with this view is that there is little recognition of the unconscious motivation behind response . . . it is difficult to say the least, to pin point why some people are more envious, or more prone to envy than others'. This critique goes to the core dilemma of emotions theorising—how do we account for the vast variation in responses that humanity manifests? To put the question/criticism into the concerns of this theses: why do some actors identify loyalty as a motivating force and others not? What particular combinations of local moral order, personal history and political economy mean that loyalty may be a force? Clarke goes on to offer an explanation of levels of envy by using psychoanalysis. I take a different view on this dilemma and turn partly to existentialist analysis, in the following section, and partly to the idea that mapping unconscious motivation is a highly problematic endeavour—especially when dealing with emotion.

In summary, a sociological approach to emotions indicates that society and culture play a central role in the creation, transmission, mediation, learning, expression and understanding of the emotions. Emotion is an expression of social values and needs and as such it is subsumed within the cultural milieu. This perspective does not require conscious knowledge or activity on the part of the actor to experience or feel an emotion, nor is the actor tied to biological manifestations of emotion as particular physical sensations. This approach generates a series of key questions in regards to loyalty and its potential place as an emotion such as:

1. How is loyalty manifested in culture? What processes transmit, re-enforce, identify and teach loyalty?
2. Is loyalty dependent upon the social values and needs of particular cultures?
3. How does loyalty manifest for the actor?
4. Does loyalty tend to occur in certain recurrent social interactions and is this a pattern across sites?

These questions have a common theme, that of human existence and how the actor is part of her social world. To complete the theoretical review I now turn to a theoretical position that critiques the rational, passion-less actor—existentialist theories of emotion.

The Existentialist Theory of Emotions

Another means of conceptualising emotion was advanced by Jean-Paul Sartre through the phenomenological tradition. Many of Sartre's comments are geared towards critiquing psychological and biological accounts of emotion (Solomon 1981: 214–5). Emotions are embodied forms of human existence, and emotion for Sartre

> has its own essence, its peculiar structures, its laws of appearance, its meaning. It cannot possibly come from *outside* the human reality. It is man, on the contrary, who *assumes* his emotion, and emotion is therefore an organized form of human existence. (2002: 12, emphasis in original)

It is his call for emotions to be returned to the reality of an individual's existence in the social world that is Sartre's greatest contribution to emotions theory (Williams, 2001: 56–7). This is similar to the social constructivist position, but reminds us that the individual is as important as the social milieu.

Sartre also posits emotions as states that are, initially, non-reflective (2002: 34). Awareness may come subsequently but is not a condition for emotionality (similar to Barbalet's 2003 position, see previous section). Part of the non-reflective status of emotions is that emotion is in flux between the object and the individual—they are amalgamated as one: 'the emotional subject and the object of emotion are united in indissoluble synthesis' (Sartre, 2002: 35). This serves to remind the researcher that the actor and the object are drawn together through emotions and subsequently that emotional behaviour can change the world and the subject. As Sartre (2002: 41) explains, 'during emotion, it is the body which, directed by the consciousness, changes its relationship with the world so that the world should change its qualities'. Emotions modify the world without acting upon the world, at least in their initial interaction. Thus, the actor uses emotion to change parts of the world around her to better suit the individual's wants, desires and expectations— often in the form of ameliorating tension from actions or thoughts that cannot be acted upon or expressed. Sartre uses the example of a bunch of grapes (2002: 41) to illustrate this point. If the bunch of grapes is beyond reach, the actor may shrug her shoulders and mutter that they 'are too green anyway'. For Sartre this is not as simple as it seems. The act of deciding they are too green is a substitution for the action that could not be completed. Thus the tension of not being able to reach the desired object is resolved because a new status has been conferred on the grapes— that of undesirability.

Sartre places particular emphasis on the emotion of fear (2002: 42–3). As discussed, many biologically based theories of emotion see fear as the quintessential bodily emotion, hereditary and fixed across culture and time. The meaning of fear, to Sartre (2002: 43) is as

a real consciousness whose aim is to negate something in the external world by means of magical behaviour, and will go so far as to annihilate itself in order to annihilate the object also.

Thus, the actor may faint—clearly a poor evolutionary choice with the lion bearing down. But from the existentialist viewpoint that fainting is explicable and obvious. The actor can 'magically' remove the object of fear, and lessen internal tension by shutting down the mind completely. The lion ceases to exist in the actor's reality. Sartre (2002: 42–3) also explains the active manifestation of fear behaviour—flight and points out that flight is not a rational, logical course of action; 'we do not take flight to reach shelter: we flee because we are unable to annihilate ourselves in unconsciousness'. Thus fleeing is the attempt of the actor to annihilate the object of tension through space and time, rather than a 'survival' mechanism in the evolutionary sense.

The central aspect of Sartre's emotion theory is that 'emotion is a phenomenon of belief' (2002: 51). The actor lives within the world, body and mind combined indissolubly, and interacts with the world. Consciousness is a 'magical' aspect of existence and it acts upon itself and the world to modify it—emotion is the magical means used to change the world (Sartre, 2002: 51). Emotions are behavioural, purposive actions and this perspective therefore encourages a sociological treatment of the emotions (Crossley, 1998: 34). A second, important contribution Sartre makes is to remind us that the emotions are 'magical' things, not easily reducible to rational discussion, measurement and analysis. As sartre (2002: 54) points out 'we have to speak of a world of emotion as one speaks of a world of dreams or a world of madness'. Sartre has been criticised for succumbing to the traditional view of emotions as irrational (Solomon, 1981: 223). Solomon (1981: 223) goes on to suggest that we must acknowledge that emotion is 'as important in sustaining *our* effective behaviour as in rationalizing our failures and our impotence' (emphasis in original).

A number of further criticisms have been made of the existentialist position. Crossley (1998: 34–5) identifies two broad areas of critique: biology and management. Biologically concerned theorists quite rightly point to the fact that emotions can be altered through drugs. Sartre would probably have countered this by saying that this is yet another example of the actor 'magically' transforming the world to suit her needs. The actor takes ecstasy as a means of modifying her interaction with others in order to enhance pleasure. This criticism reveals that the world of emotions is not just from within the individual but can be engineered by drugs from without. The second criticism that Crossley identifies is that existentialists fail to account for purposive management of, and reflection upon, emotion, such as the changing of emotion to suit particular needs. This is exemplified by Hochschild's (1983) oft-cited thesis on the management of emotion by airline stewards and debt collectors. Emotions are not just magical transformers. They are, according to Crossley (1998: 35), '"things" that we think and talk about and that we put a value upon'. This is an important caveat to the existentialist position. The emotions can be created and managed through social structures. It is not that existentialists cannot account for management of emotion—it is that the perspective has not engaged with it (Crossley, 1998: 35). A defence that existentialist inspired theorists might offer would be that managing one's emotion is a requirement of the social system/structure, is another way of transforming the social world (further, we are always 'managing' our emotions as part of being social entities). If the airline steward makes a show of pleasant, comforting nice-ness, then they have gone part of the way to making for a pleasant interaction for themselves and the passenger. It is when the views of the emotional world collide that conflict ensues, and in this case one could foresee the passengers without their baggage as needing their world to look different. Barbalet (1998), in his critique of Hochschild's position, makes a point that is very similar to the position that Sartre would have taken in response to such criticism. Stating that:

What Hochschild fails to acknowledge, however, is that the experience of the emotional feeling, in directing the subject's disposition to that object, thereby modifies the relationship between the emoting person and the object of their feelings. This emergent situation, therefore, can be described as one of emotional transformation, because this new situation will be appraised by a new emotional feeling. (Barbalet, 1998: 180)

Thus, even in the case of purposeful management of emotions, the act of engaging in a social interaction with emotion transforms the interaction. This suggests that the critique of the existentialist position as being unable to account for management of emotions is overly-simplistic.

The insights that the existentialists offer for the study of loyalty are three-fold. The first is that emotions magically transform the world. For loyalty to fit this proposition it would need to make the world a more understandable place, to transform an actor's existence and to enhance her comprehension of social interactions. As part of this magical transformation, loyalty would also need to change the world. Thus I ask whether an actor's loyalty gives her an understanding of the world and also whether this understanding projects back onto the world and thus transforms it.

The second contribution that this tradition gives to a study of loyalty is to suggest that emotions are phenomena of belief. Thus, the actor must believe in the efficacy of the state/feeling/passion. This belief component can be expanded to include membership as well, and as I show later, the denial of an actor's loyalties can have profound effects.

This brings us to a third issue that the existentialists contribute to the analysis of loyalty—that emotions are like a world of dreams or madness—that they can be irrational and difficult to study in the scientific tradition. This aids in two ways. First, that different methods of study need to be used on emotions like loyalty. Second, how do the instances of loyalty that I explore in the case studies point to emotional 'madness' on the part of the actor? Does having loyalties create a change in the actor's thoughts, perceptions and actions only on the basis of passions?

The use of Jean-Paul Sartre's view of emotions extends the questions this book seeks to address. It does this by firmly placing the individual actor back into the world of emotions and passions. A social constructivist position has a tendency to focus on structural forces and not the actor. As a consequence, I will endeavour to explore both aspects when it comes to loyalty—the social forces and the actor's response. The generation of the above research questions focusing on the individual and the way emotions change and modify their existence is an artifact of this perspective. When this is combined with a modified social constructivist position, I hope to offer a more complete picture of loyalty.

The Implications of Loyalty as an Emotion

The previous sections have been working towards a rationale for accepting loyalty as an emotion. While the debate over the categorisation of loyalty as an emotion is likely to continue, it is necessary to make some preliminary assumptions at this point and posit loyalty as an emotion.

The key advantage of recognising loyalty as an emotion is that it allows me to bring a range of theoretical tools to bear in explaining and understanding the phenomenon that is loyalty. Thus, I can use the various tools of social constructivism to explain loyalty—such as the focus on emotions being the product of social interaction and not an innate behaviour. This position informs the position I take on loyalty, namely that it is socially constructed, guides behaviour, contributes to identity, is conflicted and is layered. The proposition that loyalty is an emotion also informs my methodology, as 'knowing' when an emotion exists is a key problem in the study of emotions.

The critical question, for this study, is this—does loyalty have sufficient aspects in common with other phenomena that are generally considered to be emotions (such as love and shame) for it to be considered an emotion?

Conclusion

I have identified some key definitions of loyalty in this chapter as a way of beginning the discussion on the social phenomenon. This has resulted in is the proposition that loyalty can be considered an emotion. The implications of loyalty being an emotion are critical for my argument as this informs the theory and methods employed in elucidating the phenomena. While the definitional argument is not complete yet, and I will return at length to this question in the next chapter, I have sketched what loyalty is. This has then been followed by an exploration of emotion theory with a view to testing the validity of the perspectives against this provisional understanding of loyalty. Loyalty fits neatly within the sociological viewpoint, with an acknowledgment of the value of the existentialist position as well. This will of course be tested at length in the case studies that follow.

The next chapter continues the theoretical exploration of loyalty and theory and constructs a set of more detailed questions surrounding the nature of loyalty and how it operates. The key methodological hurdle of my argument will be now addressed—just how do I know that loyalty is *loyalty*?

Chapter Three
Elements of Loyalty

> Although scholars and lay persons alike attach a highly charged, unbending emotion to loyalty, a consistent definition has not evolved. It appears to mean different things to different people.
>
> Guido-DiBrito (1995: 223)

Introduction

The proposition that loyalty might indeed be an emotion allows me to create a set of propositions with which to approach the case studies in the following chapters. Having established the possibility of viewing loyalty as an emotion in the preceding chapter, it is now necessary to establish the purpose, role and effects of loyalty in social relationships. This will contribute to a richer understanding of a sociology of loyalty that is framed within the emotions literature.

This chapter outlines the key components of loyalty which I will explore through the case studies. My intention here is to discuss the theoretical underpinnings of each aspect of loyalty; that is, to place them within sociological theory. I will explain how each of these components of loyalty functions, although, as with any social system in reality they are intimately tied together. The case studies themselves will deal with the question of loyalty in a holistic way. The expression of emotion through language has been a long-standing argument within the literature. Consequently, I place the term loyalty within that debate and further my argument that the term 'loyalty' can denote a particular emotion. I also critique the view that loyalty may 'just' be a behaviour and not an emotion. This is necessary for reinforcing the possibility that it is an emotion. Emotion is also not value-neutral, indeed a purpose of emotion is to orient the actor to social values (consider shame). I discuss the role loyalty plays in power relationships and critique the view of emotions as being irrational.

Notes on Methodology

Attempting to analyse a concept such as loyalty raises a host of methodological dilemmas. Fortunately for this book, much of the methodological groundwork for sociological investigations of emotions has already been covered. Consequently, I draw heavily on the theorists that have already established how to 'see' emotion and I propose how loyalty may fit these methods. This section serves a dual purpose. The first is to establish that these particular methods are a relevant and acceptable sociologically informed way of investigating emotions. The second is to question how these methods will interact with a concept such as loyalty. At this stage I can only assume that this methodology will elucidate loyalty. The proof will come in the case studies and then in my conclusion when I confirm that loyalty is an emotion.

The first challenge is the proposition that emotion simmers below consciousness the majority of the time. It is only when an event occurs triggering the emotion that an actor may become aware of the feelings, cognitions and behaviours that define the emotional experience. Barbalet supports this contention when he argues that 'the emotions centrally implicated in social action operate at an unacknowledged and therefore nonconscious level' (1992: 155) and that 'many significant emotions function below the threshold of awareness' (160). A similar point is made by Carroll (1999: 29) when he argues that when emotions are generated by watching films 'it may, so to speak, fly in under the radar screen'.

The lack of awareness about our own emotional state is heightened by the contention that emotions are also constantly evolving and modifying the world; they cycle, morph, twist and change, flowing from one to another and back, in varying degrees, aspects and volumes (Sartre, see previous chapter and Barbalet, 1998: 181). Emotions also never 'finish'—they are in flux, or as Barbalet (1998: 180) phrases it: 'emotions themselves are never finished objects but always in process'. Thus, at a single point in time you can have an emotion, but then it will be gone, morphed into another, lost or changed. This lack of permanence to feeling states can make it difficult to pin-point an emotion.

If emotions do simmer below the surface most of the time, as suggested by Barbalet (1992), it makes their study problematic. If an actor does not know he or she is experiencing an emotional response how is a researcher to study and describe the nature of that emotion? Does the emotion still exist in its original form when a researcher asks about the emotion that may or may not be already in existence? This methodological issue is not new, and goes back to the heart of inquiry-based social scientific discourse—does asking about or studying intently the object of interest change the object? This question is especially pertinent when the phenomenon of study is a malleable, indistinct and fuzzy concept. Gerth and Mills in *Character and Social Structure* (1964: 50) caution us on the difficulties of emotion observation by stating that:

our feelings can only be ascribed to us by others on the basis of our gestures and appearance. We do not read these signs unerringly and thus *know* the feelings of others; sometimes, even often, we do not know directly, nor can we name, what we ourselves feel. (emphasis in original)

If, as Mills and Gerth posit (and many thinkers since, and for that matter before), that it is indeed difficult for the feeler and even the observer to know what emotionality is occurring, how can the researcher occupy the position of an informed observer—let alone be 'objective' in any scientific sense?

I flag these issues as a means of acknowledging the problematic nature of researching emotions. To adequately critique these methodological concerns is a task beyond the scope of this work. Consequently I will turn to the methods that some sociologists have successfully employed in elucidating various emotions.

Katz's (1999) influential study of emotions, *How Emotions Work*, makes a forceful case for the importance and relevance of qualitatively informed studies of emotion. The key problem with using qualitative evidence is that inevitably the researcher will rely on an example or illustration that is recorded, remembered and noted by the participant. Thus it could be argued that the example used is too sensational or out of the ordinary experience and as such, that renders it as poor data and merely a curiosity of passion. However, Katz (1999: 77) argues for the opposite: 'a qualitative study of emotions – a topic that ought to be sensually interesting – *should* feature materials that border on the sensational' (emphasis in original). It is the sensational passion events that can give the best insight into the processes involved in emoting as these events distil the emotions and make them more visible and visceral. Consequently, I will draw on many examples that are sensational in my efforts to explicate loyalty. Further, emotion is passion—examples that are clinical, unpassionate and dull are probably not a good indicator of emotionality.

The range of sources I use to illustrate loyal interactions, across time, space and social site, targeted at different entities and felt by a range of actors, is designed to show the gamut of loyalty. This adds explanatory power to my arguments around loyalty and enhances the robustness of the conclusions I draw. This approach is further supported by Katz (1999: 76) who argues that 'qualitative social research that is boring to read because it reports many similar cases is likely to be weak in its evidentiary logic'.

In understanding the nature of emotion, Solomon and Stone (2002: 428) argue that 'multidimensional appraisals rather than a single appraisal are necessary to adequately characterize emotion'. It is a range of eliciting stimuli that create and manifest emotion generally. This is even the case in supposed single emotions or emotion events. Solomon and Stone are primarily concerned with appraisals of emotion that have positive or negative affect but do offer an important point to all emotions research when they contend that:

marriage and love are both more than just two people together, and even anger is more than just one person angry at another. The object of love, despite the romantic schmaltz and cynical witticisms, is neither the dearly beloved nor the narcissistic self (*amour de soi*) but the relationship and what two people (lover and beloved) become with it. (2002: 428)

Thus, emotion is not, for example, merely the individual action of anger, but all the social connection that goes with that anger (Solomon & Stone, 2002: 430). This could also be extended to loyalty and is thus an aspect worth exploring in the case studies. Loyalty is not simply one person's connection to another or a group, but all the relationships that form that connection. An actor's loyalty is also more than the sum of their individual connection. It is, as Solomon and Stone point out with love, what they both become with it.

Then there is the problem of biology and the question of what role the human body plays in emotions. Are there innate emotions that are hard wired into humanity through a long evolutionary process? There is also the question of society, moulding and shaping emotions to fit social needs. As Fehr and Russell (1984: 483) point out:

> Emotion theorists face a dilemma. As scientists, they have sought precisely defined descriptive and explanatory concepts and definite, clear-cut answers to their questions. At the same time, they have attempted to be, or their critics have demanded that they be, true to our everyday concept of what emotion is.

This is the methodological dilemma; on the one hand, a need for 'scientific' certainty drives much theorising and research, often in the direction of ever smaller definitional segments. On the other hand, the everyday understanding of emotion is that it is malleable, difficult to define and context-dependent. Loyalty is a good example of this difficulty, as it appears to be highly context dependent and consists of a varied subset of emotions and actions. There are pertinent criticisms of studies that reduce emotions to definable and testable propositions. Harré (1986: 4) argues that it is an 'ontological illusion' that when it comes to emotions there is something concrete and identifiable: 'an abstract and detachable 'it''. This illusion then drives theorising and research directed towards physiological events and changes. This is then labelled an emotion. Harré (1986: 4) goes on to point out that 'there is a concrete world of contexts and activities. We reify and abstract from that concreteness at our peril'. Thus, Harré is calling for the social—the world of contexts and activities—to be part of the definition of emotion.

An example of the flawed approach Harré (1986) warns against are studies that attempt to reduce emotions to simple definitions with testable hypotheses. Zdaniuk and Levine (2000: 502) are representative of this trend (marketing studies are particularly prone to this) with loyalty and defined loyalty as 'staying in a group and accepting the same outcomes as everyone else, even though one could obtain higher outcomes by leaving, because staying benefits other group members'. This reductionist definition allows for testable hypothesis, amenable to manipulation in an experimental context—at least in their opinion. What it does not do is acknowledge that emotion cannot be removed from the wider social context. In the laboratory Zdaniuk and Levine (2000) manipulated undergraduate psychology students and their 'loyalty' response, but only by so narrowly defining the object of study so as to make it less valuable as a generalisable proposition.

The Language of Loyalty

A further complication in defining emotion is the issue of language. Each language has cultural nuances to the expression and meaning of a particular emotion term. This makes it difficult to be sure that researchers are communicating about the same thing. This is further compounded by cultural influence and acceptable expression of emotion in different societies. The British 'stiff upper lip' contrasts greatly to Lebanese wailing and screaming, yet both deal with loss and sadness. Indeed, cultures themselves develop certain emotion concepts to deal with their specific cultural and historical roots—for example, *amae* in Japanese and *toska* (melancholy, or a yearning sadness, Fitzpatrick, 2004) in Russian (Wierzbicka, 1990: 134–5).

The very concept 'emotion' is a cultural artifact. It is a product of the English language and consequently based around specific cultural and historical beliefs (Wierzbicka, 1995: 22–3). Other languages do not necessarily have a word 'emotions'. Wierzbicka (1995: 21) points out that German has no word for emotion but does have a word 'to feel', but this term includes physical and mental feelings. Does this mean that without language expression, emotional expression is curtailed? Not necessarily, because to experience an emotion actors do not need a word label. Frijda, Markam, Sato & Wiers (1995: 125) point out that English does not have an equivalent word for the Japanese emotion of 'amae', which is the desire to depend upon someone else. This does not mean that an English speaker can not experience the emotion, just that if they were to verbally express the emotion they lack the succinct single word label (Evans, 2001: 2). A way of reconciling this difference is to acknowledge the cultural relativity of emotion and emotion expression as exhibited through language. As Morsbach and Tyler (1986: 302) point out in relation to the Japanese word 'amae': '[t]he language seems to recognize that there is an active, conscious aspect about the desire to be loved passively'. I believe that Morsbach and Tyler have it the wrong way round, the social forces/processes inherent in a particular social milieu encourage a need for amae and the language reflects this need by having a word to describe this desire to depend upon another. As Evans (2001: 2) argues:

Why is there no word for *amae* in English? The different ways in which various languages carve up the world reflect different cultural needs. Perhaps the Japanese need a word for *amae* because the emotion it designates accords with the fundamental values of Japanese culture. Unlike the situation in the English-speaking world which prizes independence, self-assertion, and autonomy, in Japan it is often more important to fit in with others and live in harmonious groups. *Amae* is an emotion that helps people to comply with these values. (emphasis in original)

Another limitation of employing language as the signifier for the presence of emotion is that emotional states and feelings are communicated through a range of medias, from tone of speech, to bodily movement and expression, and it is thought by chemicals such as pheromones (Turner, 2000). All these mediums defy the use of language as an arbiter of emotions (Turner, 2000: 126).

What does this mean for an emotion like loyalty? Firstly, it must be acknowledged that loyalty is an English language cultural artefact and as such when using the term 'loyalty' I refer specifically to that construction of the term. However, the feelings and behaviours associated with loyalty occur across many cultures.

The Japanese notion of loyalty, like the western one is a product of their feudal history. As Benedict (1991: 29) points out: '[e]very man's immediate loyalty was due to his lord, the *daimyo*, and, beyond that, to the military Generalissimo, the Shogun' (emphasis in original), very similar to the European feudal system of Lord-Duke-King for example. Similarly, the Japanese notion of familial loyalty is very strong, perhaps stronger than the western notion and incorporates the principle of reciprocal obligation to family for all that is done for a child, almost a form of indebtedness (Benedict, 1991: 99–104). To return to the issue that 'amae' raises, what this term illustrates is that the English language, as an expression of culture and society, needs a word to denote the connections and obligations surrounding 'loyalty'. The language has the term 'loyalty' because of its need for a succinct expression to describe that emotional purpose. Consequently, the presence of the term 'loyalty' in the language is indicative of its importance and relevance to the culture using the term.

This issue of cultural relevance regarding types of emotion and expression is also illustrated by the Gururumba tribes people of Papua New Guinea and their wild man behaviour (Newman, 1964: 1–19). This behaviour is often exhibited by men in their mid 20s to 30s and results in them running amok within their society, engaging in what is called 'wild pig' behaviour. They steal and destroy things, attack bystanders and generally cause mayhem. The tribe eventually re-introduces them into the village by a complex series of rituals. This action is a response to the social pressures that men in this age group are under in relation to family and clan responsibilities and is a way for them to draw attention to their difficulties in a culturally acceptable way. As Newman phrases it: '[c]ulture becomes a determinant of behaviour in that it supplies a pattern of action suited by its form to the individual's needs' (1964: 13). Averill (1980: 46) points out that: ' "being a wild pig" is a consequence of – and not antecedent to – socialisation. No child or infrahuman animal could engage in such complex behaviour, only a highly socialized adult'. Thus we have an emotional behaviour that is clearly learned in a cultural context as a response to the specific pressures, obligations and expectations of a society. Evans (2001: 18) also supports this viewpoint, arguing that:

for emotions like 'being a wild pig', then, it really is the case that you would not feel them unless you had first heard about them. It is this that distinguishes them from basic emotions such as fear or anger, which you would have the capacity to feel even if you had never heard of them.

While Evans' use of basic and complex emotion terminology is problematic (see chapter two) the basic point stands—that you cannot feel some emotions unless you have been socialised to the emotion, and the language and expression that are part of that emotion. Thus we have strong evidence for not only the cultural specificity of some emotions but also the need for social learning to understand and express emotions.

This discussion of language and cross cultural emotional expression has a particular point for loyalty. The loyalty that this book explores is a particular emotion originating from feudal relationships. I take feudalism as the start point because that is where the first usage of the term is recorded in English and by staying true to the language arguments above, until we can enunciate the emotion it is not socially relevant. I do not mean by that that loyalty has not existed before we had that particular term for it, of course the connection to kin as been around for as long as we have, but that the particular social relationship that our current term 'loyalty' denotes are specific to a western, Anglo, Judaeo-Christian society. Or, in other words, specific to the British Diaspora. Ultimately, I would have great difficulty drawing the myriad of examples that I use in the later chapters together if there was not a term to denote what was happening. However, terminology is never value free, and the origins of the term loyalty point to a very specific and exploitative class and productive relationship.

Emotion(al) Discourse—Gender, Power and Control

Emotion is power laden and in many ways emotions are the expression of power, control and coercion in society, both between individuals as well as individuals and social structures. Emotions can also be seen as irrational states that require management and control. This inherent tension regarding emotions runs through the various theories of emotion and in part explains some of the difficulties each meta-theory has in elucidating a theory of emotion. This section tours the claim that emotion is about power and coercion and concludes with the implications of these tensions for loyalty.

Emotions are often characterised as irrational states, out of balance, unhealthy, animalistic and feminine. As Lutz (1996: 151) argues:

As both an analytic and an everyday concept in the West, emotion, like the female, has typically been viewed as something natural rather than cultural, irrational rather than rational, chaotic rather than ordered, subjective rather than universal, physical rather than mental or intellectual, unintended and uncontrollable, and hence often dangerous.

Lutz's argument is that emotion in western society has been construed as an irrational, feminine 'other'. Thus emotion is the opposite to the western ideals of rational scientific thought. Lutz also identifies a tension within emotion discourse, that emotions are 'paradoxical entities that are both a sign of weakness and a powerful force' (1996:152). Thus the actor can be a victim of emotionality and be reduced to a gibbering wreck or can be impelled to action, forced into a behaviour that may cause harm but is unavoidable as the result of emotional influences. Averill (1980: 46) points to a similar problem within Western society and intellectual tradition—that emotion is irrational and dangerous: 'rationality and freedom of will have been considered the hall-marks of humanity; irrational and compulsive responses have therefore tended to be viewed as animal-like, brutish, and the like'. It is this conception of emotion as a 'lower' order of existence that has encouraged either its marginalisation in western intellectual discourse or its problematisation into 'disorders' or 'pathologies' which need to be 'managed' or 'cured'. Lutz posits that this trend is primarily a result of the need for social control and that problematising emotion into 'managed' fields is a means of achieving control, particularly over women (1996: 166–7).

Hochschild argues that emotions are being managed in the workplace by employers for customer support purposes: '[w]hat was once a private act of emotion management is sold now as labour in public-contact jobs. What was once a privately negotiated rule of feeling or display is now set by the company's Standard Practices Division' (1983: 186). Companies seek to utilise the emotional output of workers to make customers happier and thus likely to buy more and return later for other purchases. Furedi takes this proposition further and argues that emotion management has reached a point today where we are addicted to individual psychological well-being and are trapped in a 'therapy culture'. He argues (Furedi, 2004: 197) that the

cultivation of certain emotional attitudes and the repression of others is systematically pursued by institutions and professionals devoted to the management of how people ought to feel. . . . Today's cultural elite may lack confidence in telling people what to believe but it feels quite comfortable about instructing people how and what to feel.

This criticism is firmly within the constructivist theory fold, in that Furedi is arguing that our emotions are being increasingly managed and manipulated for the benefits of others. This can only occur when it is acknowledged that emotions are socially defined, created and constructed.

Barbalet (2002:1) makes a similar point in relation to the emotions and the pathologisation of their expression:

The conventional opposition between emotion and reason typically leads sensible people to reject emotion and to regard it as an inappropriate category of analysis, unless in accounting for psychological and behavioural pathology, in which case the emotions are held to predominate.

The two extremes that Barbalet identifies, either the inappropriate rejection or the predominate position (psychological pathology) build further on the points already made by Furedi, Lutz and Hochschild. Emotion is rejected as it is not a 'real' rational object that can be studied or when it does exist it is managed and rationalised.

This sort of criticism and discussion of emotions in society is not new. The rationalisation of existence was discussed at length by Weber. Elias also identifies the rationalising processes in modernity (Williams, 2001: 20–23). This idea of rational, calculable emotions has also infused modern marketing schemes that take advantage of emotions, such as loyalty in frequent flyer schemes. A whole field of marketing has developed, called Customer Relationship Marketing (eg Newell, 2000), designed with the express aim of creating and manipulating customer perceptions, feelings and behaviour. Or to put it into other terms, these marketing methods are designed to tell people how to feel and thus act.

Loyalty can also be viewed as a mechanism of social control. A key aspect of loyalty is the way it can guide and inform behaviour. This makes it a mechanism of social control as it furnishes obligation, rights, responsibilities and reciprocities upon an individual. As Grodzins (1956: 5–6) points out:

society – social structure of every sort – rests upon loyalties: upon attitudes and actions directed at supporting groups, ideas, and institutions. Loyalties sustain and are sustained by mutual rights and duties, common beliefs, and reciprocal obligations – all essential ingredients of social life.

These obligations have a social value and are backed up by coercive social relations—often supported by state apparatus. The divisive loyalty oath debates held during the McCarthy period of the 1940s and 1950s in the USA (Schrecker, 2002) demonstrate how a state can be caught up in societal discourse around loyalty and employ its coercive power to control and enforce a particular view of the emotion and its expression. I discuss these events in Chapter Five.

In discussing the potential irrationalities of emotion we must remember that reason, choice and the facts can and do underlie emotional expression. Planalp (1999: 187) phrases it thus: 'facts and reason *do* underlie emotion, and this is easy to demonstrate. Anger changes to embarrassment when you find out that your boss did not call you in to give you more work, but to give you a surprise party'. Thus it can be an error in fact that leads to 'irrational' displays of emotion, not that the emotion itself is in error.

This oppositional or binary thinking of emotions in general (rational versus irrational, feminine versus masculine, natural versus cultural and so on) has also suffused itself into emotions specifically. Thus, we often see emotions as binary opposites – loyalty or disloyalty, hope or despair and the quintessential binary opposite love and hate. Solomon and Stone (2002: 432–433) argue that the

reason for rejecting the notion of polarity and emotional opposites doesn't depend on ridicule. It follows from the analysis of emotion and emotion concepts. If an emotion is multidimensional then it immediately follows that the notion of 'opposites' is confused. Opposites depend on polarity, and polarity is just what is not available in even the simplest emotions.

This is a note of warning from Solomon and Stone for the common sense (in Mills' typology) usage of loyalty and disloyalty. Often the emotion of loyalty is seen as a binary opposite but this obscures the very real differences within the emotional expression and feeling of actors. While loyalty can become disloyalty there is no requirement for it to convert in this manner. Loyalty can just dissipate into nothing. This is when the loyalty connection slowly expires over time as it lacks reinvigoration and relevance to an actor's existence. There is also no restriction on loyalty transforming into other emotions, or being subsumed by other emotions. To use a gendered and stereotypical example, the loyalty of the personal assistant can easily develop into love. Loyalty rejected or spurned does not necessarily create disloyalty. The spurner may have thought there was never a loyalty relationship and thus rejecting displays of loyalty from another does not create disloyalty—hurt, anger and disappointment are the more likely outcomes. Thus it is important to acknowledge the direction of the loyalty to begin with in understanding what may be the outcomes of loyalty interactions.

A further difficulty with characterising positive and negative emotion states (another way of seeing binary opposites) is that we can have mixed feelings of both positive and negative emotions at the same time. When an actor chooses between two friends there is both loyalty and disloyalty being experienced. Sullivan and Strongman (2003) point out the difficulties of studying emotions that are mixed, especially when contradictory. They cite the example of a father expressing both pride and grief at the sacrificial actions of his son and the bittersweet experience of achieving one amazing feat but falling just short of another at the same time (2003: 212–3). How does a researcher separate the feelings? Is it indeed even plausible to try and separate the component parts from the overall feeling? What this does is sound another cautionary note to the study of any one particular emotion—such as loyalty. When isolating loyalty as a key component of the emotional life of the individual I am not discounting the other emotions that are in play, rarely will you see a 'pure' single emotion functioning.

A further complication arises with value laden emotions, like loyalty, which have a tendency to have a moral aspect attached to their feeling, value and expression. Tumin (1970: 150–151) argues that we have theorised truth, honour and loyalty as if they were cardinal values, passed down from sacred sources. This raises the spectre of moral judgement in the analysis of an emotion such as loyalty. It is essential to step beyond one's moral basis and look at loyalty critically. As Tumin (1970: 151) points out: 'the language of moral discourse is such that neutral sociological analysis is made extremely difficult at the outset'. This can be readily seen with loyalty by the attachment of the negative qualifier 'dis' – which as Tumin (1970: 151) points outs leads to 'feelings of anathema and condemnation'. My argument accepts the moral difficulties of loyalty by moving beyond a 'right' and 'wrong' analysis and recognising the functional aspect of the negative side to loyalty. After all, there is no loyalty without an other and no potential for loyalty without the ever present threat (real or otherwise) of disloyalty.

When the moral dimension is included in the judgements on loyalty, a complex and difficult picture emerges. I will side-step the issue of moral value and cultural, ethnic and religious values here and only deal with a few clear cases where loyalty is obviously present and enhancing the well-being of the individual. However, upon reflection after the fact, from the perspective of the informed observer it may not be considered in the best interests of the individual and society that this loyalty was so strong. The Nazi Party engendered fantastic loyalty among its adherents, the rallies, spectacles and rituals used are still among the most effective invented to create, inspire and affirm loyalty to a cause. One only has to watch Triumph of the Will by Leni Riefenstahl (1934), the great propaganda film featuring the Nuremberg rallies to perceive the fervour created. While for the individual this loyalty gave all the aspects of emotional succour, such as identity and reason for action, it also supports the constructed nature of loyalty. This loyalty was, however, ultimately horrendously destructive for the social fabric of Germany and the world, not to mention the treatment of Jews and other minorities. For the individual, the violence, death and destruction that ensued from this loyalty with its expression in war is obviously, from a moral perspective, wrong and bad. But it would be selective and remiss of the social theorist to ignore some constructions of loyalty because they result in 'evil'. For many of the Nazis and ordinary Germans their commitment to the party was a comforting membership that gave meaning. Hence the individual gains from this loyalty, at least initially, while the social fabric of world society and the position of minorities was severely compromised.

Seeing Loyalty

These points are a caveat to my argument. It must be noted that the preceding definitional discussion acknowledges the inherent contradictions of trying for a definition and discussion of an emotion concept as complex as loyalty. Loyalty will be explored in its social context and not reified in the abstract. It is only by placing loyalty in its social, cultural and historical milieu that an elucidation of the emotion is possible—akin to the example of the Gururumba people and 'being a wild pig' (Newman, 1964: 1–19). This is the significant point that Harré (1986) offers researchers on emotion—you cannot control for the extraneous variables—those variables are the emotion and not including them in the analysis is intellectually restrictive.

Consequently, in arguing that loyalty may be playing a role in the interactions I discuss, I will adhere to a simple rule—the protagonists within, or commentators upon, must use the terminology of loyalty. Firstly, if the word loyalty is used to describe an event, the behaviours or the feelings a loyalty event may be occurring. Secondly, a loyalty event may be occurring when there are references to 'negative' loyalty concepts such as disloyalty, treason and betrayal. Lastly, I consider that a loyalty event is occurring if the event has the effects of loyalty, that is, if it invokes loyalty through actions or words—even if not explicitly using the word loyalty. The identification of loyalty in these situations will be made by using textual analysis of books, movies, television, newspaper reports, magazine articles, web discussion and even comic strips. In short, if the research materials speak about loyalty then it is worth investigating whether there is an emotional engagement occurring and if this fits into the paradigm of loyalty that I am exploring. This approach to researching emotions is supported in the literature (for example, Ahmed, 2004).

The media I analyse have some distinct advantages in explaining the emotion of loyalty. Popular culture, by which I mean books, films, magazines, television, newspapers, the internet and radio, is not merely a means of entertainment in modern society. Popular culture is an essential aspect in creating, reinforcing and propagating values, beliefs, feelings and understandings. Docker (1994) develops this idea in his work on television, arguing that the representations in popular culture

> ...must appeal to popular traditions. Such traditions are always open to the new, in technology and form, and at the same time go back deep into the history of centuries and even millennia of popular culture ... back to thousands of years of folk cultures. (1994: 276)

Loyalty appears to be a social emotion, created from and reinforced by society. Social systems need a means of communicating what emotion is and how and when it is appropriate to feel and express it. Consequently, popular culture provides a powerful medium of communication and reinforcement. The use of these sources means I will be able to explore a plethora of examples and not be limited to a particular type of loyalty interaction. Consequently, I will have heeded Katz's (1999) and Solomon & Stone's (2002: 430) warnings on method and not be vulnerable to the charge that my material is not compelling.

A potential criticism of my use of these sources is that they are merely illustrative and not actual evidence. Thus it could be argued that all these sources are merely reporting on various social occurrences and, as such, are vulnerable to not only errors in observation and communication but also in meaning. The sources I use are also vulnerable to the charge that they are self-selecting and biased. The authors, writers, directors and discussants must have a pre-determined belief in the presence and action of loyalty to write about it. This means that I am already relying on a self selecting sample with no means of controlling for a null response. It is plausible that loyalty is only spoken of by a few distinct individuals and/or groups with a particular agenda or background. Consequently it could be argued that I am basing an argument for a general theory of loyalty on a limited sample of specific cases.

The charge that the material I use is illustrative and not evidence can be challenged on a number of grounds. Firstly, the very nature of 'fact' and 'evidence' is ambiguous to begin with and, as I have discussed, this becomes particularly problematic in the study of emotions when the only way to know about emotions is to take the observations of onlookers or the originator at face value. While you can measure some physiological changes (blood pressure, heart rate and skin conductivity being among the more popular) these still do not tell you what emotion is occurring. The researcher relies on the subject communicating what emotion is occurring, observations about it from an outsider and/or various elicitation mechanisms. However, again, how does one know for certain that anger is being fashioned? Stearns and Stearns (1985: 814) discuss how anger among the Utku Eskimos is suppressed through socialisation, yet they beat their domestic animals as a response to provocations from others. To the Utku there is no anger, while to an observer with a different emotional socialisation there is. While these are serious difficulties it does not mean that one can not study emotion with these mechanisms.

The second key defence of my evidence is its broad and wide ranging nature. The material comes from a variety of sources through a range of media. It can be conceptualised as a broad approach as opposed to a specific example approach, or an in depth approach in a specific instance. The range and depth of the material I investigate offers this defence: while isolated instances in the case studies may not be loyalty, the chance that a significant proportion of the examples discussed in the studies are not loyalty is very slim.

The difficulty of knowing when emotions are occurring and which happens to be the most salient at a specific moment of time is a problem that all emotions researchers face. My approach to knowing loyalty is based upon other's work on similar emotions and emotions theory in general. I will be drawing on a host of sources across a range of time from a mix of media. This approach allows me to argue for a broad understanding of loyalty. However, in an attempt to focus the discussion in each of the case study chapters I will now propose a set of loyalty elements that will guide my theorising. These elements appear to be common across different loyalty instances.

Loyalty Layers: An Individual's Multiple, Competing Loyalties

There are many different possible targets for loyalty in society, spanning the micro—family, friends and local area, to the macro—church, nation, ethnicity. A concept that helps describe these differing targets is the notion of 'loyalty layers'. By loyalty layers I refer to the multiple targets of loyalty that operate on individuals, spanning the micro to the macro levels of social structure. Layering also raises awareness that there are multiple loyalty influences being placed upon the actor.

The concept of layering does not imply a particular hierarchy of loyalties. A focus of this book is how an actor negotiates these layers and consequently how to identify an individual's hierarchy of loyalty. The way a particular layer of loyalty becomes the current dominant layer for the actor occurs through a number of processes, yet these remain under-theorised. I suspect that the current social milieu of the actor helps to determine the layer of loyalty that is most dominant. War, international sports and patriotic festivals are probably likely to elicit a nationalistic layer of loyalty. A threat to the family may foster familial loyalty and an ethnic food festival could reinforce the actor's ethnic loyalty. Layers also interact and overlap, they are not exclusive. The case studies explore loyalty in particular layers and why some actors engage and others do not. This will give some insight into how particular loyalties become the salient loyalty at a specific point in time.

The longevity and intensity of loyalty feelings appears to be a very individualised process. While I propose that social forces have a central role to play in eliciting loyalty, the role of the actor should not be denied. I postulate that an actor's professed loyalty historically would increase the likelihood of exhibiting loyalty in the future.

The socialisation of the actor also appears to be a key component of loyalty. If this is the case then I would expect the case studies to show that some actors are more likely to express loyalty than others, based upon their social milieu. I also expect that loyalty can not be elicited if the actor has not learnt that that particular target can be a focus of loyalty. Further, if society dictates that loyalty must not be shown to certain targets then the actor will have a very difficult time developing a loyalty relationship.

Layering reminds us that the actor is imbedded in multiple sites, structures and relationships, all of which impinge upon his or her actions. Barbalet makes a similar point in relation to emotion and class when he argues that 'emotion inheres simultaneously in individuals and in the social structures and relationships in which individuals are embedded' (1992: 151). Shklar (1993: 186) argues that 'conflicts are common between obligations, commitments, loyalties, fidelities and allegiances. Moreover, each of these has to endure internal conflicts as well. Loyalties clash'. This idea of a conflict between differing loyalties is, as Shklar (1993: 186) points out, a storehouse of literature. That it is such a popular source of conflict for characters only points to its existence in real, everyday interactions.

Leading from the proposal that there inevitably will be conflict between layers, I suspect that there is an inherent loyalty layer management system within social structures. I will investigate the case studies for evidence that indicates how particular social forces/institutions have built into them mechanisms to reduce the likelihood of inter- and intra-layer conflict. This process is present because it is recognised that conflict between layers can be extremely destructive and that it is in the best interests of a loyalty group to maintain that group over-and-above competing layers.

These clashes in loyalty seem to point to loyalty requiring an 'other' to define itself against. The causes to which the individual is loyal must be balanced by alternative causes to which the person could be loyal (Hirschman 1970: 82). It is not necessary that this prospect be a viable one, merely that it is present. The family, like all loyalties, requires an 'other'. Despite the fact that the other, for example, the family across the road, is not really an alternative, it represents a competing target for loyalty. In other words, loyalty needs competition, because one cannot be loyal to a cause if there is no other cause. This helps explain why the layer of national loyalty is stronger than a conceptually broad concept, such as humanity. Without an other it is difficult for the individual to conceptualise such a loyalty.

A source that gives an insight into the hierarchies of loyalty layers are the decisions made by actors under duress. When tortured, the order of betrayal by the actor of their loyalties can give an insight into the hierarchy of layers (a literary example is Orwell's *1984*). Koubi, Israel's former Chief Interrogator for their General Security Services (Bowden, 2003: 14), formed a view on the order of betrayal from his extensive experience with interrogations. Bowden (2003: 14) quotes Koubi as saying that 'the hierarchy of loyalty under stress is 1) self, 2) group, 3) family, 4) friends'. Koubi argued that

[w]ith older men the priorities shift slightly. In middle age the family often overtakes the group (the cause) to become the second most important loyalty. Young men tend to be fiercely committed and ambitious, but older men – even men with deeply held convictions, men admired and emulated by their followers – tend to have loves and obligations that count for more. Age frays idealism, slackens zeal, and cools ferocity. Abstractions lose ground to wife, children and grandchildren. (Bowden, 2003: 15)

While I will side-step the moral and ethical question of using an interrogator's reflections on humanity, Koubi makes two points worthy of exploration in the case studies. His hierarchy needs to be tested with other available evidence. From Koubi's observations it appears that loyalty operates in a relatively set hierarchy, and that people will choose one type of loyalty over another more often than not when required and that the one that is more often chosen may well be the prototypical loyalty. Thus, establishing how people make choices between loyalties under conditions where there is a conflict and whether these choices tend to favour self and the family over other loyalties will indicate a hierarchy.

Koubi (Bowden, 2003) points to a construction of responsibility based on age; that is, the older we get the more important family becomes and the less important other causes. It is difficult to separate this observation from the prevailing social norms of age based behaviour; it seems to be a given that we expect the young to be 'idealistic' and the old to be 'conservative'. When it comes to loyalty, this points to the construction of the emotion. Indeed if it is considered odd that a very old person could be strongly committed to a cause then we have social norms influencing what is considered appropriate age-based loyalties. This points to an age-based construction of loyalties.

To summarise this section, the actor has multiple layers of loyalty, and these layers generally act in a fixed pattern of hierarchies. A layer is by no means a monolithic construct like geological patterns, but a useful heuristic to highlight the differing and often competing loyalties that an actor feels.

Identity and Loyalty

The second aspect of loyalty is that it may help to furnish an actor's identity. That is, our connections to other people and institutions, as mediated by a loyalty relationship, help to constitute our individual and collective identities.

Mills and Gerth offer an insightful view on identity and role of the actor in our social world. They argue (Mills and Gerth, 1964: 80) that the person is

predominantly a creature of interpersonal situations. Indeed, this integration of person with others – that is to say the roles that persons play – is the key to the understanding of the concept: the person is composed of the combination of roles that he enacts.

They go further and posit that 'our total self-image involves our relations to other persons and their appraisals of us' (1964: 80). Thus it is the connection the actor has with others that informs their identity, both to the observer and reflected back to the actor. Our roles in life are informed by a plethora of social activities and postions, from class, gender and ethnicity to hobbies, beliefs and memberships. Role is the pattern of action (and inaction) that an observer expects of the actor. Gerth and Mills (1964: 83) argue that a 'person is composed of an internalisation of organized social roles . . . we have defined role as a conduct pattern of a person which is typically expected by other persons. It is an expected pattern of behaviour'.

One means through which our roles become valuable to us in an identity-furnishing way is when we develop emotional attachment. Loyalty is one of the emotional markers that signals the importance of a particular role. This is because it marks our membership and connection with a role, that role being anything from mother, to football fan, to soldier, indeed, any and all social personas that are taken on. Loyalty signals that the actor is part of that role, and it compels the actor to defend and work within the role. This becomes the expected pattern of behaviour, just as you know an avid Manchester United fan will comment on the team's victory the following day. This is the predictive aspect of roles and how it reflects back upon the actor from the observer.

Mewett (1999: 2) argues that in understanding identity, and, in particular, national identity, it is not the top-down elite driven view, fostered by national leaders and other figures of importance, that is of most value. It is the ordinary person and their view of the nation and nationalism that should be studied in an attempt to understand how this creates identity:

> ... if we are to develop an understanding of the emotive power of national identity, it is necessary to move beyond elites, intellectuals and nationalist mouthpieces and look, instead, at how ordinary people affirm the idea of nationhood. (Mewett, 1999: 2)

This position emphasises that the actor's feelings, beliefs and actions are critical in understanding the construction of their identity. This does not diminish the need to understand the macro-sociological processes at work, such as power and ideology. It highlights the importance of looking at both. Consequently, I use the musings of 'ordinary' people, as Mewett phrases it, to explore whether they play a role in affirming loyalties and test the value of the proposition that we must move beyond a focus on elites and the messages they present.

A further perspective on identity is offered by Jenkins (1996), in his Mead inspired tract. He posits that:

> all human identities are in some sense – usually a stronger rather than a weaker sense – *social* identities ... if only because identity is about meaning, and meaning is not an essential property of words and things. Meanings are always the outcome of agreement or disagreement, always a matter of convention and innovation, always to some extent shared, always to some extent negotiable. (Jenkins: 1996: 4, emphasis in original)

In short, identity is a negotiated understanding of one's place in the world. Jenkins tries to bring the argument between the social identity and the individual identity together by arguing that the '*individually unique* and the *collectively shared* can be understood as similar ... that the processes by which they are produced, reproduced and changed are analogous; and that both are intrinsically social' (1996: 19, emphasis in original). This view is a soft form of social constructionism in that it allows individual negotiation with identity. Jenkins' view has been critiqued by Vogler (2000) as being too reliant on the external social interaction and for not taking into account the individual's internal dimensions. Specifically, Volger (2000: 21) attacks Jenkins for omitting 'the unconscious and emotional dimensions of identity entirely'.

This criticism is not limited to Jenkins' work, but can equally be applied to nearly all discussion of identity within the sociological literature (Volger, 2000; Craib, 1998). Emotion seems to be a curiously neglected aspect of identity formation. For example, affection, care, loyalty, love and pride (to name just a few) help regulate who our friends are and if there was not an emotional attachment, complete with feelings and cognitions, then they would not be friends. Volger (2000) offers a psychoanalytically inspired answer to this curious absence of emotion within identity theory. In short, Volger (2000) building on Craib (1998), argues that identity is emotional, and that this emotionality is part of our social interaction, indeed even central to it. As Volger (2000) points out, the central contention is:

> the psychoanalytic idea that the primary and most basic form of inter-subjectivity between individuals is emotional rather than cognitive as it is in sociology. In psychoanalysis, human beings are seen as being linked to each other by a profound emotional intersubjectivity or emotional communication in which they continually give and receive emotional messages, although this is usually unconscious and not recognised by those involved.

Thus, emotion can be seen as central to identity formation and maintenance within this perspective. Note the similarities between these claims and those of the existentialists and Barbalet on emotion. This view could be characterised as a strong claim for the importance of emotion in forming identity. The view that interaction is key to emotion is borne out by the need to personalise impersonal means of communication such as email and newsgroups/bulletin boards. The increasing use of 'emoticons' [☺ :-p ☹] is evidence of the desire for people to have more 'authentic' emotional interactions with others even when the medium is impersonal and their physical presence completely removed from one another.

The views of Volger and Craib offer a useful base from which to start an exploration of identity and emotion. I would like to postulate a weaker view (one that does not require a psychoanalytic grounding as it does not need unconscious processes and intra and inter psychic conflict). This is the idea that emotional engagement with others in society (others being both other people and social institutions—which are merely construed by people anyway) helps to dictate how we feel about ourselves and the world. Which in turn, provides identity markers (for example, I feel good when Australia wins the cricket and therefore I am probably a cricket fan and Australian).

I am therefore compelled to ask how does emotion helps to construct identity? Thus, in the context of my argument, I will examine instances of identity constituted through emotions—specifically loyalty. The second component is the view that our identities are constructed through social interaction and that one of the key components of these interactions is our emotional experience, before, during and after said interactions. Emotions help mediate the perception of these interactions which goes on to confirm, deny, modify and/or enhance our identity.

Our loyalties furnish identity. Actors construct and are constructed by their emotional experiences, and identity partly arises through this emotional process.

Motivation to Action

The last aspect of loyalty to consider is that the phenomenon motivates action (or inaction). What is of interest to my argument is the question of when loyalty is called on as an explanation or justification for action. If there is a pattern is it consistent across loyalty layers? Does this point to something specific about loyalty as opposed to say love, shame or trust? These questions lead us to a key question within the emotions field—what forces influence actors' actions, thoughts and feelings?

Loyalty provides an indication of what one should do in a particular situation—it guide behaviour. For example, consider the tradition of Catholicism calling upon my loyalty to Christ and his teachings to oppose sex outside marriage. The Church calls on the actor's loyalty to engage in certain behaviours; as part of their identity as a Catholic the actor may consider this call and possibly undertake the action under consideration. If the actor does not, then they could suffer a crisis in faith and identity. Can loyalties make decisions easier? The marketing literature certainly indicates that a 'loyalty' to a product can increase the likelihood of its choice over a competing one. Does this premise hold for more challenging interactions such as: which employee do I feel is most loyal to me and consequently promote? In the case of familial conflict how does an actor choose? These examples give an idea of the sort of dilemmas that I explore in the case studies to show that loyalty helps motivate action.

Another way of conceiving of action and loyalty is to consider if loyalties provide simple schemas of how the world should function. By knowing of my or another's loyalties I can more accurately predict behaviour. Perhaps loyalty provides emotional certainty (faith) about a difficult and uncertain world. It allows the actor to assume behaviour, thought and values on their part and on the part of others (others being people and social institutions). Thus, it is an emotional heuristic device that allows functioning at/on an assumed level. It would be patently impossible to renegotiate social relations each time they are entered into. Consequently, the presence of loyalties allows predictions about the future. One means to explore this proposition is to look at when loyalties are supposedly not returned or acted upon, for example, when the actor perceives a disloyalty. This can be conceptualised as the breaching of an expected loyalty outcome—which if present in the case study material would indicate that actors do use loyalty to predict future actions.

The previous two claims hold true for any emotion. For example, love guides our behaviour and gives us a predictive tool in managing interactions with the social world. The more interesting question sociologically is: does loyalty predispose our actions in particular ways? Or to phrase the question differently: when loyalty is acknowledged as being important in a particular social exchange, are there certain behaviours, thoughts, actions and other feelings elicited? Do these common properties (if indeed the evidence bears it out) hold true across the various layers of loyalty?

I have primarily raised the issue of motivation in this section, but there is another way that emotions, and loyalty in particular, can inform an actor's activities—as post hoc justification. Thus in the case studies I want to also explore and question whether the use of loyalty is as a justification for behaviour after the fact as opposed to motivation for action beforehand. Methodologically this is challenging as the case studies rely on post-event reporting of the events and loyalties—thus inevitably having a taint of justification.

If loyalty does play a role in motivating or justifying an actor's actions, often value judgements are placed upon the behaviour as negative, bad or irrational. However, what I argue for is a far more nuanced understanding; namely that loyalty (and, for that matter, most emotions) can have different positive and negative outcomes depending on what perspective is being taken. It is not the emotion *per se* that is negative but the outcomes as judged. Two lovers completely consumed with each other will not feel any problem with their embrace in the physical and mental sense, but family and friends may see it as a dangerous dependency. This might also apply to loyalty, as a loyalty seems to require an 'other' to be defined against. Hence the actor is inevitably choosing one over another. The idea of breaking down emotions into positive and negative, or immoral and moral is highly problematic and Kristjánsson (2003: 362) argues that 'to put it bluntly, there is no such thing as a *negative emotion*' (emphasis in original). Consequently, I see loyalty as a motivating force, rather than inherently good, bad, moral or immoral.

Is It Just a Behaviour?

Before moving to the case studies there is a remaining issue that I need to discuss; is loyalty merely a behaviour? In other words, is loyalty merely a meta-category of action/response/trust/expected behaviour. Some claim that it is not an emotion in and of itself but a pointer to which emotions should be elicited in a given event; akin to an emotional marker or script. This section examines the argument and offers more evidence that loyalty is more than merely an act. It is necessary to challenge the view of loyalty as a behaviour in order to move into the case studies confident of the plausibility of the contention that loyalty is an emotion.

Building on Durkheim's work, Fisher and Chon (1989: 6), point out that intense group activity is designed to elicit an emotional response from the individuals involved. The individuals themselves can be engaging in a mere behaviour at first, but inevitably in times of intense activity this develops into real emotion. As Fisher and Chon (1989:6) phrase it: 'the function of intense group activity is to create the conditions under which individuals spontaneously experience the emotions that are necessary and constitutive of group life'. In relation to loyalty, the rituals associated with the emotion are created and enacted to manifest genuine emotion in the actor, irrespective of the actor's initial intention. Gerth and Mills (1964: 55) make a similar point when they argue that 'the reactions of others to our gestures may help define what we really come to feel... Moreover, our gestures may elicit or impose feelings which at first were not present'. Gestures for Gerth and Mills (1964: 49) are the observable behaviour and appearance of the actor.

The case studies will highlight this aspect of loyalty repeatedly and across different social contexts, but it is helpful to cite one example here. The ritual of national loyalty illustrates the point. Governments are constantly creating ways and means of inculcating a loyalty response in citizens. We have national holidays, usually celebrating a day of significance for the nation—such as Australia Day or Independence Day and Loyalty Day in the USA. There is the associated flag waving and celebratory aspects to these events as well. While at one level citizens can be seen as engaging in a behaviour during these celebrations, at a deeper level what the ritual is arousing is an emotional response, and in the case of one's country this emotional response can be defined as loyalty. This generates clear manifestations of emotionality on the part of the actor, be it a tear in the eye, cheering one's country on or a sense of pride. In Chapter Six I argue that patriotism is the act of loyalty in specific social contexts, and that loyalty is the underlying emotional state.

Much of our existence as social actors is at the level of habit or behaviour. This is no different for the many and varied loyalties that we possess, nor for all the other emotions that guide us through life. To take the example of love; while it is accepted that we should love our partner always, we do not register the emotional response of love for our partner all the time. The love feelings that we consciously appraise are often only elicited by certain events; anniversaries, attending a romantic wedding, recovering from illness or accident and the like. To return to the psychological terminology; these types of events make our love feelings salient. Thus, it could be said that love can be a habit or behaviour—this is true for much of the time but that does not mean that it is not also an emotion. If we imagine an existence where all emotions were triggered simultaneously this would be a recipe for emotional overload. Consequently we have them simmering away, waiting to be drawn out by internal or external factors.

Another way of illustrating this idea of simmering and salience is to consider the act of supporting a sporting team. Often this occurs at the level of behaviour and habit—you might wear the team jersey, go to the game, you may always pick your team in the office tipping competition regardless of the chance that it may win. In discussion and banter you will back up the team. The majority of these acts will not generate a manifest emotional response, yet the emotional connection, or the sporting loyalty, is always there and ready to be drawn out. An extremely close finish to a game will elicit anxiety, hope and expectation and if the team scrapes through, undoubtedly pride will surface. When there is an external threat to the continued existence of one's club then there will be an emotional response. Loyalty is called upon and anger may well be revealed. As I explore in Chapter Seven, the exclusion of the South Sydney Rugby League Club from the Australasian competition sparked precisely this response from its fans—a massive outpouring of support and loyalty such as the club had not seen in decades (nor since). The threat to the continued existence of this club aroused the passions of all who identified with the club. It required an external threat to its continued existence to summon the fans to action.

Thus, the actions of loyalty can be construed as habit as well as a behaviour, but this does not diminish the fact that it still may be emotion that underlies this habit. There are often acts associated with particular emotions—such as the clenched fist for anger—but that act does not discount the existence of an emotion behind it.

Conclusions

As this is the final of the chapters dealing with issues of theoretical approach, methodology and argument it is appropriate to summarise my case. At the deepest level, I am questioning whether loyalty is an emotion; how it is created, re-enforced and structured through social interactions and relationships; and whether it helps the actor establish and maintain identities and belongings. I am also questioning how it operates across a number of layers of social interaction, from micro to macro processes. Further, I will explore if loyalty is also a component of motivating the actor to (in)action, both before an event and as a *post hoc* justification.

This chapter has also been important in defending my approach to researching loyalty. My use of popular culture sources, in the widest definition of the term, offers a valuable way of 'seeing' loyalty in social relationships across space and time. It is this breadth of material which allows me to generalise beyond limited examples and argue for a universal definition and understanding of loyalty in western, English-speaking societies. This approach is supported by many of the leading theorists within emotions research. I have also questioned the perspective that suggests loyalty is merely a behaviour, rather than an emotion.

The empirical test of my approach to the evidence is in the case studies, and it is to the first, family loyalty, that I now turn.

Chapter Four
Family Loyalty

So much of what is best in us is bound up in our love of family, that it remains the measure of our stability because it measures our sense of loyalty. All other pacts of love or fear derive from it and are modelled upon it.

Haniel Long, American author, 1888–1956

Introduction

The purpose of this chapter is to explore the manifestation of loyalty in the context of the family. I will be using a myriad of sources to illustrate the way loyalty is dealt with in discourses on the family. My definition of the family is wide and includes both the traditional concept of the nuclear family, as well as extended family and intimate relationships.

The initial question to be explored is how loyalty and the family have been theorised in the literature to date and if these approaches fit within the framework for loyalty that I established in the previous chapter.

The first of these case studies is a range of first and third person accounts of events within families that have been partly explained or justified by the use of loyalty. The nature of this evidence is two-fold: first, it illustrates the popular understanding of loyalty; and second, it provides evidence for my arguments around loyalty. The next set of cases is of a somewhat different order, being non-family relationships that are characterised by the actors and observers as being family-like. This discussion will look at crime gangs and small military units.

This exploration of family loyalty will also consider the issue of the base or quintessential emotional expression of loyalty—is family the prime site for loyalty that all other layers of loyalty are built upon? It is to this question that I now turn.

Family Loyalty—A Primordial Relationship?

The family is a vast and well theorised area of sociology, beginning with the founding sociologists. My argument is concerned with only a limited and particular aspect of familial relationships—when loyalty is specifically invoked and spoken of, and, accordingly, what can be drawn from the use of loyalty in this institution in explicating the emotion. Consequently, in this section I will explore a range of arguments that incorporate both the family and the discourse of loyalty. There are only a few theorists who deal explicitly with this combination. This approach serves two purposes. The first is to test if loyalty is an emotion by considering what other thinkers who have dealt with the concepts of family and loyalty claim. The second purpose is to set up questions with which to approach the examples I draw upon in the second half of the chapter.

The definition of family is not only controversial, but extremely problematic in the modern era of blended, separated, divorced, de-facto, same-sex and extended 'families'. For my argument here the legal definitions are not important. What is important is that to be a family there needs to be an emotional bond created through birth, marriage, commitment and their equivalents. Dizard and Gadlin (1990: 6–7) offer a definition of familism, which they define as:

> a reciprocal sense of commitment, sharing cooperation, and intimacy that is taken as defining the bonds between family members. These bonds represent the more or less unconstrained acknowledgement of both material and emotional dependency and obligation. They put legitimate claims on one's own material and emotional resources and put forth a set of 'loving obligations' that entitles members of the family to expect warmth and support from fellow family members.... Familism embraces solicitude, unconditional love, personal loyalty, and willingness to sacrifice for others.

This definition points to a number of loyalty manifestations. Dizard and Gadlin see the family as an entity that can, at times, be relied upon by its members, pointing to a motivation for action. They also point to the reciprocity involved in loyalty, that is the expectation that there is a return on loyalty given. A problem within this definition is that family and familism could well be two separate entities, with family merely being anyone with a blood or legal connection, and familism also being family, but in addition, the members have the shared sense of dependency and obligation as described by Dizard and Gadlin.

In support of the argument that family is a natural, automatic and proto-typical loyalty, that plays out irrespective of the amount of care and connection, Spark (1977: 170) argues that:

> Whether the quality and quantity of the caring has been minimal or maximal, loyalty ties exist and indebtedness occurs. A family member may be caught in a denied or otherwise invisible loyalty bind and so inevitably may find himself in a guilt laden position, which may interfere with his involvement and commitment in his marital and parental relationships.

Spark's contention is that loyalty to family is so primal that regardless of the extent of care received, the family member will still feel the pull of loyalty, a distinct difference to the definition offered by Dizard and Gadlin (1990). This is a strong argument that is worth exploring in the following examples. What confirmation of this contention would point to is that family loyalty is indeed the prototypical loyalty. This does not necessarily point to a biological base to the emotion. It can also point to the strong socialisation process that occurs with the primacy of family, and as a consequence of the dominance of family loyalty, even when there is no sense of shared commitment, cooperation or intimacy, there can still be the effects of loyalty bonds on the actor.

Royce argues that the 'first natural opportunity for loyalty is furnished by family ties' (1908: 220) and that 'family ties, so far as they are natural, are opportunities for loyalty. . . . after all, fidelity and family devotion are amongst the most precious opportunities and instances of loyalty' (221). The construction of the family as a site of nurturing and primary care lends itself to this proposition of Royce. The most relevant point he makes is that the family is a site where loyalty often occurs.

This 'precious opportunity' identified by Royce was a vice to Plato who argued that the family should not be limited to blood-like relation but that the family must include everyone. One's spouse is everyone's spouse and children belong to all. Runkle (1958: 131) points out that Plato worried that 'separate wives and children, it is feared, would transfer their loyalty from public matters to more private matters' and Runkle explains that the 'Athenian philosopher distrusts the family unit as being dangerous to the larger social unit' (131). This fear accords with Koumi's (Bowden, 2003) observations regarding the loyalties' of his interrogation victims (see previous chapter). The Bible and the some church hierarchies take a similar view in that they see marriage, and by implication family, as a threat to the divine calling of worship (Runkle, 1958: 132). Runkle (1958: 132) quotes Corinthians 7:33 as a prime example of this approach. Here the Apostle Paul speaks of how marriage is a distraction from the affairs of the Lord:

I want you to be free from anxieties. The unmarried man is anxious about the affairs of the Lord, how to please the Lord; *33* but the married man is anxious about worldly affairs, how to please his wife,
34 and his interests are divided. And the unmarried woman or girl is anxious about the affairs of the Lord, how to be holy in body and spirit; but the married woman is anxious about worldly affairs, how to please her husband.
35 I say this for your own benefit, not to lay any restraint upon you, but to promote good order and to secure your undivided devotion to the Lord. (RSV, Corinthians 7)

What this concern with family loyalty shows is that it has been historically recognised as a strong influence on people's behaviour (i.e. it guides action). The Apostle Paul points out that loyalties heighten one's concerns about the mortal world, which mean that the actor becomes anxious about such 'mundane' considerations as pleasing the wife. The invoking of the concept of divided loyalties and interests also speaks to the conflicts that loyalty provokes. While Paul might suggest that the Lord comes first, the mere presence of competing loyalties can create conflict. The idea of loyalties creating conflict is a common theme across all layers of loyalty, and, as I theorised in the previous chapter, an essential component of loyalty.

In an attempt to explain why the Church has such a problem with family loyalty, Runkle (1958: 133) argues that 'we owe duties to people in certain relations to ourselves that we do not owe others'. These certain relations are those of kin, which have a particular connection to the actor over and above, for example, a priest's flock. Thus, our local milieu tends to command greater loyalty and connection than larger, more global phenomenon—hence the threat of the immediate familial loyalty over religious loyalty. The prohibition on priestly marriage in the Catholic Church (besides being to maintain church property) is an acknowledgement of this conflict. Boszormenyi-Nagy and Spark (1984: 132) make a similar point regarding the clash of religion and family, arguing that:

> split loyalty commitments were observed as crucial factors in the family lives of men of clergy... God should never have to take second place behind any loyalty to humans. However the wife and the children tend to test the clergymen's comparative loyalties as a husband and father.

This indicates that loyalty can guide some behaviour by indicating social obligations, and this in turn dictates to whom and how we owe or can expect loyalties. Here Boszormenyi-Nagy and Spark point to a conflict between the different layers of loyalty felt by a married clergyman. The motivation for action that loyalty provides may see the clergyman put his family above the service of God, because of this familial loyalty.

The loyalty shown within families has been blamed for backwardness within social organisations. Banfield (1958), commenting on why economic development was stymied in Southern Italy and Sicily, argues that amoral familism can hold back a village's (and by extension a society's) prospects of economic development. According to Banfield (1958: 9–10): 'the inability of the villagers to act together for their common good or, indeed, for any end transcending the immediate, material interests of the nuclear family' results in economic and social backwardness. This loyalty to family over and above all else creates a situation in which people 'maximize the material, short-run advantage of the nuclear family; [and] assume that all others will do likewise' (Banfield, 1958: 83). According to Banfield, this approach is irrational and likely to lead to continued economic disadvantage. However, from an emotion perspective the family members are merely fulfilling their emotional duty within the family. This primacy of family will be explored at length in the following examples. Banfield's theory is a useful reminder of what is beneficial for a family unit, at least in the short or immediate term, can hinder social development more generally.

In a similar vain, Boszormenyi-Nagy and Spark (1984: xiii) argue that family connection

> develops as a result of loyalty commitments which become evident in a prolonged period of living and working together, whether the commitments are recognized or denied. We can terminate any relationship except the one based on parenting; in reality, we cannot select our parents or children.

Thus, again family loyalty is characterised as an underlying loyalty that is difficult to avoid. Boszormenyi-Nagy and Spark (1984: 42) also turn to the hereditary connection as an explanation for this commitment, pointing out that family 'loyalty is characteristically based on biological, hereditary kinship. In-law relationships usually have weaker loyalty impact then ties of consanguinity'. In the context of the family, Boszormenyi-Nagy and Spark (1984: 52) summarise the way they perceive loyalty to function:

The invisible fibers of loyalty consist of consanguinity, maintenance of biological life and family lineage on the one hand and earned merit among members on the other. It is in this sense related to a familial atmosphere of trust, built on reliable availability and proven desserts of the other members.

In this conception loyalty is an implicit connection from the biological given of reproduction and the social given of marriage. It is mediated or tallied through an invisible ledger of earned and called upon 'loyalty'. Loyalty is an extremely powerful motivator in Boszormenyi-Nagy and Spark's (1984: 84) theorising and it is worth quoting them at length as their position deals with aspects of the question I am posing in relation to loyalty, particularly in regards to conflict and motivation for (in)action:

Loyalty to the family's value system constitutes an invisible, yet very important, dynamic regarding the accounting of merit in any individual member. Loyal adherence may balance the scale for many transgressions. The family as a whole tends to incorporate into its ongoing bookkeeping of merit the prejudicial definition of their values at the expense of the scapegoated outsiders. However, a particularly strong reinforcement of familial value myths can occur through the scapegoating of one member of the in-group. Through the shared condemnation of the disloyal member, the rest of the in-group can reinforce their commitment to the shared value system.

The authors assert that loyalty to the family is an assumed emotional connection, that has particular effects in the family context. They use the concepts of 'earned merit' and 'proven dessert' to characterise the role of loyalty. Alternatively, I construe these effects as reason for action, conflict generation and identity formation/maintenance.

Boszormenyi-Nagy and Spark (1984) also argue that loyalty requires an other; indeed the very definition of loyalty to something has to be loyalty against another object. It is the 'loyalty against' that seems to be the critical point in family loyalty; that is, it is the outside threat that drives family connection so strongly. They hint at this dynamic by referring to how the in-family can reinforce its loyalty by excluding the wayward member. Family mythology generates the identity aspects of loyalty, or, in their terminology, the myths of family. This strong claim by Boszormenyi-Nagy and Spark (1984) posits a powerful role to familial relationships. Is it this influential, or merely one of many aspects of an actor's existence and emotional life? This claim also accords with my argument from the previous chapter, namely, does loyalty require an other to be functional?

Importantly, this position of Boszormenyi-Nagy and Spark (1984) does not indicate a biological basis to the emotion of loyalty. The way they use loyalty and family recognises that biological bonds form the building block of family life. In effect, they are postulating that while biology gives you the child, the bonds that may or may not follow are social.

An alternative way of approaching this idea then is to acknowledge the primacy of the parent-child bond in family loyalty. It is here that we can see a 'natural' loyalty. Doherty (1999: 4) comments that historically:

> Parental loyalty to children has been seen most often as a 'covenantal' commitment as opposed to a 'contractual' commitment of quid pro quo. Rich in religious tradition, the idea of covenant conveys irrevocability . . . Parents must always love, and do right by, their children, no matter how they behave. This is as close to a universal moral norm as we have in our world, a norm honoured in every culture and expounded in fields as disparate as evolutionary psychology and theology. Indeed, parental loyalty—the unbreakable, preferential commitment to one's children—is so taken for granted that it is not even included in the Ten Commandments.

This proposition of Doherty—that parental loyalty to a child is the prime loyalty site—is worth investigating further in the examples, if only to question further the taken-for-granted assumptions that underlie it. The investigation can be framed by these questions: does the primacy of family loyalty, especially the parent-child bond, represent the strongest form of loyalty and the prototypical manifestation of the emotion?

If, as Doherty (1999) suggests, family loyalty is the quintessential loyalty, the fear and/or appropriation of the concept by the Catholic Church and Plato discussed earlier becomes more understandable. Loyalty to family poses a threat to other social institutions. Rothstein (2001: 3), drawing heavily on Doherty (1999), argues that:

> [p]art of understanding loyalty issues is realizing that loyalty requires prioritising our commitments to the people in our lives, favouring those we are linked to by nature and nurture. Commitment alone is not enough; without loyalty, the emotional building blocks of family life – feeling loved, nurtured, protected and cherished – have half-lives shorter than some subatomic particles. Loyalty is what allows us to say 'my' child, 'my' parent or 'my' spouse within a thick web of morally laden expectation. It is not just a feeling or sentiment. It is demonstrated in our behaviour and our choices.

Rothstein argues that loyalty provides the central building blocks of family relationships by creating and denoting expectations. I suspect that this set of expectations provides reason and motivation for (in)action. Feeling loved and nurtured falls under the identity-forming and sustaining aspects of loyalty. If it is the core site of the emotion, it will inform all other uses of loyalty across the layers and give a particular insight into the effects of loyalty. This is because one would expect the derivative loyalties to contain aspects of the primary type.

According to the perspectives on loyalty and the family that I have discussed, loyalty in the family appears to be an automatic relationship that occurs even without ties of commitment. The definitions and discussions of loyalty and family also suggest the primacy of this layer of loyalty over other layers, particularly when conflict between loyalties occurs. There is also an undercurrent that familial loyalty is potentially a dysfunctional emotional connection and something that compels the actor into poor choices and actions. This is curious; if family loyalty represents one of the most important emotional connections then why is it sometimes perceived as a vice? I will explore this conjecture of 'dysfunction' in more depth in the examples—my view is that loyalty per se is not 'bad', 'wrong' or 'dysfunctional', although the consequences of acting from loyalty connections may be. Further, given Kristjánsson's (2003) challenging observation that there is no such thing as negative emotions (see previous chapter), it is valuable to test this proposition.

Blood Is Thicker than Water

Family loyalty is often claimed to override all other competing layers of loyalty. This in part explains why nations and religions often extend their call for loyalty to include familial like relationships, the use of 'Fatherland' by the Nazis and 'Motherland' in the USSR during World War Two are prime examples of this (see the next section and the following chapter). Runkle (1958: 134) points out that it is no coincidence that the Catholic Church uses terminology like Father, Brother and Sister. This primacy, however, often results in family loyalty being derided as unhealthy and a vice. Undoubtedly there is a moral and social component that determines appropriate loyalty displays/manifestations and this very determination of appropriateness indicates the social construction of the emotion.

Potts (1999: 4), in his work with abused children, continually confronts family loyalty and finds that:

> [a]bused, neglected, frightened sometimes for their very lives, the children I worked with refused to 'betray' their families by giving me information which, ironically, I needed to help their families. There is something so powerful, so pervasive in being family that it superseded even these children's need for physical safety. Blood really is thicker than water. Deny it, resist it, there is a bond of loyalty to one's family that is difficult, if not impossible, to break. We may feel misunderstood, abused, betrayed, rejected by our families, yet we will remain loyal. Our loyalty can be so binding that we deny any family failings, or our own pain and anger at them.

What Potts shows is that family loyalty has moulded these children so strongly that they behave in a certain way regardless of the cost. This familial loyalty provides these children with an indication of who they are and how they should act. The intervention of the state, even on entirely reasonable grounds, creates a threat to their loyalties and the response is the same one that loyalty under threat often generates—a defensive mentality. This example also points to the negative implications of loyalty, binding family together when, to the observer, they need to be parted. This also supports the contention that loyalty is an emotion as there is passion.

The *Gloucestershire Echo* (2002) reports on a 15 year old girl who was arrested for trying to stop police arresting her sister. The defending solicitor is quoted as saying 'the girl accepted she had tried to put herself as a barrier between police and her sister, because of misguided family loyalty'. Similarly, the *Birmingham Post* (2003: 3) reports that the relatives of a murderer 'may have been acting out of 'misguided family loyalty' when they provided him with an alibi' and the prosecutor in the case commented that '[t]here is nothing, in one sense, like family loyalty, especially when you are faced with endless protestations from someone you want to believe and support'. It is not surprising that the solicitor and the prosecutor have a particular view on loyalty in their respective cases. This case exemplifies the idea that familial loyalty can over-ride other moral responses in certain situations.

The brother of the infamous Unabomber also had to struggle with competing loyalties. Sniffen (1996) reports that 'David Kaczynski was torn between duty to country and loyalty to family before he pointed investigators toward his older brother'. An investigating FBI agent is quoted as commenting that '[h]e was torn, as anyone would be, between doing what is societally right and loyalty to his brother' (Sniffen, 1996). In the end he made the decision to turn his brother in, as the moral necessity of preventing further deaths over-rode the brotherly loyalty. The effects of his loyalty were to create internal conflict for him.

These examples could be construed as merely invoking loyalty as a justification for morally reprehensible behaviour. However, the labelling of the actions as motivated by loyalty indicates that the observers see that sort of loyalty behaviour as justified and within the broad expectation of what loyalty is. Further, this shows the strength of loyalty in familial relationships, and the conflict that can ensue from acting out loyalty.

One outcome of loyalty conflicts in families can be the total exclusion of the wrong-doer. O'Dell (1998: 14) reports on the experience of Maria Hines who has 'struggled with the conflict between her opposition to the death penalty and loyalty to her grieving family, all capital punishment supporters'. Hines lost her brother, a State trooper, when he was shot during a traffic stop, but had since befriended the killer and forgiven him. In the process however she lost her family. O'Dell (1998: 14) quotes her nephew and the son of the trooper as saying: 'She's come to know and love Dennis Eaton [the killer] more than she ever did her brother, or us . . . We don't consider her part of the family'. In another example, the brother of a serial rapist who turned him into police has been ostracised by his family. One letter to the editor argued that the brother 'put his duty to the public, and women in particular, above that of family loyalty, and I hope his family and friends will see where his duty lay and welcome him back' (Arkinstall, 1999: 23).

The most obvious effect of loyalty in these last two cases is the creation of conflict within families. The families involved feel aggrieved at the disloyal behaviour of one member and respond with exclusion. To the families in these cases it is clear that first loyalties should be to the family, supporting the primacy of family loyalty contention (and is an example of the in-group scapegoating that Boszormenyi-Nagy and Spark (1984) note). However, the families had members which did not believe this and in the case of Hines, her beliefs about crime and punishment were more important, and, in the second case, duty to society overrode family loyalty. These examples add further support to the claim that loyalty has layers and it is the social, moral, political and economic forces that draw out each particular layer. There is also an identity and membership aspect to these examples as the families themselves are re-affirming their loyalty to each other and their place within the family by excluding the rogue member. They have the 'other' to define against, as noted by Boszormenyi-Nagy and Spark (1984). There is also motivation and explanation for action in these examples—the families respond with particular behaviours as a consequence of the perceived shift in loyalties. The 'disloyal' member is also motivated by differing feelings and thoughts, or perhaps another loyalty layer.

Other family forms, such as step and foster families offer another rich site of loyalty conflict, and thus possible theoretical exposition. The following examples explore the conflict within these family structures. Doherty's (1999: 2–3) view on stepfamilies is that they 'enact unique morality plays, with plots involving divided loyalties, betrayal, heroic commitment, and Solomon-like discernment'. The key dilemma is the addition of a competing loyalty target in the guise of a step-parent for the children, or step-children for the new spouse. This results in a myriad of conflicts, as Doherty (1999: 4) remarks: 'loyalty struggles abound in stepfamilies because of the unbalanced triangles their members encounter'. In conventional families the loyalty obligations are relatively balanced. There is no love competition because as Doherty (1999: 4) puts it: '[I]f you are my spouse and caring for our children, you are indirectly caring for me'. Conversely, with multiple 'families' the scope for conflict increases and, as Spark (1977: 169) points out, the 'loyalty ties are even more confused and are far more complicated than it might have been in the first or second marriage'. This creates a range of competing targets for loyalty.

A key issue is that the actor can feel torn between the families, feeling like they are betraying one side by being with the other. Doherty (1999: 4–5) recounts the case of a six year old girl in therapy who said, 'in a whisper', that she did something she felt bad about after visiting each of her families. She 'said she always said something 'a little mean' about what happened in the other family, often something the stepparent did or said. Sometimes, she confessed, she kind of made things up' (Doherty, 1999: 4–5). This child is trying to manage the competing claims on her loyalty by demonstrating her commitment to whichever family she was with. This is an indication of the internal conflict that can occur with competing loyalty targets.

Leathers (2003) explored the connection between emotional and behavioural disturbances in foster children as a function of how strong their loyalty bonds were to their biological and foster parents. Leathers (2003: 62) found that after controlling for extraneous variables, loyalty conflict experienced by the foster children was significantly associated with anxiety and defiant behaviour. Thus, when the foster children were identified as experiencing a loyalty conflict, their behaviour and anxiety levels were worse than foster children not experiencing the conflict. Leathers (2003: 63) also found that children who 'were reported to have strong relationships with both [biological and foster parents] were more likely to experience greater loyalty conflict'. A stronger loyalty attachment also predicted greater emotional and behavioural problems. Leathers (2003: 63) points out that 'loyalty conflict is an important indicator of adjustment problems'. This suggests that the children involved are often caught in the bind of family loyalties that prescribe a commitment to family. These children exhibit behavioural problems because they are breaching the social norm of family loyalty, which, as the examples to date indicate, is a singular commitment. This conflict between loyalties leads to the behavioural problems Leathers identified. This provides good evidence for my argument that loyalty not only can create conflict, but that it creates this conflict partly out of the way it helps to furnish identity and belonging. While Leathers (2003) does not explore questions of identity and belonging with the children, on the basis of the evidence, these foster children often experience an identity crisis, lacking the fixed identity that membership of one family often gives. Consequently the foster children do not know how they are meant to behave due to the conflicted loyalty ties they possess, and exhibit the behavioural disturbances Leathers reports. This is similar to Doherty's (1999) account of the conflict a step child felt between her two families.

Family loyalty also has an intergenerational component. Spark (1977: 167) argues in the context of family therapy that to 'concentrate only on the needs of each spouse would be to ignore the primary loyalty ties, indebtedness and obligations that exist with each one's family of origin'. Thus the loyalty to parent can conflict with the loyalty within the marriage. This can impact on action and identity formation. The identity transition from son/daughter to wife/husband/spouse is the key shift in this case. Spark (1977: 168) points out that 'leaving one's parents even for marriage, can cause undue distress. Facing these feelings and concurrently changing one's behaviour to shift the primary loyalty ties to the new spouse is a demanding task'. Because loyalty has an identity forming aspect, when primary loyalty ties change, as in the case of marriage, the actor can experience tension. Further, while before marriage the loyalty ties and obligations are clearer, with another layer of loyalty added conflict can become more likely. This creates the possibility of conflict over identity—is the actor a son or husband first?

The Sena family offers more evidence supporting the influence that loyalty can have on identity and motivation. The Senas, consisting of parents, four children and eight grand-children is reported as being 'proud that loyalty bonds the family together' (Baca, 1996: A–01), Baca comments that the 'Sena family may disagree, but it hasn't broken down. Like all families, they have their differences. Don and David [sons] may criticize each other, but loyalty transcends their conflicts'. Teresa, a daughter notes

loyalty to the family, loyalty to each other, and loyalty to their parents. 'Loyalty is the unconditional acceptance of each other,' she said with a warm smile. 'It's about loving each other without judgement'. (Baca, 1996: A–01)

This family characterises loyalty as the emotional glue and belonging that keeps them together. Being part of the family is intrinsic to who they are and how they act, and despite conflict they still feel a deep attachment to each other.

When people were asked by a reporter if they think their friends or family are more loyal they gave these types of responses (The San Francisco Chronicle, 1992: A19):

Family is more trusting, because there's a bond there. They're your own flesh and blood, so I don't think they would do anything to hurt you. It's a different type of bond than you have with friends.

Family, definitely, unless it's real dysfunctional. A good friend, a true friend, is hard to come by.

Probably family, I've had friends who have kind of fallen off, but I have family members who would jump for me even though I haven't seen them for a while. If I was done and dirty, there wouldn't be any questions asked by family.

Family. It's hard to establish that same kind of relationship with friends. Friends' loyalty can change radically, given unfortunate circumstances, whereas there is always a family connection.

Usually family. They go through the rough times and the undesirable times with you. Friends, a lot of times, are there for the good times only.

The story of loyalty that these vignettes construct is that family can be relied upon to maintain their loyalty. These respondents indicate that there is something special about the family relationship. It has been constructed to be the quintessential unbreakable form of loyalty, the layer that others build upon. This seems to be because the respondents assume that it is an automatic, assumed connection. Merely saying 'it's family' is enough to invoke the notion of reason for action and a clear belonging and identity. These comments also point to the layered aspects of loyalty and place a distinction between family and friends.

Hoggard, a *Guardian* newspaper columnist, argues that women seek loyal men as partners not just because of the faithfulness loyalty implies but also because 'loyalty is damn sexy. . . . Part of the erotic power of a loyal man derives from his steadfastness' (2003: 2–3). While Hoggard is taking a humourous approach to the issue of loyalty, she does touch on a key component of the emotion: this idea of steadfastness, or, in other words, belonging and commitment. This supports the family loyalty examples discussed so far, particularly in regards to making a commitment. This reliability, to use yet another synonym for loyalty, implies commitment to the family. The decision by the columnist to use loyalty in this particular way, to denote a steadfast relationship that as a consequence is 'sexy', points to the popular conception of loyalty in the family that all the selected comments/cases speak of. This type of commentary offers further evidence of the role popular media plays in the transmission and continuance of loyalty as a particular social relationship (which I discuss at length in Chapter Seven).

Financial planners often lament the influence that loyalty has on their clients' financial decisions, because of the social obligations that flow from the relationship. Rothstein, in the *Journal of Financial Planning* (2001: 1) complains that when '"Clients" decisions or actions are not making sense, many times family loyalty is responsible. Loyalty issues befuddle many of us in the helping professions'. He then argues that financial planners should ask their client to codify the loyalty relationships at work and points out that planners 'need to understand the emotional ledger in every client's history' (Rothstein, 2001: 4). What this demonstrates is that loyalty influences decision making, even when it is meant to be a rational, calculating choice (as is the supposed ideal in financial planning). Family loyalty can affect the way clients choose to manage their finances and distribute their wills (Rothstein, 2001: 1). This is the micro version of Banfield's (1958) amoral familialism. This phenomenon gives more weight to the contention that family loyalty guides behaviours, which at least to the observer, can often be in strange and irrational ways.

Another area where blood ties are prevalent is in the experience of migration. The introduction of new kinship systems in another country can also highlight the importance of family loyalty. Immigrant groups often maintain strong family ties as a bulwark against the majority view, creating the potential for discrimination and a lack of acceptance. However this in itself can lead to familial conflict, as Woelz-Stirling, Manderson, Kelaher and Benedicto (2001) argue in relation to Filipino women growing up in Australia:

kinship systems and sense of family are sustained with immigration. . . . This has advantages for new settlers, insofar as kinship provides new arrivals with a sense of identity, support and loyalty, and a place of refuge when encountering social discrimination. But at the same time, young people are expected to be loyal to, respect and obey all blood and affinal relatives-all persons older than them and related through their parents or through marriage.

This family network offers the supports of loyalty but also points to the conflict that this loyalty can create. The family loyalty ties may be at odds with prevailing/dominant cultural norms which can create conflict between staying 'true' to the family or accepting new ways of interacting. There are also layered loyalties at work in these instances, often exemplified by the clash of 'homeland' values with new cultural values. I discuss the issue of migrant loyalty at length in the following chapter and draw out a host of examples dealing with the conflict in loyalty that a migrant often faces can create. However, it is worth introducing the idea here because of the role familial loyalty plays for the migrant experience.

The evidence presented thus far indicates that conflict can be generated over the actor's loyalties. Family loyalty does appear to be conceived of as an underlying loyalty or the most compelling loyalty. Loyalty mediated through family relationships also appears to have an influence on the identity of the actor. These conclusions are very tentative at this stage and I will wait until I have explored more of the case studies to ascertain the veracity of these propositions further.

Family-Like Loyalty

Crime gangs and military units, would, at first glance appear to have little in common. Significantly for this study they do have a common theme of loyalty. The loyalty within gangs and the military has some striking similarities to 'traditional' family loyalty. In this section I will use a number of case studies and examples to explicate the use of loyalty in these relationships and how and why it mirrors family loyalty. Like religious orders, these sites of loyalty also invoke family nomenclature in the discourses of membership and this aspect is an important one that I will explore in the following examples as it may demonstrate that family is indeed the primary loyalty. I will also use these examples to show that management of inter- and intra-layer conflict takes place. Further, these case studies will allow me to further explore if loyalty is an emotion.

Examining family loyalty that *isn't* family offers a number of excellent ways of exploring the emotion. The first issue is why and how is the family nomenclature invoked and whether it matches the use of loyalty in the preceding examples. Are the social relationships identified in the examples by the use of loyalty akin to all of the other relationships that have the 'loyal' tag? If the use of loyalty in these examples is similar, and if I can draw out sufficient examples of emotionality (i.e., loyalty as an emotion fitting within the definition of emotion and loyalty that I offered in the previous chapters), it points strongly to the contention that family relationships are the emotional base of loyalty with which all other layers of loyalty are based upon. The null hypothesis is that the use of loyalty within these social interactions is merely lazy/inaccurate use of language, and not meant to denote an emotional connection.

As I noted previously, nation states are another entity that are often referred to using family nomenclature. While I will explore nation loyalty at length in the following chapter, I want to flag here the theoretical underpinnings of the use of family terms as this applies to the following discussion and the next chapter. Vogler (2000: 30) argues that:

> the reason why nation states are seldom referred to as 'it' but are revered and personified as primal authority figures such as mother or father is not only cultural but also because of the close connection between national identities and processes of splitting and projection characteristic of early infancy.

Vogler's psychoanalytical approach points to the formation of basic understandings of attachment in early infancy, and these attachments then form the basis of the myriad of social connections that we develop throughout life. Thus, in Volger's view, nations, gangs and military units then take the language and feelings of the early emotional attachments and apply it to the new ones. Thus one is taking a primordial, basic and early feeling (or passion) and connecting this with later emotional bonds by giving them the same significance through the use of familial terminology. This perspective offers an explanation for the use of familial terminology that is worth exploring in the examples remaining in this chapter, and in dealing with national loyalty in the next chapter.

The use of familial honorifics also shows the primacy of family loyalty and then subsequently the value placed on the relationship that receives the honorific. For example, Dizard and Gadlin (1990: 225–6) note that:

> when especially close ties develop with non-family members, it is not uncommon to assign family titles or use familial references to acknowledge the closeness. Thus, we describe a very close friend as being like a brother or a sister. And we will extend emotional or financial support to such fictive kin, in much the same way we would to blood relatives. Similarly, children are often taught to refer to significant friends of their parents as aunt or uncle, simultaneously acknowledging both the respect due to elders and the intimacy that goes along with family.

These honorific titles provide an emotional short-hand to explain the complex historical, emotional and relational connections that result in a non-family member being elevated to family status. It labels the relationship as having loyalty ties and connections. It is a clear signifier of an emotional bond.

Gang Loyalty – A 'Brotherhood'

Gangs often use the rhetoric of loyalty to explain their commitment to each other and the 'creed', likening the gang to family. Donaldson (1995a: A21) argues that to understand a gang feud in Utah that led to a number of deaths,

> one must understand the unwritten code of ethics that gangsters adhere to as religiously as main-stream society adheres to its laws. Their credo demands loyalty and revenge from its young members, most of whom seek acceptance and respect in return. A 'snitch' and a traitor are the worst things one can be. Dying or killing for the cause, even if gangsters themselves can't articulate what that is, earns the most respect.

Another gang member, according to Donaldson (1996: B1):

> was drawn to gangs because there is a closeness and a loyalty among members. It was those people, he said, who offered to help him when he was down, offered to help him with family problems, and stuck by him when he got caught doing something everyone else saw as horrible. It is that loyalty, which many young people are willing to die for.

These comments point to the how loyalty is a connective force that helps to create expectations about future action for the actor. Further, they provide more evidence of the role loyalty can play in identity formation and belonging. Katz and Jackson-Jacobs (2004: 98, 115), in an academic exploration of gangs, point out that testing loyalty and membership is an important symbolic act designed to maintain gang mythology.

One member of a different gang, who sees his gang as his family, refused to testify against another member in a murder trial (Powell, 1996: 1). Powell (1996: 1) quotes the gang member as saying that 'loyalty was a major reason he refused to testify in the trial'. This gang member explains his connection to the gang thus: 'A while ago I got kicked out of my house, and the gang was the only people who were there for me . . . They took care of me, gave me a place, helped me get food, all that stuff. So I have a lot of love. I have no regrets for being what I am' (Powell, 1996: 1). Another gang member in jail for shooting a man commented that his gang is 'my family and I love them' (Donaldson, 1995b: A22). Donaldson (1995b: A22) argues that the gang 'loyalty runs so deep it pushes gangsters to not only fight for each other, to steal for each other and to lie for each other, but sometimes to kill for each other'. This is very similar to the examples of traditional family loyalty in the previous section. Here we have gang members behaving in the fully committed ways of some families—you are loyal or disloyal. These examples also point to how the loyalty relationships within gangs dictate actions, such as lying for other gang members in order to protect them. This is similar to the examples of family members who lie to protect each other, as the previous section discussed.

Asian triad gangs have a similar approach to the western gangs discussed above. Basham (1996: 12) argues that 'loyalty or death' characterise triads and that this brotherhood mentality makes them:

far more dangerous – and more difficult to prosecute – than most criminals . . . Triads are 'autocephalous' sworn brotherhoods; that is, they are 'self-headed' or autonomous cells composed of initiates who have sworn loyalty to the death to their particular group and its principles. The cell-like nature of individual Triads, and their tendency to recruit members from the same speech group and locality, and through ties of kinship and long-term acquaintanceship, make them extremely difficult for outsiders to penetrate.

Of interest in this characterisation of gangs is the use of already-in-place loyalty to kinship groups, speech groups and locality as a basis from which to form a stronger gang loyalty. It indicates that layers of loyalty can be used to enhance a particular loyalty. This is done by recruiting people of the same ethnicity, speech group and or locality. The multiple layers that the actor then shares with the gang helps to re-enforce the gang membership and loyalty. It is probably easier to create this sort of mentality when there are already strong ties (speech, ethnicity etc) in existence. It is also noteworthy that gangs use the rhetoric of familism such as 'brother' to denote this close tie. The use of familial terms points to the way loyalty conflicts are managed within gangs. By reducing the threat of 'real' family loyalty, the gang layer of loyalty becomes the strongest.

This section has offered further support for the proposition that family is considered the primary loyalty. It also supports the contention that family loyalty is meant to be a whole-of-being commitment. Loyalty is also contributing to identity formation and reason for action for these gang members. Such members explicitly acknowledge how their gang identity and loyalty intertwine and provide them with a way of viewing, and acting in, the world.

A Soldier's Loyalty

The military is a site where loyalty is strongly invoked and re-enforced. While I will deal with some aspects of military loyalty in the following chapter on the nation state, this section deals with small unit cohesion. It is a truism that small groups of soldiers fight for each other first, and higher ideals second. But, as the following discussion shows, it is through the rhetoric of familial loyalty that this bond develops, or, to borrow from Ambrose (1992) the bond of brotherhood. Winslow (1998: 345) phrases it thus: '[i]n particular, strong interpersonal relationships and small unit cohesion are seen to be necessary aspects of land warfare. Loyalty is encouraged at all levels as military values and structures grant primacy to collective goals'. This inculcation of loyalty happens in all armed forces at all levels. For example, a former Australian Governor-General (Hollingworth, 2003: 1) made these comments at the passing-out parade of new recruits for the Army claiming that:

Qualities such as courage, confidence, mateship and teamwork; loyalty, integrity, mental and physical toughness, self-discipline and the will to see the task through to the end. These are qualities that were evident in the original Anzacs, and which generations of other Australian soldiers have displayed.

Goffman (1991: 372) identifies this phenomenon of unit cohesion and loyalty through his concept of the total institution:

[t]otal institutions are also incompatible with another crucial element of our society, the family. Family life is sometime contrasted with solitary living, but in fact the more pertinent contrast is with batch living, for those who eat and sleep at work, with a group of fellow workers, can hardly sustain a meaningful domestic existence.

Thus the soldier's bonds to the family that they have grown up within weaken and the soldier becomes part of a new family—the unit. This inevitably leads to a forging of new loyalty bonds. The reason for the military to inculcate loyalty as strongly as possible is to make that layer the most salient for the serviceperson—to filter out competing targets. Fukuyama (2004: 87-8) makes a very similar point when he writes of the organisational culture of military units and the problem of motivating soldiers to risk their lives:

Military organizations solve this problem not by increasing individual incentives but by replacing individual identities with group identities and reinforcing group identities through tradition, ceremony, and group experiences that are meant to bond soldiers emotionally . . . The strongest bonds are not to large organizations or abstract causes like the nation; rather they are to the immediate group of soldiers in one's platoon or squad, before whom one would be ashamed to be a coward.

This small unit cohesion is not without its risks. Fukuyama (2004: 89) argues that 'group identities and loyalties tend to crowd out consideration of other interests, including the interests of the organization to which a group is nominally subordinate' and further, that 'people see loyalty to groups and group values as a good thing in their own right and are loathe to abandon them when they prove dysfunctional'. While Fukuyama is speaking of groups in general, the military offers an excellent example of this overriding of super-ordinate goals and loyalties when a small group becomes the dominant layer of loyalty. The following examples deal with documented cases of unit loyalty overriding all other layers.

The strength of unit cohesion, while essential in combat, is often characterised as problematic. Winslow, writing about the Canadian Army in peace-keeping operations, (1998: 246) argues that 'exaggerated loyalty to the primary group can lead members to work at counter purposes to the overall goals of a mission or even of the Army' and the primacy of this layer 'of fierce group loyalty, w[as] counter-productive in these peace operations'. Brotz and Wilson (1946: 374, cited in Winslow 1998: 353) argued that unit bonding was so strong that 'covering up for, defence of and devotion to one's buddy was expected'. Winslow (1998: 353) reports that one of her subjects, a Canadian soldier, stated that:

We're so connected physically and mentally, that if there's one person that we admire . . . the others will group around him. If he incites his group to racist behaviour, they'll follow, even if they don't agree, because the group's all you've got. If you're in battle, no one else is looking out for you. You can't count on your family.

This points strongly to the contention that loyalty is essential to the small military unit in the sense that it is like family, and therefore, they are the only ones that can be relied upon for assistance if the need arises. An emotional belonging is being created.

An Australian SAS (Special Air Service) member was convicted of plotting to help kill a fellow soldier's unborn child, and in his defence his lawyer commented that their 'training placed an emphasis on loyalty that was essential to a soldier's survival and desensitised him to aggression and violence' (Banks, 2004: 1). This is similar to the role and power of the family already discussed in this chapter and is very similar to other incidents of loyalty inspired behaviour (such as in the examples connected with illegal behaviour). The actions of the individual are being justified by reference to loyalty bonds. This case further shows how military training is designed to suppress other loyalty layers, indicating that layers can be purposefully managed to reduce the likelihood of conflict. Further support is also offered for my hypotheses that loyalty bonds consist of shared identity and motivation for (in)action. These forces often influence the soldiers' behaviours.

The military, like gangs and many religious organisations, also uses the nomenclature of the family. According to Winslow (1998: 357), in the Canadian Army the 'Regiment is often referred to as a "family" and the family nature of the system is underscored by nicknames such as "old man" for the CO and "auntie" for the second in command'. A Canadian Army manual states:

The soldier must want his Regiment, his comrades and those around him to survive. The Regiment is his family, where he is not alone . . . He fights for something more than himself; he fights for his comrades and the Regiment; and indirectly, for his home and his family. (Winslow 1998: 357)

Even though this is the 'official' rhetoric of the military (and thus a claim of what is real, as opposed to evidence of it in operation) there is further evidence that supports the contention that this is how many soldiers feel. Another Canadian soldier is quoted by Winslow (1998: 32) as saying:

Guys 'il (sic) stick together. They won't rat on anybody. But the other commandoes are like that too. What goes on inside, stays inside. You have to belong. If you don't, well it's just too bad. It's your family. You have to live with them.

And another commented thus:

The pressure is so strong that beyond the group, right or wrong lose their meaning. Only the group matters.

This intense loyalty to the group is not confined to these units, but to a pervasive trend in most military units. Rule (1996) reports on an exchange that occurred at a funeral service for the Australian SAS (Special Air Service) after two helicopters had crashed killing 18 servicemen. Two members of the Regiment from 25 years ago were at the service and had been thanked for coming. One said 'We had to, sir. Had to. The family's well spread, but we care for each other' (Rule, 1996: 2). Rule (1996: 3) reports that 'little is known about the SAS [because] fierce loyalty fostered in the service extends to keeping the silence years after soldiers leave it'. Thus the bonds of being a member of the unit and feeling those loyalties can extend beyond the immediate existence of the unit. These 'old soldiers' still feel the tug of loyalties and behave accordingly.

These reports indicate the importance of loyalty to the soldiers involved and that they relate to the unit as a family. The identity-forming aspects of this connection appear strong, as is the motivation for action. The soldiers are encouraged to behave in certain ways because of their loyalties—whether this be through not reporting contrary conduct or by attending funerals 25 years after leaving the service. These examples indicate that loyalty helps to denote the complex web of social forces that impinge upon a soldier. The examples I cite are cases where the protagonists justify behaviour with reference to loyalty to their mates and/or unit. Like all complex social systems this is not always the case; there are examples where loyalty has no bearing on behaviour in the military. I offer this caveat then—loyalty can sometimes have a profound impact upon an actor, but not always.

Family the Quintessential Loyalty?

The significant point regarding family loyalty that the pseudo-family examples of gangs and military units raises is the use of family loyalty as an ideal type or quintessential loyalty. Each of these use familial terminology or stipulates that the relationship is one of family. This suggests the primacy of the family in the construction of loyalty. In terms of my argument regarding the elements of loyalty, these sites offer evidence that the emotion contributes to identity formation, reason for action and conflict generation. The case studies of this chapter hint at the power of loyalty to motivate people, especially in conflict situations. The strength or power of this motivation appears to be substantial, but ascertaining a formula for the influence is beyond the current state of emotions literature. As I discussed in Chapters Two and Three, measuring a single emotion and its strength is exceedingly difficult as we rarely have just one emotional influence acting upon us. Thus, identifying that loyalty does play a role and the mechanisms through which it is created and invoked, as well as defining how it manifests, is a significant contribution to the emotions literature.

When loyalty and family are theorised together a particular perspective emerged; that family loyalty was a primordial or quintessential loyalty—as Long's opening quote indicates. This contention has been moderately supported by the case studies. Often the actors would talk of the importance of the family and how that bond (or layer in my terminology) is the most important. The use of family nomenclature to denote relationships in non-familial contexts provides good supporting evidence. This idea of family loyalty being the prime site is hardly surprising given family units are an initial site of socialisation. However, family bonds do not provide a solid, unbreakable connection. Some of the examples point to how even familial loyalty can be lost, subsumed under another layer or changed. These occurrences did offer more support for my argument that loyalty can lead to or justify conflict. This conclusion informs the remaining sites or layers of loyalty that I explore in the following chapters. If this contention is to be further supported then the construction of loyalty outside of the family should be similar to the way loyalty is within the family. This is a question I will return to over the course of the following chapters.

Loyalty provides reasons for action, the examples have shown that loyalty is invoked as a justification for behaviour, and at times an excuse. This use of loyalty as an excuse leads to another conclusion—that family loyalty is potentially dysfunctional. The evidence I explore does support the proposition that loyalties can be a negative influence on the actor. However, it is the misguided (at least in other's opinions) use of loyalty bonds that is the negative aspect, not, it seems, the loyalty itself. Thus, if loyalty makes it difficult for the actor to inform on their criminal sibling, it is the fact that it is hard, not the existence of a family loyalty, that is at fault. This is an important and fine distinction that returns my argument to the proposition that emotion cannot be inherently negative or positive in and of itself. It is the activity that is associated with the emotion that provides a value judgement.

An actor's identity appears to be influenced by their loyalties, and familial and pseudo-familial loyalties play a role. Actors defined who they were by reference to their kin connections as mediated through loyalty. The way that the actors spoke of their loyalties also indicates that loyalty is an emotion. The examples had similarities to love and hate in the way the relationship was construed and reported. There was also an indication of the irrationality of loyalty at times (though emotion as irrational is highly problematic) which is another marker of emotions in western discourse.

This chapter has also begun to accumulate evidence that loyalty denotes certain social relationships, and that within these relationships are issues of identity, belonging, action and conflict. There is also emerging evidence of the social construction of the emotion, as shown by the differing sites of loyalty discussed in this chapter, such as in gangs and the military.

Loyalty in the family, gangs and in small military units represents a micro site of emotional feeling and expression. In establishing that the emotion of loyalty operates across a range of layers it is essential to show that the same feeling and expression is present in other social relationships and interactions. Consequently I will now move to a much wider site of loyalty, the nation state, and the implications for the actor of having a loyalty bond to a state.

Chapter Five
National Loyalty

A man's country is not a certain area of land, of mountains, rivers, and woods, but it is a principle; and patriotism is loyalty to that principle.

George William Curtis

Introduction

The loyalties a nation's citizens express are critical in understanding the identity of the country and its people. This loyalty can form part of the emotional existence of the actor, whose well-being can be closely tied to the fortunes of the nation. When politicians, media commentators, generals and sports teams call on national loyalty, what are they actually attempting to invoke? Is this layer of loyalty different from our loyalty to family?

In this chapter I explore the way loyalty is used and invoked in the context of the nation state. I have chosen to limit this chapter to three areas; the debates regarding conscription in Australia during the World Wars and Vietnam, the experience of migrants living in Australia negotiating their 'dual' loyalties and a brief exploration of how loyalty was used during the McCarthy period in the USA. I have limited myself to these three themes as they serve to illustrate quite different areas of nation-based loyalties. I am not attempting to review or critique the wealth of literature on nation states or migration, a task well beyond this book. I am analysing the role of loyalty within the emotional interactions that occur, something that is lacking within both literatures.

The case studies in this chapter also serve to illustrate historical constructions of loyalty, especially with regard to the conscription and McCarthy era debates. What this allows me to look for is the way emotion has motivated, or justified, social movements and action historically. Thus, I can explore how loyalty, as an emotional state, mobilises collective action. This endeavour has been called for by Barbalet (1998: 28) who comments that:

what remains under-represented in the field as a whole, though, is the significance of emotion in large-scale or macroscopic social processes, and the role of emotion in not simply social interactions of a face-to-face nature between individuals, but in the mobilizations of collective social actors in historic contexts.

The case studies of this chapter will show how loyalty has inspired collectives of actors to think, behave and emote in certain ways that accord with loyalty interactions at other layers of operation. This chapter also illustrates how loyalty can adhere, as Barbalet (1992: 151) suggests, simultaneously within an actor and the social structures of a society.

The second area that I explore in this chapter, that of migrant experience, will show how the concept of national loyalties can serve to exclude those who are born outside that country. I will be exploring how this exclusion occurs and its possible effects on the actor. I contend that some actors are excluded from the emotional succour of national loyalty because of the way loyalty is constructed and manifested. This can have a profound impact on the individual actor.

Lastly I deal with the McCarthy period in the USA. This exploration serves to highlight how loyalty can be ritualised through oaths—further indicating the passionate qualities of loyalty. Second, I show how important the acknowledgment of loyalty is for the actor by analysing the case of a McCarthy victim who eventually cleared her name. A motivation of her case was to secure her own loyalty position within the nation-state and all that that connection offers the actor. It is to the importance of national loyalty generally that I first turn.

A Loyal Nation?

National loyalty is the connection that one feels towards a particular nation. Generally it is to the nation of one's birth and one's allegiance is assumed, as merely being born in a country is *usually* enough to make one part of the nation. This loyalty is an emotional relationship that functions from the individual to the collective and vice versa. National loyalty fosters a sense of identity and belonging for the actor, helping to define who and what a person is. Conversely, national loyalty is expressed by the actions and behaviours of the people who make up the nation. There would be no nationalism but for the individuals and groups that engage in activities to support and encourage a sense of national identity.

National loyalties are particularly strong because of their close relationship to the social milieu of the nation (Grodzins, 1956: 24). Common language, geography, history, traditions, suffering and sorrow all combine to further the cause of national loyalty. There are remembrances and celebrations, such as ANZAC Day in Australia and Loyalty Day in the USA, which give individuals a sense of their country's history and character. Sporting events also play a significant role. The Sydney Olympics, for example, was one of the most nationalistic events that has occurred in Australia.

War, diplomacy and trade all reinforce the notion of nationality and the desire, requirement and need for loyalty. As Grodzins (1956: 20) argues: 'The whole social structure tends to promote the relationship, binding human satisfaction to national welfare'. This human satisfaction is an integral component of loyalty, as the individual and the nation strive for a mutually supportive relationship that can enhance each other. These factors are mediated by social institutions and, as Grodzins (1956: 20) states: 'national loyalty is built strong as the result of the active role taken by social institutions in building a firm, direct tie between individual and nation'. The institution of government is central to this process through its control of law, education, and the military. Grodzins' claim is a strong one that will be tested in the following case studies. These social structures play an integral role in the promulgation and maintenance of loyalty.

Loyalty differs from patriotism in several specific ways. Loyalty is an emotion, where as patriotism is an act, or, to put it into social psychological terms, we have a behaviour and an affect. Patriotism is the manifestation of loyalty, such as wearing the flag and singing the anthem. This separation will be examined and demonstrated in the following examples.

The importance of loyalty to nationhood is shown by the questions asked in a security vetting package for security clearance in Australia. The first question asks: 'Do you have any feelings of loyalty or allegiance to any country other than Australia?' and the ninth asks 'is there anything in your personal life that could cause you embarrassment or reflects badly on your character, loyalty or trustworthiness?' (Australian Protective Services, circa 2003). The questioning indicates the importance in which loyalty to country is held and that loyalty is not merely a connection but also a state of being, almost a belief of the actor's. By asking twice, this case shows the importance in which security vetting organisations hold loyalty. This supports the view that an actor's loyalties can influence behaviour, otherwise the vetting organisation would not be interested in loyalty.

Feelings of national loyalty wax and wane, and compete with other loyalties; the family, work, religion, friends and the myriad of other connections held by individuals are often more powerful. It is also important not to overstate the power of loyalty itself; the individual has a range of emotional influences guiding her behaviour at any one time. Further, as Chapter Three discussed, I conceptualise the complex mixture of loyalties felt by an individual as interacting loyalty layers. Which layer or combination is predominant at any particular moment depends on the situation, but every loyalty held by an individual influences identity and values in a consistent and ongoing way. As Willis (1993: 20) points out: 'trying to think of oneself without any nationality is quite difficult'. Just because one has not been proud to be an Australian, American or Canadian in the last week does not negate the power of that loyalty. Nor does it negate its influence on identity.

Nation, Identity and Loyalty

Having established the importance of loyalty to the nation, and for the individuals within it, I want to turn attention to how identity may enter this equation. Loyalties appear to give the individual access to identity, belonging and reason for action. We develop our sense of self in order to function in society. The question is, does loyalty help to create and sustain our identity and maintain emotional connections? Oldenquist answers in the affirmative, saying that: 'humans find emotional satisfaction in social identities, group loyalties, and cooperative endeavours for a common good' (1991: 97). Importantly, the creation of one's identity, while intensely personal, is constructed within the social milieu, as Jenkins (1997: 142) puts it, paraphrasing Marx: 'actors may make their own identities, but they do not do so in circumstances of their own choosing'. In my argument within this chapter the circumstance is the construction of loyalty, and the way it allows some but not others access to the emotional succour of attachment.

One of the main avenues for this type of identity is belonging. Loyalties can provide us with a sense of connectedness and belonging. Loyalties can help define how individuals act in social situations and the groups they identify and belong to. Hence the often asked question of migrants and the children of migrants—'no, where do you really come from?'—is a query geared to separating the migrant and questioning her loyalty. Loyalties operate in a reciprocal pattern—the objects of an individual's loyalties set her apart and make her distinctive. Thus the individual affects the object of her loyalty by giving loyalty to the cause, while the cause responds by helping to define the individual and giving her social cachet (Fletcher, 1993: 8–9).

A key aspect of the construction of loyalty is that it requires an 'other'. The causes to which the individual is loyal must be balanced by alternative causes to which the person could be loyal (Hirschman, 1970: 82). It is not necessary that this prospect be a viable one, merely that it is present. Ethnicity provides an obvious other, obvious not only in physical appearances but also in the ease of identifying that other as a threat to one's loyalties.

This claim will be explored in the case studies by seeking to explain the process by which some can feel excluded from national loyalty by the conduct of others. This may help explain why the layer of national loyalty is stronger than a conceptually broad concept, such as humanity. Without an other it is difficult for the individual to conceptualise such a loyalty.

However, where there is an other there is often conflict and exclusion. It is this claim that loyalty creates a site of conflict and exclusion that I test in the case studies. As Baines (1998: 2) points out: '[t]he past has shown that the assertion of a single national identity has precluded the assertion of others. National identity is invariably defined by the dominant group which excludes others from the locus of power'. If the case studies support this claim, I suggest that the construction of the emotion within this exchange, that of loyalty, is what asserts a singular identity. This is the key theoretical contention of the chapter. Which is not without controversy.

One of the means of exclusion rests in the origin of loyalty. How do you 'get' loyalty? Where does it come from and why do some migrants feel like they do not have it? Wolff (1968: 60–61) argues that loyalties differ in their origins across two axes, that of contractual loyalty and that of natural loyalty. Natural loyalty arises out of human interaction and is almost a non-conscious act. The primary example of this would be family loyalty, such as the bond between parent and child (as was discussed at length in the previous chapter). Contractual loyalty arises out of pledges of commitment. National loyalty can be considered a natural loyalty, but critically, only for those born in a country. In fact, to renounce one's country of birth is often characterised as treason. This raises a particular problem for migrants as they cannot have a natural loyalty to the adopted nation. They are locked out of this emotional space by the place of their birth. Thus, they can only inhabit the contractual space of national loyalty, considered by Wolff (1968) to be an inherently weaker emotional site because loyalty must be proven, rather than a taken for granted assumption. This distinction is similar to the often used distinction of ethnic versus civic nationalism (see for example, Smith 1991). Ethnic belonging, like natural loyalty, is something you are born to, while civic nationalism is a contractual arrangement, mediated by identity papers and naturalisation ceremonies.

The way national loyalty is fostered and reinforced can offer another site of exclusion. Loyalty is engendered through shared experience, collective memory, celebration, language and tradition, to name just a few sources. Clarence (1999: 201) argues that:

individuals are constantly reminded – whether it be by the flag hanging over a national building, or other unobtrusive, 'banal' symbols – of their nation and their identification with it. The language spoken by the government and in the media, the images created and perpetuated all serve as powerful reminders of who belongs – and who does not; thus the idea of a 'true Aussie' . . . implies that there are 'untrue' Australians'.

This is a two way process. The negotiation of who does and does not belong is not merely situated within the sphere of macro structures such as a government, but also within the small, local interactions of the citizen. Ong (1996: 738) summarises this when she argues that:

I use 'cultural citizenship' to refer to the cultural practices and beliefs produced out of negotiating the often ambivalent and contested relations with the state and its hegemonic forms that establish the criteria of belonging within a national population and territory. Cultural citizenship is a dual process of self-making and being made within webs of power linked to the nation-state and civil society.

One of the key linkages in this process is our emotional life, and I will illustrate these linkages in the case studies by exploring how loyalty to the nation is construed. The contention that follows from this is that to be part of this process of citizenship the actor must have the necessary cultural capital, and in Australia's case this is a question of race, colour, ethnicity and religion. As a loyalty relationship requires an other, the other is constructed as the 'foreigner'.

Hage (1998) identifies a further problem of belonging within Australia when he argues that there is a schism between formal acceptance and informal, or communal, acceptance. He (1998: 50) states:

there is an important, and historically growing, incompatibility between the state's formal acceptance of new citizens and the dominant community's everyday acceptance of such people. This is especially so when there is a clearly dominant, culturally defined community within the nation. In such cases, the acquisition of formal citizenship does not give any indication of the level of practical national belonging granted by the dominant cultural community. This is largely because the basis of communal acceptance remains determined by questions of cultural descent far more than by state acceptance.

Thus, for this perspective, the question of 'no, where are you really from?' is geared to the informal acceptance of the migrant by the dominant community. While Hage ignores emotion within this exchange and as a basis for the exchange, the invoking of loyalty and the inability for the migrant to be loyal is about excluding them from the space of national loyalty. Or to again use Hage (1998: 51–5) and consequently Bourdieu, the cultural capital of having loyalty must be defended and used against those who do not. For this book I use the term emotional capital (Cahill, 1999) to describe having access to and the ability to use and understand emotional scripts, feelings and behaviours within a given social milieu that can advance the actor's position in society. Migrants can lack access to the symbolic order of Australian nationalism, further estranging them from the emotional capital required (see Ahmed, 2004 for a mechanism by which this exclusion can occur). Thus in the context of Australian national loyalty, the emotional capital the citizen can gain by having access to the emotion of loyalty is belonging, identity and acceptance within the nation. This can also be converted in the field of social conflict to aid or detract from social success, by allowing the possessor to gain an advantage. If this is the case, then excluding the migrant from this emotional capital maintains its relative value to the excluder.

The War(s) Around Loyalties

This section deals with the conscription debates that occurred in Australia during the two World Wars. I will be focusing on World War One as it offers a well documented historical example of a conflict that drew heavily on the rhetoric of loyalty. I draw on examples from World War Two and the Vietnam conflicts to show that the themes are enduring. The key themes that I draw out in this section are the ways in which loyalties motivate actors and help sustain collectives and wider social action. I will also draw out more evidence for other elements of loyalty, particularly family loyalties. The first part of this section shows how the Australian Government and various actors responded to the call to arms in each conflict, and illuminates the way loyalties are fashioned. It also points to the way loyalty is used by wider social institutions to motivate and justify behaviour as well as create or reinforce an identity. Loyalty, in the following examples, operates beyond the actor and within social collectivities, at a macro-sociological level.

When the First World War began in 1914, Australia responded rapidly to the call to arms from its imperial benefactor, Great Britain. The Prime Minister, Joseph Cook, immediately supported Britain's declaration with the words: 'If the old country is at war, so are we' (McKernan, 1980: 7). This declaration was greeted with euphoria, to the point of rioting in the streets of Melbourne (Beaumont, 1995: 2). This rioting was an overt display of some Australians' zealous support of the declaration. Much of this response was due to the fact that Australia was very much part of the empire, a 'child' of Great Britain, and it was expected that most, if not all, Australians would rally to the cause. As Beaumont (1995: 3) noted: 'Britain, the centre of the empire, former home of the vast majority of immigrants and the source of Australia's cultural and political traditions, commanded a profound loyalty and affection'. There was little conflict over this apparent dual loyalty. As McKernan (1980: 182) argued: 'willingness to enlist in the AIF [Australian Imperial Force] quickly became the ultimate test of loyalty anywhere in Australia'.

Despite federation and self government (1901), successive governments perceived that the nation needed some form of imperial benevolence to protect a vast, but empty country, too close to Asia for its comfort, and, at the time of World War One, Great Britain remained this protector (Kelly, 1992: 1–18). Therefore, when Great Britain needed help, Australia would come to its aid. As the editorial for the *Sydney Morning Herald* proclaimed on October 6, 1914: 'Britain is at war, and that is now the condition into which the Empire has been flung. For good or ill, we are engaged with the mother country in fighting for liberty and peace'.

Similarly, at the outbreak of the World War Two, Prime Minister Menzies stated: 'It is my melancholy duty to inform you officially that, in consequence of the persistence by Germany in her invasion of Poland, Great Britain has declared war upon her, and that, as a result, Australia is also at war' (Menzies, 1939). Again, Australia was at war beside the mother country, or imperial benefactor. Little had changed since World War One for Australia's loyalty as a nation nor for the loyalties of most of its citizens. Perhaps the addition of melancholy was a result of Australia's experience in World War One.

During the Vietnam conflict, Australia did not make a formal declaration of war. However, a similar kind of commitment was made. Then Prime Minister, Harold Holt, pledged Australia's support for the USA in the Vietnam War in July 1966, on the White House lawns, with the now immortal phrase 'all the way with LBJ' (Pemberton, 1987: 323). This statement is very similar in its feel to the formal declarations of war made in both World Wars. There was an automatic assumption that Australia would join the conflict based on the ANZUS treaty and Australia's reliability as an ally. This is an indication that the nation's loyalty was shifting to the United States. This shift originated in World War Two.

The fall of Singapore in February 1942, combined with the fact that Australia came under direct under attack for the first time ever by the Japanese, sent shockwaves through the country and initiated this shift in benefactors. There were calls to bring all the 'boys' home from the Middle East and overseas to defend the country. There was also the beginnings of conflict between the Australian Prime Minister and the British government about how the war in the Pacific should be fought (Inglis, 1968: 52). Some in Australia blamed the British for the threat now manifesting in the Pacific, questioning in particular the competence of the British command at Singapore.

Australia began to assert itself as an independent nation. In terms of loyalty, there was the development of tension, particularly at the higher levels of the military and government, between loyalty to Australia, and loyalty to the greater Allied cause. The Australian military felt the need to seek a different direction in the Pacific from the British. At a deeper level, Australia suddenly found itself with another nation, the United States of America, providing the support that Great Britain had previously supplied. Prime Minister Curtin acknowledged this publicly during a speech in December 1941 and Inglis (1968: 52) argues that it was 'historic for its public recognition that Australia's security depended henceforth not on the Royal Navy but on the armed might of the United States'. This is an indication of conflict within a loyalty layer.

During World War Two, the connection to America was one of a desperately needed 'big brother' in a time of crisis. Australians' loyalty to Great Britain can be viewed as a natural extension of the nation's colonial history. Yet the nation was suddenly asked to put its trust in a different country, one that comparatively did not have strong historical ties to Australia. Holt's exhortation that we would go 'all the way' is evidence that this change was firmly established, at least at the level of government, by the 1960s. It has been maintained since, and has been consistently reinforced by successive Australian Governments (for example, Australia's involvement in the 'war on terror'). There has been a continuing ambivalence amongst the public to this new loyalty, in part because it does not have the historical basis of the former loyalty to Britain. Loyalty is important in establishing identities, and this shift removed one place of identification.

In current political parlance, the invoking of various layers of loyalty can be seen as a form of 'wedge' politics. Protagonists in the debate call upon a particular loyalty in the same way as occurred during the conscription debates, be it family, nation, empire or mateship. In so doing, advocates seek to unite the population but the result is that they actually divide it. Once a side is chosen, it appears to be difficult for the individual to change position. This is due to the emotional investment the individual makes which is a result of her belief in the importance of her commitment to the layer of loyalty being accessed. The following case studies will explore if an actor can easily switch.

The question of Australia's loyalty as a nation has been an enduring theme throughout the 'war on terror'. The visit of Australia's Prime Minister to Washington in 2002 was intensely scrutinised by the media and political commentators. Some media commentators were scathing of Prime Minister Howard's approach: 'Sycophancy isn't the word, Try psychophancy, wherein obsequiousness becomes a medical condition and the volume of piss in the presidential pocket suggests a complete collapse of bladder control' (Adams, 2002). Others were more supportive of the stance. As Henderson (2002) pointed out: 'Australia has little alternative but to retain close alliances with traditional allies'. What is not at doubt is that the Australian government is continuing to pledge and affirm its loyalty to the US, which it views as the modern version of an imperial benefactor. Successive Australian governments have always felt that Australia has needed a benefactor and protector, be it the British Empire or the United States (Kelly, 1992). This loyalty to a benefactor has been crucial to Australia's image of itself throughout its history and consequently the nation's role as friend and ally has been a significant part of Australia's identity as a nation. The past predicts the future, and loyalty is a means of predicting the future based on past connections and belonging. Cartoonists are particularly apt at identifying this trend with the illustration by many of Prime Minister Howard as a small deputy, clutching at the coat-tails of President Bush (Moir's cartoons in the Sydney Morning Herald, 'Axis of Justice ... The Vigilantes, 23 April 2002).

The Australian government's immediate support of the US actions in Afghanistan and Iraq and its willingness to commit troops to the conflict again illustrates this loyalty to another nation. Given the limited nature of the war and Australia's troop commitment to it, the question of conscription has not arisen, yet the anti-war in Iraq movement had mobilised significant sections of the Australian community. What these recent events illustrate is the continuing conflict that arises in Australia over the country's loyalty to other nations. Thus, I can plausibly suggest that the historical debates I explore in the following case study have laid the groundwork for the current approach to national loyalty in Australia. This suggests that the themes and conflicts that I will elucidate are crucial in understanding loyalty today and that loyalty plays an enduring role in the maintenance of the imagined space that is a nation.

Conscripting Loyalty

The debates in Australia over conscription and national service that took place during World War One, World War Two and the Vietnam War provide compelling evidence to illustrate the contested nature of loyalty and the way different layers of loyalty interact. This section will focus on how and why loyalty was invoked in these debates to support both sides of the argument. The use of loyalty by each side will also illuminate the layered nature of the emotion, with appeals not limited to nationalistic concerns but also encompassing family, religion and ethnicity. What is of particular interest in examining issues of loyalty is not the wars as such, or even necessarily conscription itself, but the way conscription campaigns were run, and, in particular, how different layers of loyalty were invoked to support both sides of the campaign. Before looking at the events in detail, I will briefly canvass how the debate was formed in each of the conflicts. I will use a thematic analysis of loyalty in war and consequently move between engagements with the themes.

The conscription debate during World War One was a divisive public campaign fought across two referenda. During 1916, army recruitment became a pressing problem for the Australian Government and the possibility of conscription was raised (Withers, 1972). Opposition to the proposals began almost immediately with the formation of anti-conscription organisations and an eruption of public debate. Both referenda were narrowly lost by the pro-conscription side.

The debate in World War Two was largely confined to Parliament and the internal machinations of the Australian Labor Party. Much of the argument which occurred in this forum concerned the question of whether the militia could be compelled to serve overseas. The parliamentary debate was divisive, with the appeals made to issues of liberty, morality and loyalty (Main, 1970: 108–28). This time however, the pro-conscription side won and conscripted troops were sent overseas to a limited extent, fighting mainly in Papua New Guinea. With Australia under direct threat of attack, the opposition to sending the conscripts 'over there' was not as compelling as in World War One and there was no groundswell of public outcry, either for or against this national service.

The next time that conscription became an issue, during the Vietnam War, it caused intense public division. As with World War Two, there were no divisive referenda. National Service came into law on 24 November 1964, based on a lottery system of compulsory service for young men (Main, 1970: 136). In April 1966, Prime Minister Holt announced that conscripts would be sent to Vietnam and in May the first conscript death occurred (Forward, 1968: 126). However, unlike World War Two, a huge public outcry over this parliamentary decision would follow.

Curiously, during the Vietnam War the opposition to conscription was much slower to mobilise than in World War One (Hamel-Greeen, 1983: 102–112). The RSL expelled two members for supporting an anti-conscription association in 1969. Street protests and ceremonial draft card burnings began. These protesters were often harassed and arrested by police, but given that the twenty year old men subject to the draft could not yet vote, protest was one of the few avenues of available. In April 1969 a series of protests were held that the media labelled the 'Battle of Sydney'. In this series of protests, sit-ins and occupations 302 people were arrested (Hamel-Green, 1983: 114).

To use the terminology of loyalty layers, at the time of World War One, loyalty to Australia was expected, as was loyalty to the empire. These two layers were mutually supportive. Australia was a nation with a deep connection to Britain, both on a national level through institutions such as inherited parliamentary structures, but also on the personal level through family and immigration. The fact that these two loyalties, while closely aligned, were indeed different layers opens up the potential for conflict, and this conflict arose as the war progressed, particularly in relation to the issue of conscription.

Opponents of conscription were labelled traitors to Australia and empire, willing to stab 'mother' Britain in the back; or shirkers, unwilling to lend a hand in a time of need. Appeals to national loyalty and the loyalty of mateship were enduring themes of the debate. One argument used by pro-conscriptionists was that there existed an obligation of citizens to contribute to the nation's defence, and many extended this duty to King and empire (Withers, 1972: 6). A powerful cartoon depiction is of Lindsay's ape-like Hun, standing over slaughtered mother England while little, lost boy Australia looks on forlornly. The caption reads: '"YOUR TURN NEXT." Help to prevent this by voting "YES."' (Lindsay, 1917). As Beaumont (1995: 46–7) points out: 'the forces proposing conscription saw the campaign in many senses as a moral crusade, to be waged against the forces of disorder and disloyalty'. These appeals are highly emotive and were designed to shock and then compel the Australian people to support conscription, the threat being the loss of the motherland, and perhaps, even Australia.

Themes such as national and imperial loyalties were heavily relied on by the pro-conscription camp. These appeals were designed to utilise that layer of loyalty and inspire citizens to fulfil their patriotic duty. However, while national loyalty is a powerful motivator, it is also a contested motivator. Australians could fulfil their national loyalty by staying at home and farming, mining and manufacturing for the war effort, and some anti-conscription propaganda made this very point. This theme of service to the nation was repeated during the conflicts that followed.

The Vietnam war resulted in similar appeals. It was argued by those in favour of participation in the war that the key to containing communism in South East Asia was stopping the spread in Vietnam, and that if one country fell to communism, all would be under threat (Pemberton 1987: 161). Similar to the calls to defend Europe and Great Britain in the world wars, the implication was that if they fell, Australia could well be next. Again, calls to duty and obligation were made. Professor McAuley argued in 1966 that '[t]he duty of service. . . . is one of those duties like paying taxes or serving on a jury which a good citizen loyally accepts when it is put upon him, though he may dislike it' (Main 1970: 150).

During the debates of World War One and Vietnam, the loyalties of the anti-conscriptionists were often questioned. Of particular interest during World War One were the attacks by the pro-conscription camp against the loyalties of one of the most vocal opponents in the second conscription referendum, Archbishop Mannix, of Melbourne, an Irish Catholic.

Mannix was attacked over his ethnic heritage (Irish) and the role he played in the Catholic Church, and asked how could he be loyal to Australia with these other loyalties. Many saw his opposition, in particular, as a continuation of the conflict between Catholics and Anglicans, and the Irish and English. As Prime Minister Hughes argued: 'the forces arrayed behind the campaign against the Government's proposals could be divided into three sections — the Germans of Australia, the Sinn Fein, and the I.W.W [Industrial Workers of the World]' (Jauncey, 1935: 291). Thus, Hughes was happy to cast Mannix as an Irish separatist and thus a non-believer in Australia and empire. Others went even further. At a pro-conscription meeting in Melbourne a resolution was passed: 'that this meeting of loyal citizens views with grave concern the disloyal and seditious utterances of prelates of the Roman Catholic Church . . . It urges the Commonwealth Government to take action without respect of persons to repress all such treasonable utterances' (Jauncey, 1935: 291). Invoking treason and sedition are powerful attacks, illustrating the strength of the nationalistic layer of loyalty.

Mannix himself did not shy away from his anti-empire position. He called on Irishmen to seek home rule and continued his appeal to Australians more generally: 'To you Australia is first and Empire is second' (Jauncey, 1935: 275). Mannix also called strongly on moral values, specifically the dangers to liberty that conscription represented (Charlesworth, 1968: 244–5).

During the debates on national service for Vietnam, almost identical rhetoric was invoked. Often anti-draft groups were labelled as disloyal, traitorous organisations that were controlled by communists bent on the destruction of Australia (Main, 1970). Communism was the great fearsome 'other' of the time, just as the Germans, Sinn Fein and the I.W.W had been during World War One. In a parliamentary debate in March 1966, a Liberal member, Dr Mackay, argued in the context of Vietnam that 'the most virulent opposition can almost always be traced fairly and squarely to the communists' (Main, 1970: 144–5).

The common loyalty theme that runs through these examples is the notion of sacrifice for one's country. The rhetoric of loyalty was being used to invoke an actor's connection with, and obligation to, the nation. This is an example of macro-sociological processes directing individual action. What these examples have shown is that the commentators in each case believed that appeals to loyalty could sway behaviour. This supports my argument that loyalty can motivate or justify action. However, this motivation is often highly contested, especially across layers, and I explore the complexity of layered loyalties and how the family can clash with the nation next.

As I established in the previous chapter, loyalty to the family represents a powerful, even underlying, layer of loyalty. Families are often internally loyal, not because of blood relations, but from the shared experiences that each family has (Barth, 1951: 3). Loyalty arises from shared commitments, living together, interacting with each other and the outside world as well as the rituals of the family; anniversaries, birthdays and celebrations (Royce, 1908: 220–8). Each family has its own idiosyncrasies and rituals and these can help inspire loyalty. Thus, it is not surprising that family appeals were strong during the conscription debate. The Australian Labor Party released a poster with a young boy imploring his mother: 'Vote No Mum, they'll take Dad next' (State Library of Victoria, date unknown). Another anti-poster asks:

> Why is your face so white Mother?
> Why do you choke for breath?
> O I have dreamt in the night my son
> That I doomed a man to death . . .
> They gave me the ballot paper,
> The grim death warrant of doom.
> And I smugly sentenced the man to death,
> In that dreadful little room. (Jauncey, 1935: 203)

But appeals to motherhood were not restricted to the anti-conscriptionists. A recruitment poster asked: 'Whose Son are you?' and depicted one son, not in uniform, as a 'shady' character in a close embrace with his mother and a second one in uniform, his mother beaming while sending him to war (McKernan, 1980: 39).

Like the anti-conscription campaigners of World War One, Vietnam anti-draft organisations made calls to familial loyalty. For example, the Draft Resistance Movement called on parents to act on their sons' behalf to challenge the policy of conscription. The 'Save Our Sons' movement was organised by mothers to oppose war and conscription (Guyatt, 1968: 181).

These specific examples demonstrate the point that loyalty is a socially negotiated emotion that can be called on by different sides in a debate. They also show how different layers of loyalty can be called upon. Did the average Australian believe the appeals to empire and Australia or were they more swayed by appeals to religion, morality or family? This is a question that cannot be easily answered (Beaumont, 1995: 54–7), but it is important to consider as it helps highlight the multi-faceted nature of appeals to loyalty.

The preceding discussion of conscription and Australia's need for an imperial benefactor has elucidated some of the principles of the emotion of loyalty. How loyalty informs identity can be inferred from the attacks made on individuals and groups in the campaigns. The layered nature of the emotion is demonstrated by the appeals to differing types of loyalty, be it the family, church, nation or empire. Each appeal strove to change the voters' minds or entrench a decision by invoking a salient loyalty layer. Lastly, the issue of an imperial benefactor shows how a country's leaders can only marginally direct the loyalties of its citizens when an historical connection is lacking. As loyalty reflects connection and reciprocity, it is not surprising that the alignment of Australia with the USA is still being questioned by a significant proportion of the population. This connection component suggests the process by which identity can be informed through loyalties.

I have used the case studies of Australia's involvement in conflict over the last 100 years to illustrate how loyalty has been invoked to influence the perceptions, beliefs and actions of the actor. This section has provided strong evidence that loyalty can create intense conflict, particularly when competing layers of loyalty make calls upon the actor, such as familial, religious and ethnic layers. Further, the case studies confirm the role loyalty plays in helping to form identity. It is to the question of migrant identity and loyalty that I now turn.

Dual Loyalties – The Immigrant's Conflict

For much of Australia's history, the non-British immigrant has had his or her loyalty questioned. Part of this questioning of the foreigner's loyalties comes from the nation's past. Australians were inculcated with a fear of the foreigner from Sydney Cove onwards and the White Australia policy was a significant pillar of the Australian settlement from federation in 1901 (Kelly, 1992: 1–18). A common experience associated with ethnicity and migration is the clichéd 'so where are you from?', often followed by the supplementary question: 'no, where are you actually from?' (Perkins, 2004: 13). What this leads to is the often reported occurrence by migrants and the children of migrants of never feeling at 'home' in Australia. While this is not the case for all, there is a significant body of literature and commentary supporting this feeling that I explore in this section. I examine the basis and context of this question and what it means for the individuals involved in the exchange. This question operates as short-hand that encapsulates the position of the migrant versus the 'real' Australian, as the question queries the other's connection to place and people.

The following discussion of immigrant experience is designed to draw out the contested nature of loyalty and the impact these dual loyalties have for the individual. This will further illustrate how loyalty orients social action and its importance in shaping the actor's identity. I will also further explore how loyalty helps to provide identity and motivation by assessing whether loyalty can only exist when it is reciprocated by the object of loyalty. Or, to phrase it another way, can a migrant who consistently has her loyalty questioned feel loyal?

The central sociological question within this section is: does the social construction of loyalty to the nation-state deny some citizens access to the emotional succour of attachment? And, if this is the case, what is the explanation for this exclusion? Ang (1998: 2) encapsulates this question when she argues that

> in a world in which the modern nation-state still forms the dominant framework for cultural identification and construction of imagined community, the question of 'where you're from' tends to overwhelm and marginalise that of 'where you're at'.

Why is where you are from more important than where you are at? As I will explore in this section, loyalty is about where you are from—past connections and beliefs—and not about where you are at, unless you intrude upon another's loyalty space. Loyalties help the actor predict the future on the basis of past connections. Consequently, the actor may look at another's history of loyalty (i.e. the connection to a different country) and assume that that loyalty will be the strongest.

My examples show how some migrants and children of migrants feel that they never belong, are not allowed to belong and that they do not feel part of the nation in the sense of being loyal Australians. The advantage of drawing on an historical example from World War One is to show that the issue of loyalty to country is an enduring one that predates the mass non-English speaking migrant influx after World War Two into Australia. This example in combination with more recent experiences, such as the current debate over religious loyalties, also highlights that the rhetoric and use of loyalty is not confined to war times, but exists irrespective of 'threat' to the nation. While it is important to acknowledge that many migrants never experience this difficulty, I am focusing on those that do as a way of understanding the influence of loyalty.

The common sense notion that national loyalty needs to be a singular connection has been questioned at times. As Richard Boyer (quoted in Zubrzycki, 1991: 126) argued at a naturalisation seminar in 1954: 'Indeed, it is true to say that the people who have only one loyalty are a nuisance to themselves and to everybody else'. Boyer was calling on immigrants to maintain an affection for their homeland and not to be singularly loyal. However, within each layer of loyalty there is the potential for serious conflict. Consider the issue of blended families that I explored in the previous chapter. That family structure is renowned for the conflict that can occur between 'new' mothers and fathers and step offspring. It is this duality I now explore and, specifically, how immigrants negotiate the notion of otherness and twin, often conflicted, loyalties.

It must be noted that prior to World War Two dual loyalties for immigrants were only a problem for most of Australia's history if one was not British. In fact, for much of the nineteenth and twentieth centuries it would have been considered disloyal if an individual did not have a loyalty to Great Britain as well as Australia—especially considering that all Australians were considered British Subjects until World War Two. This changed markedly after World War Two, partly as a result of the influx of non-British migrants and partly from Australia shifting its alliances and, as discussed already, partly from finding a new benefactor. British immigrants are now equally lambasted for their dual loyalty (Smolicz, 1991: 48–9). Interestingly, it is the post World War Two British immigrants who have made appeals for their different stories to be told as distinct narratives from those immigrants who came from elsewhere (Hammerton & Colebourne, 2001: 86–8). What this indicates is that a loyalty to Great Britain and Australia was for a considerable period of time a given. It is only recently that British connections and loyalty have come to be questioned.

No, Where Do You *Really* Come From?

I now turn to the specific examples that illustrate cases of migrant exclusion. These examples take the form of migrants' and children of migrants' own commentaries upon their feelings, as well as archival material. I have drawn these from a wide range of articles, books and web pages and they are representative of the phenomenon I am describing as they form just a snapshot of the large literature that speaks to this phenomenon of exclusion. I acknowledge the contested nature of this literature and that not every migrant feels excluded. However, I am drawing on Katz's (1999) argument on seeing emotion that you need to look at the out-of-the-ordinary, different and challenging events to adequately theorise emotions (see Chapter Three).

The first example is drawn from history and regards the treatment of Germans in World War One. Sourcing accurate statistics on residents of German birth and heritage for the period of the First World War is challenging. The 1911 census recorded 32 990 (0.89% of the population) people as being born in Germany but did not track the ethnic heritage of Australian born residents (ABS, Australian Historical Population Statistics 2004). Another estimate from the beginning of the war in 1914 claims that approximately 100,000 people of German heritage lived in Australia, making up about 2.25 per cent of the population (Nutting, 2002). Notwithstanding the difficulties of sourcing accurate figures, we do know that several thousand were interned during the war, with no trial or means to clear their name. Most were locked up on the basis of unfounded suspicion. Hermann Homburg, Attorney General in South Australia, was forced to resign, despite being born in South Australia and having never left the colony. National loyalty even went far enough to overcome sporting loyalties. St Kilda Football club changed its colours in 1915 from red-white-black (the colour of the German Imperial flag) to the black-gold-red of allied Belgium's flag (Nutting, 2002). Town and street names did not escape the anxiety of a nation at war, with the South Australian Parliament legislating to change German place names (McKernan, 1980: 167).

German Australians were denied the right to vote in the second conscription referendum, partly as they were blamed by pro-conscriptionists for the loss of the first vote. One soldier with a German background was incensed by the denial of his mother's right to vote:

Now this has hurt me very much. She has two sons fighting for the Empire, one in France (myself) and one in Palestine, her brother also was refused a vote; he had two sons fighting, one killed in action on the Somme last year, and the other serving in the _th Battalion. More, mother was bred and born in Australia and a more loyal woman never lived. She worked hard in every respect towards assisting the troops on this side . . . I am really hurt that much I can hardly explain the position to you, to think that me and my brother are away fighting for our country and she treated like that. From the *British-Australian*, 7th March 1918 (McKernan, 1980: 167)

Being of German extraction denied these Australians a belonging to Australia. The dominant group (those of British descent) excluded them because it felt they could not be trusted in wartime. This points to the role loyalty plays in motivating action. Importantly, at this time one could still be excluded from belonging even if one was born in Australia, as was the Attorney General of South Australia. Loyalty was structured around an unwavering commitment to Australia and Empire, and German descent barred these Australians from rights during the war. The soldier invoked the rhetoric of emotion to explain why he is so hurt: 'I am really hurt that much I can hardly explain'. To the soldier there was an emotional component to his response—he sees the loyal behaviour and actions of himself and his family as being ignored and vilified. While there are a range of emotions involved, the use of loyalty in his appeal indicates that this is the key emotion in the exchange occurring. This plea is also a good example of the separation between loyalty and patriotism, the soldier is engaging in patriotic acts (fighting for his country), yet laments the feeling that this overt act is not being rewarded by the recognition of his feelings of being loyal. This case supports my argument that loyalty is a social emotion and that it needs to be validated within social exchanges. The soldier's loyalty was not recognised and consequently he expresses emotional anguish at the lack of reciprocity.

The soldier and his family were also being denied their identity as Australians. Price (1991: 161) has argued that 'some families of German origin undoubtedly felt a deep conflict of loyalties . . . though working for the Australian war effort, felt very torn at this struggle between their two identities'. This reinforces the point that loyalty is important to identity, and when the clash between the two becomes salient that it is not the individual who chooses which is paramount (or 'who they really are'). It is others, or the social milieu, that imposes the identity. In World War One, German heritage meant disloyalty and threat to the majority. Much of this treatment was because Australians needed an enemy whom they could see, touch and point at. Immigrants and Australians of 'questionable' heritage provided this target (McKernan, 1980: 150–178).

The same thing occurred during World War Two, with the Japanese subject to universal internment. Some 1,043 people of Japanese descent were interned; the low number of Australians of Japanese descent a testament to the success of the White Australia policy. While not subject to universal internment, considerable numbers of Germans and Italians were interned, on nothing more than suspicion based on their heritage (Priesnitz, 1987: 10).

The experience of being accused of disloyalty is not confined to immigrants during wartime. The policy of assimilation followed by the government after World War Two actively denied the possibility of dual loyalties.

The influx of new migrants after World War Two created an identity and loyalty problem for Australia. For a predominantly white, British population the arrival of people from a diverse range of non-English speaking places threatened their values about what it meant to be Australian. Consequently, immigrants were to be assimilated, give up their old loyalties and identity and become Australian. As discussed in Chapter Four, an individual's loyalties are an essential aspect of the self, informing the individual of who they are, where they have come from and thus they help shape identity. Loyalty furnishes significant meaning to existence. These immigrants were asked to leave those meanings behind.

The commentaries from migrants over the last 50 years point to the ubiquity and continuation of this phenomenon.

It's hard in Australia, because I'm not seen as Australian. I'm not. Even though I have no accent, I was born here, but because my parents aren't Australian, I'm not Australian. And I'm not your typical blond-haired, blue-eyed Skippy. I've got dark features. I mean, you look different to them. Plus my background is different to them. (Zevallos, 2003: 82)

If you go overseas – this is the really contradictory thing about living in Australia – you go overseas, someone asks you where you are come from, you say 'Australia. Born there.' And they go, 'Oh okay.' But when you're in Australia, when you say, 'I'm Australian', they go to you, 'No, what *nationality are you?*' Then you go, 'oh, Chilean.' So in the end, I think a lot of people just cut out the 'Australian' and just go straight to the ethnicity. (Zevallos, 2003: 89, italics in original)

When you go back to your country you're not a Greek, you're an Australian! I went on holidays and tried not to speak any word of English because I didn't want people to ask me where I come from, I had enough of that in Australia. (Markus & Sims, 1993: 10)

I've been out here 40 years. That's a long time. I served in the Australian Army during the War. And they still call me a dago bastard. My family has been brought up here but I'm still sort of foreign. (Markus & Sims, 1993: 11)

These commentaries indicate how important it is for one's identity to be recognised and acknowledged by others. These migrants and children of migrants lament that they are still seen as foreign and not Australian. Their Australian-ness is challenged as they are not seen to be Australian by many Australians. The layer of loyalty and belonging that is most relevant is ethnicity, not nationality. It seems that they cannot have a loyalty to Australia as it is denied them by others to the point that they give in, no longer saying 'Australian' but instead acknowledging their ethnicity first. This points to the contention that some cannot have a loyalty to Australia.

However, some theorists and some self reports point to the advantages of having a dual loyalty and thus dual identity and existence. The empowering nature of dual identities occurs when the actor can play one existence off against another. For example, Zevallos (2003) explains how young women of a South American origin use their Australian identity as a means of resistance, especially in enhancing gender equity and freedoms. Noble and Tabar (2002) report that Lebanese youth also take aspects of Australian identity, especially when it comes to dating behaviours, as a means of resistance. One sociological question is how do they take advantage of this and is it really about dual or hybridised identity? In the following commentaries this question of dual identity is commented upon and again the reports point to the emotion-laden aspect of national belonging and the exclusion that is often felt.

By the time I was a teenager, a certain conflict of interests was beginning to dominate my life. Allegiance to two cultures was dividing my intellect from my emotions . . . But being Ukrainian was not always so easy. At school, on the television, amongst Australian friends, the assumption was that there was a definable quintessential Australian culture which was at the centre of our lives. And yet for my family, the Ukrainian community was the pivot of our existence. I longed to belong to the first but was inextricably part of the second, and the problem of dual allegiance only increased as I got older. (Mycak, 2003: 4)

This commentary points to the conflict that dual loyalties creates. It is clear that this child of a migrant feels that there is an Australian culture and value system, yet they are drawn into the local, family based culture of being Ukrainian. Her identity is Ukrainian, but there is a longing to be Australian. This prioritising of one identity over another is borne out in the following quotes:

I've had this conversation before. Like, are you determined by where you're born, or where you've grown up, or what are you? What are you exactly? I don't see myself as South American *living* in Australia. Australia's my home, but my culture's very much South American . . . I don't see myself as Australian. I see wherever you're born, that's where your culture comes from. *But* there's also influences, definitely, from Australia. But yeah, absolutely, I would say I'm not Australian. (Zevallos, 2003: 82, italics in original)

At home you're in an Italian culture. At school or with friends you were in a totally different culture. You don't fully realise the difference until you marry someone and go into another household. (Foley, 2000: 2)

The social construction of identity is highlighted by these two commentaries. They discuss the nature of 'knowing' who you are and note that not only do you need to see yourself as Australian but you need to be recognised as such. Often the realisation only occurs on reflection with an other.

Using the understanding of loyalty that I am developing in this book can help to explain the process of exclusion and explain how some migrants do feel as if they do not have access to an Australian identity. Loyalties are reciprocal; if there is no return or acknowledgment of an actor's loyalty then maintenance of that loyalty becomes difficult. Consequently, the actor can then be excluded from what loyalties can provide, such as identity. The following quote illustrates this contention:

I blushed that lovely shade of crimson which I had developed over the years in response to revelations concerning my other life. A blush which expressed all the pain and embarrassment of living a dual existence in a seemingly singular country. I looked quite normal, I sounded like everyone else, but I had a surname which no-one could ever pronounce, and a grandmother who wore a scarf around her head and flowered ankle-length skirts, who spoke not one word of English, and insisted on coming right up to the gates when she picked me up from school. I remember the tears in my mother's eyes when I asked her to tell Babusia to wait for me around the corner where no-one could see her. (Mycak, 2003: 2)

For loyalty to fit within the emotions framework I have sketched, there needs to be reason or motivation for action and identity formation. In this commentary we see that as a response to others' shock at a dual loyalty this actor tries to separate her dual existence even more so as to avoid the question of motivation. The commentaries and historical events illustrate these three components.

I do not want to overstate the power of this one emotion, loyalty, as we have a range of emotions impinging upon us. Also, it could be argued that these examples do not point to loyalty per se but to a range of other emotions and behaviours. Using loyalty as a means of explaining and analysing these comments from those that do feel excluded allows me to suggest that loyalty is indeed important in identity formation. However, within a nation state not everyone has access to the 'imagined community' as a result of being seen as different and not accepted. In the following discussion I explore why I think loyalty is at the core of these exchanges, as loyalty is central to the construction of the nation state. Consequently, if this can be established it provides strong evidence for the argument that loyalty is a socially constructed emotion.

As discussed, loyalty requires an other. Migrants can have their loyalty questioned as the other for the national layer of loyalty is another nation. Immigrants often challenge the assumption of natural loyalty to Australia and some Australians assume that they must still have a stronger connection to the nationality of their birth than the adopted loyalty to a new country, as shown by the question 'no, where are you really from?'

With the advent of multiculturalism (formally in 1975), non-UK immigrants were allowed to renew their long distance loyalties, to homeland, culture and religion and celebrate their heritage. This continues to create some interesting conflicts in Australian society. For example, one former Ukrainian celebrates two birthdays, his actual birth and his 'rebirth'—landing on Australian soil. He was naturalised at the first opportunity. However, as an ardent Ukrainian nationalist, he works hard to maintain the religion and culture of the Ukraine amongst Australians of Ukrainian descent (Markus & Sims, 1993: 9). While this is a successful strategy in regards to the maintenance of an individual's identity, it can create conflict and suspicion in the minds of some as he has a dual loyalty.

This manifestation of long distance nationalism (Anderson, 1991; 1992: 3–13) that this Ukrainian-Australian demonstrates is quite common across ethnic, religious and nationality groups (Skrbi, 1999). As I have argued, the fear of the other, particularly in wartime, is an enduring theme of Australian history. This poses a problem for a modern multicultural society; namely, with such a history of fear how does the country negotiate the diverse backgrounds of its individuals? As Smolicz (1991 :61, emphasis in original) argues: 'Before multi-ethnic societies can successfully pursue policies which seek consensus and avoid strife, it is necessary that the dominant group reconcile itself to the *pluralist reality* of the country'. This is a call to open up the way national loyalty is defined, especially in relation to the 'other'. However, given the case I am making for the role loyalty plays in maintaining an other, I cannot see how you could enforce an acceptance of the pluralist reality.

The question of immigrant loyalties has also come to the forefront of public debate with respect to the Iraq conflict and issues of terrorism. The loyalties of a section of the Australian community have been questioned by some members of the public, as well as by the media and politicians. Mosques have been firebombed and Muslim women attacked in the streets. Australia's Muslim communities face two loyalty challenges, much like the Irish-Catholics did during World War One. They are perceived to have not one, but two, competing layers of loyalty that challenge their Australian loyalties: religion and ethnicity. This suspicion of the immigrant can be seen as a repetition of issues raised during the two World Wars and the policies of internment. It is significant to note that opposition to refugees has been associated with the fear of terrorism and the concept of a threat to the nation's security and sovereignty.

The continued use of the term 'un-Australian' in contemporary discourse perpetuates the notion of a singular commitment to the country. It is a singular loyalty relationship. In their study of 'un-Australian', Smith and Phillips (2001), using a questionnaire, found that ethnicity and foreign identification were rated highly as un-Australian and 'reflect a continuing suspicion of the ethnic other' (2001: 335). They go on to argue that 'despite a quarter century of official government policy, Australians are still operating within an assimilationist logic' (2001: 337). This discourse serves to perpetuate the notion of one Australian loyalty, something that the commentaries highlighted with the turmoil that migrants felt about having dual loyalties. Thus, loyalty is fostered by the state and considered extremely important for its continued existence. The evidence that I have discussed in this chapter supports this contention, as do the secondary sources that demonstrate the active role of the state in the creation and maintenance of national loyalty.

These 'migrant' commentaries indicate the exclusion from the mainstream of Australian culture that the individuals are feeling. I emphasise the caveat on my own argument. This exclusion is not universal and it does not matter to all people of an 'ethnic' background—we have a myriad of forces impinging on identity. What I am showing is that for some it does matter and they are excluded from this part of emotional life. One's identity must be validated by others (Wong, 2002: 451). Wong (2002: 451) argues the case this way: 'recognition of one's identity is necessary for one's sense of self and that the harms of non- and mis-recognition are on a par with those caused by other injustices'. The emotions the actor have must be validated and reinforced through social interaction, and loyalty is a social emotion. Denying the legitimacy of another's emotional existence denies them existence. This points to the social construction and actor-mediated theses being an explanation for loyalty, and for loyalty fitting within the framework I sketched in Chapters Two and Three.

In terms of loyalty, the question is how these immigrants negotiate dual loyalties. Much like the various layers of loyalty, ethnicity and national heritage will interact with a new loyalty towards Australia. The power of each will depend on the particular social circumstance. What this section has shown is that migrants can feel excluded from the emotional succour of national loyalty by other actors. This is done through the questioning of heritage and commitment that suffuses questions like 'where did you really come from?' The questions that follow from this proposition are, under what circumstances do migrants feel excluded and how does this occur? It is beyond the scope of this book to address the mechanics of exclusion, but it is sufficient for my argument to establish that some do, and that the rhetoric of loyalty is often invoked.

McCarthyism—Rampant National Loyalty

Senator Joseph McCarthy lends his name to a period of United State's history that witnessed intense debates incorporating loyalty. This period, primarily in the 1940s and 1950s, pitted the US Government against the communist party and its sympathisers (Schrecker 2002: 1). Communism was considered a mortal threat to the USA during this period and this resulted in the imprisonment, banning and harassment of thousands of US citizens. For many, their only crime had been to be a member of the Communist Party (Schrecker, 2002: 1–5). Of interest to my argument is that the rhetoric of national loyalty was an enduring and constant theme within the discourse of the time (and since). This section will briefly explore the use of loyalty by the various actors. Its purpose is to illustrate that the themes I have identified already in this chapter are not limited to Australia, nor to the areas of war and migration.

In 1947 President Truman set up the Loyalty-Security Program, designed to impose a loyalty test on all federal employees and exclude those that had or had previously had connections with subversive organisations (Schrecker, 2002: 43–5, 171). The Executive Order that created this program begins with: 'There shall be a loyalty investigation of every person entering the civilian employment' of the Federal Government (Number 9835, re-printed in Schrecker, 2002: 172). The term loyalty or dis-loyalty appears a number of times throughout the rest of the order (Fried 1997: 28–30). This order also encouraged loyalty oaths and blacklistings. Employees could be found to be dis-loyal by acts of sabotage, espionage, treason, revolutionary behaviour, aiding another government, and crucially for many investigated, having an affiliation with a group deemed by the Attorney General as in-appropriate (Fried, 1990: 68). Particularly disturbing is that an overt act was not required, as Fried (1990: 70) points out 'tendencies or potentials in employees' associations or thinking' were sufficient. The problems with this are obvious.

Loyalty 'oaths' were another oft-used device during this period. As Schrecker (1998: 271) points out 'there were loyalty oaths for teachers, lawyers, entertainers, and all sort of public and private employees'. Slightly absurdly, perhaps, anglers had to sign a loyalty oath before being granted a permit to fish in the New York City reservoirs during the 1950s (Schrecker, 1998: 154). The need to 'swear' an oath is an intriguing addition to national loyalty, which for the native born is an assumed loyalty. This almost appears like a contractual loyalty (in Wolff's 1968 typology). However, in these instances the oath is a process of affirmation of continuing loyalty—similar to a patriotic act. The swearing of an oath acknowledges the actor's previous loyalties, and is designed to secure their future loyalty. In the context of the McCarthy era, the oath was designed to counter threats to the national layer of loyalty. Oath-taking is a ritualistic action that is designed to elicit passion and feeling. The primary emotion involved is self-evidently loyalty. As feelings help guide action, explicitly drawing upon that emotional state in the furtherance of state interests, is designed to maintain an actor's feelings of identification and belonging.

When an individual's sense of belonging was challenged in this period, for example through blacklisting (e.g. Schrecker, 1998: 211–212), it was disastrous for the named party, and sometimes resulted in years of legal wrangling to clear their name. In one such case, Beatrice Braude was fired from the Federal Government because of claims that she had associated with people supposedly of dubious political beliefs (Loose, 1996: A01). It took 43 years for her to clear her name (and then only posthumously). Of particular note is the wording used in the judgement and the response of her family. The judge noted that she 'cared about others deeply and was loyal to her friends, family and country' (Loose, 1996: A01). Her niece commented that 'It's what we were after: to have someone acknowledge that she was a regular loyal American and that she was treated shamefully by the United States government' (Loose, 1996: A01).

Of interest here is the continued use of loyalty by the judge and the family. The family felt this need to have the loyalty of Braude vindicated. This points to the social construction of the emotion and how it is an all or nothing commitment. The actor can be loyal or disloyal and once labelled it is very hard to escape that tag. In this case, the rhetoric of loyalty is being turned back against the use of the term during the McCarthy period, again illustrating the contested nature of the emotion. The long battle that Braude undertook also illustrates the importance of the loyalty label to the actor—to be called disloyal was painful and required action to change this characterisation.

Loyalties are the justification for action used by the social actors in this period. Identity and nationalism are also part of this equation, to be a loyal American you could not be a communist, nor even have acquaintances who were. This debate mirrors the dual-loyalty debate of migrants, except that in this case it is an acquired loyalty that is the threat, not an assumed one the actor is born into. This indicates that even membership/joining based loyalties can be considered a betrayal to the nation layer. It also indicates that Wolff's (1968: 60–61, see this chapter) typology of contractual versus natural loyalty and their motivational power is problematic.

The hunt for communists in the McCarthy period was as vehement as any hunt for 'naturally' dis-loyal actors, such as those born in another country.

Conclusion

As a socially negotiated and contested emotion, loyalty is created, reinforced and enacted by the individual through the social structures of a given society. As the arguments and conflicts around the concept of loyalty illustrate, it can be a motivating emotion. Loyalty also plays a role in the construction of self and identity. This is illustrated with the inner conflict and turmoil many immigrants feel, with loyalties towards their country of origin and Australia. Loyalty also operates at several layers, from the family to religious and national loyalties. It is often the tension between layers that causes conflict. Loyalty is also a concept that is used to explain connections between nation states. This was illustrated by showing how the loyalty of Australia has expanded to include the United States of America as well as the traditional benefactor, Great Britain. While a nation state cannot experience an emotion, this did serve to illustrate how and to whom the actors within a country can be loyal and thus manifest the emotional response.

Two enduring themes in modern Australia have been war and immigration. These helped illuminate the emotion of loyalty. They showed how and why loyalty is contested in society and how important the emotion can be to the individual. While this chapter has necessarily glossed over much of the in-depth historical understanding of these concepts and events in Australia's history, what it has done is show the importance of these issues in relation to loyalty in Australia, and that these themes continue today.

The debates surrounding conscription illustrate the socially contested and emotion-like nature of loyalties. Both sides of the campaigns made appeals to loyalties from various layers, including family, mateship, empire, religion and country. The power of loyalty labelling, especially in terms of dis-loyalty and treason, is also shown by this case study. Loyalty was invoked as a motivation for action in these cases, irrespective of the layer that was being called upon. The discourse of loyalty during the conscription debates also shows how macro-sociological events can be explained by reference to the emotional experience of the actors involved.

Migrants, by their nature, cannot be naturally Australian and thus their loyalty is sometimes questioned, partly because they were not born here (or are not Anglo Celtic enough) and partly because they embody the other: the non Australian. They are locked out of the emotional experience of national loyalty by some gatekeepers in Australian society, but also by their own actions of self exclusion and lack of participation in and understanding of the symbolic rituals around nation loyalty. This results in that sense of never feeling quite at home that so many migrants report. They lack the sense of belonging and thus comfort with and in Australia. The experiences of 'ethnic' Australians in the world wars offers further evidence to support this contention.

It is perhaps not even possible to open up national loyalties to allow full participation from migrants. A possible solution to this dilemma of non-belonging is to open up the emotional manifestation of national loyalty to be inclusive of multiple countries. The nature of the other that loyalty requires needs to be redefined and, in Australia, the way members of our society who are not Anglo-Celtic enough must change to be inclusive and avoid the 'but where are you really from' question. Perkins (2004) offers one means to reconstruct ethnicity, and as a consequence national loyalty, by acknowledging the fact that Australia is a mixed race and ethnicity country, there is no one *ideal Australian*, but a bunch of Australians. However, Ong (1996) and Hage (1998) remind us that it is not just the state that constructs this but that it is a complex web of local interaction as well. The 'unofficial' problem is that some are still questioned about their heritage and consequently belonging, as this chapter has shown.

The brief analysis of the McCarthy period and the use of loyalty serves two purposes. First, this case illustrates the universality of loyalty debates in English, Judeo-Christian nations and allows me to claim that my Australian examples, while unique, are representative. Second, the response of those accused of dis-loyalty during the period illuminates how passionate loyalty is. To fight to clear one's name for forty years is far beyond any rational response—the passion is the motivation. It is telling that part of the reason for action in the Braude case was for acknowledgement of her loyalty to the country. This further supports my contention that an actor needs their loyalty acknowledged by others and when it is not it creates an emotional tension.

This chapter has advanced my case for the consideration of loyalty being an emotion by demonstrating that nation-based loyalties have a feeling component. Of particular note is the similarity of national loyalty to familial loyalty—this offers further weight to my claim that loyalty operates in a similar manner across layers. The appeals to loyalty are the same at each layer. The use of loyalty at the familial and nation layer is for the creation and maintenance of identity and motivation for action.

I have also contributed to the theorising of emotions by explaining the way loyalty works in macroscopic social processes—war and immigration—and connecting this with the experience, motivation and feeling of individual actors. This addresses the call for this type of research and analysis that Barbalet (1998) made.

The evidence for the social construction of loyalty to a nation is strong and I have shown that national identity does require a singular commitment that is mediated by actors. This mediation is maintained by dominant groups in society for particular purposes. In the case of conscription this was for the purpose of mobilising the war effort. For ethnicity and migrant loyalty, it is about maintaining an other with which to define oneself against. The concept of cultural capital helps to explain the benefit that accrues to the 'gatekeepers' of national loyalty.

National loyalty is generally the broadest loyalty experienced by the actor and encapsulates many macro-sociological processes. Familial loyalty is the most representative micro-sociological process. Sport, the case study of the next chapter, bridges these two layers of loyalty.

Chapter Six
Sport and Loyalty

The fan is the one who suffers. He cheers a guy to a .350 season then watches that player sign with another team. When you destroy fan loyalties, you destroy everything.

Frank Robinson

Introduction

Sport has a major impact on many people's identities and social interactions. Sporting fans are known to go to great lengths in support of their teams. As the *Evening Herald* (2003: 61) commented 'loyal fans are inclined to ignore all past history, current form, the opposition and various other obvious, slap-in-the-face facts and back their team unswervingly. Well, life would be pretty rubbish if you never thought your team would win'. It is these themes of identification and support—encapsulated by the notion of loyalty—that this chapter explores.

An enduring criticism of the literature on Australian sport is that it is descriptive and congratulatory. Rowe and Lawrence (1998: 159) argue that it has been 'characterised by a celebratory and descriptive – rather than a critical and analytical – approach'. In this chapter, I offer another way of reading sport. Sport and loyalty have a strong relationship, be it from fans to the club, players to the colours or a nation to the team. I draw out various case studies and examples linking sports to loyalty, with the aim of answering these questions: how are sporting loyalties fostered, maintained and extended? What purpose do strong sporting affiliations play for the actor and for society? When conflict between loyalties occurs within the sporting arena how is this negotiated? While I outline an explanation of these issues in the chapter, the overriding issue that I explore is this: what is the social circumstance of loyalty in sport?

This chapter adds more evidence that loyalty is an emotion and has certain aspects to it that operate across different layers. I will draw out a number of striking similarities in the way sporting, family and national loyalties are discussed. In many ways this chapter, and the next, fill the gap between the macro level of nations and the micro level of families.

In discussing the social circumstance of sport it is imperative to understand the globalised nature of professional sport in the modern era. Not only has the ownership of sporting teams and brands become the province of multinational companies, the broadcast and the ownership of the means of broadcast is becoming a key component of how, and when sport is played. The influence of capitalism and globalisation cannot be divorced from the individual experience of barracking for a sporting team. It is to this issue of the global that I first turn.

Product, Spectacle and Marketing

Global consumption patterns and capitalism cannot be removed from the analysis of sport-related loyalty. The sport production process, primarily as a result of professionalisation, has resulted in the commodification of sports, which has ushered in immense changes in the way sport is watched, played and managed (Rowe & Lawrence, 1998: 159–164). The production and consumption of sport is big business, and like all businesses, it needs to expand and create new markets. This often leads to conflict between the owners of the sporting codes and the team fans.

Rowe and Lawrence (1998: 164–167) offer an illuminating case study highlighting the change in sport from amateur organisation to one of production and consumption for profits' sake. In the mid 1990s, the Australian Rugby League (ARL) competition suffered a major split due to the battle between two major media owners (Murdoch's News Limited and Packer's PBL) for control of the sport. This fight was primarily about gaining control of the television rights for the rugby league and thus access to the lucrative television advertising the game attracts. The result of the split was the formation of two separate competitions and a large amount of animosity between the rival camps. In terms of ownership, the media in Australia was also split between the Murdoch and Packer camps, ensuring that the way the events were reported (or in some cases whether they were at all) was largely determined by which paper, radio or television network was reporting. Eventually the Australian Rugby League (ARL) was forced into a compromise with Super League (News Ltd's rival competition created in 1995) after the ARL's media backers, the Packer-led conglomerate, cut a deal with Murdoch's News Limited over the television coverage (Rowe & Lawrence, 1998: 165). Due to the merger of the two competitions, a 20 team league was inaugurated during 1998 with plans to reduce this to 14 by 2000. This reduction in teams, as a result of the split, forced the South Sydney Rugby League club out of the competition—the key case study of this chapter.

Of note to my argument, and a point made forcibly by Rowe and Lawrence (1998: 164), is that 'the recent events surrounding rugby league demonstrate how a simultaneous understanding of the global and local processes is imperative for any kind of adequate analysis of sport'. Thus it is both the global imperative of capitalism and the local interaction that can help inform sport sociology and create a more complete picture of the events under study, especially when it come to loyalty. At the time of the split there was continued talk of mergers and amalgamations of clubs, which had a profound impact at the level of the local. As Rowe and Lawrence (1998: 166) note, clubs threatened with amalgamation 'resisted any economically-driven reorganisation, with "loyal" supporters forcefully declaring their unique, place-based identity'. What this indicates is that even under pressure from global capital, such as that of competing media barons, the local fan still attempts to assert some degree of power and influence. How this fan resistance is played out is a focus of this chapter. My examples suggest that sport still needs to be grounded in fan loyalty and support. Its 'foundation . . . must be local, regional and national culture' (Rowe and Lawrence, 1998: 166). I will explore this assertion in the chapter by exploring just why some fans keep their club and others have lost theirs.

The fans themselves point to the importance of the local and the tribal. One sports commentator was concerned that there may be a strong and a weak competition and commented on the wash up after the battle for control of rugby league in Australia:

In the post-mortems by the winners and losers after the Super League court decisions, there remains one constant – very little reference by either side to the ultimate stakeholders in the game of Rugby League, the now long-suffering fans. . . . The last thing I want to see is a decision by clubs or players to field less than full-strength teams in whatever form of competition that eventually gets underway. That would be nothing less than a sell-out of the long-standing loyalties of the supporters upon whom the game ultimately depends. (Mulcair, 1996: 45)

Mulcair, from the dual position as commentator and fan, is identifying the key component of Rugby League, the loyal fan. The loyal fan is the bedrock that maintains a strong code and support base, as well as—critically for the owners—the revenue. This is highlighted by the cause of the split, namely the fight for pay television rights and the lucrative income this can generate. However, without a strong supporter base the television rights have little value.

As part of this battle between the media owners Murdoch and Packer, the ARL imposed what they called 'loyalty agreements' on clubs wishing to stay within their competition. They also had 'loyalty' contracts for individual players (Master, 1996: 4). The ARL, as the original administrator of the sport, was desperately trying to keep clubs and players in their camp. Invoking loyalty to the code and local heritage was one way of trying to encourage them to stay within their competition. Despite this, the allure of considerably more money tempted many of the best players and better organised clubs away to the Murdoch consortium.

Edwards argues (2002: 127) that the increasing commercialisation of sport has resulted in sport becoming 'a façade for getting ratings and making money'. This has resulted in the decline of community ties and identification. To quote Edwards (2002: 127), 'children were raised to be loyal to a particular club and felt part of a football community. When the game became commercialised . . . it became manufactured entertainment to be sold to customers'. Thus the market, and its globalised, corporatised profit imperatives have taken over what was once an emotional relationship and commercialised it.

In Rugby League we can see another side of the globalisation processes through the battle for television rights and control of the international competition between Australia, New Zealand and Great Britain. The increasing corporatisation of the clubs is occurring as many are becoming fully fledged business enterprises as opposed to player and fan owned and managed co-operatives. The Canterbury Bulldogs Rugby League Club exemplify this. For much of their history they have been known as a 'family club' (Byrne, 2004: 2). Increasingly, a corporate management style culture has crept in, including attempts to develop a $800 million resort complex attached to their club. This change in the way sport is organised and played has, according to Edwards (2002: 127), had a profound impact on a variety of relationships: 'the relationships between players, clubs and supporters all shifted from community relationships to market ones'. This has inevitably led to conflict between the loyal fans and the loyalties of management and owners. This conflict will be explored in depth in later case studies, but the experience of Soccer Australia highlights this point.

Soccer in Australia has had a difficult history in establishing a competitive league and challenging the traditionally dominant winter sports of Rugby (League and Union) and Australian Rules. A key problem has been the ethnic tribalism that has been associated with some major clubs. Hughson (1998: 171–2) identifies clubs in Melbourne and Sydney as being particularly associated with ethnicity. Two prime examples, but by no means the only, were Sydney United (formerly Sydney Croatia) and South Melbourne (Greek). In an attempt to 'clean up' what was perceived as an ethnic violence problem at games, soccer's governing body forced these clubs to change names and/or venues and banned national flags and symbols of ethnicity from games (Hughson, 1998: 172). The fans responded with subversive displays of ethnic allegiance. These include 'secret identities' as members of fanclubs, or the wearing of baseball caps with country insignia (Hughson, 1998: 176). Hughson (1998: 176) quotes one fan as saying that 'without our colours we don't stand for anything'. The fans are intensely loyal to their club and ethnic identity—to them they are intertwined and not separate layers. The attempts by administrators to remove one aspect of the fan's identity impinges upon all of their self. We can see their subversive responses as part of the way loyalties motivate behaviours.

This conflict between soccer's sports governing body and the fans is similar to the problem the Australian Rugby League has been facing. While the governing body is intent on commercialising and expanding the game, the fans are there primarily for the personal connection they have with the team and what it represents. In the context of European soccer fans, de Ruyter and Wetzels (2000: 403) have found that: 'membership of a social group (i.e., the fan club), peer expectations and social sanctions are pervasive normative influences that are frequently stronger than personal norms'. The following case studies will problematise these claims as I question the motivational power of fan loyalty.

Notwithstanding the critique of sport as a marketing exercise useful to capitalism, sport has another aspect to it—it is a ritual. Building on the work of Durkheim on religion and Goffman on ritual, Birrell (1981), argues that sport can be seen as one of the everyday occurrences that maintains social bonds. Sport is 'a social ceremony structurally capable of fulfilling social functions comparable to those of religious ceremonies' which serves the purpose of 'reaffirming the values of the social order' (Birrell, 1981: 356). I contend that loyalty is part of this affirmation of social order. Hence, as we are ritualised to be loyal to sporting teams we are also reaffirming the social value of loyalty.

South Sydney Rabbitohs

The South Sydney Rugby League club, affectionately known as the Rabbitohs or Souths, was excluded from the Australian Rugby League competition in October 1999. With the amalgamation of the two rival competitions the number of teams was reduced from 20 to 14. The code management instigated a review of all clubs and assessed them on a range of factors, including sponsorship, on-field success, product marketing, and game attendance. South Sydney was one of the teams chosen to be excluded by the game management and owners—News Limited and the Australian Rugby League (ARL). Just two and a half years later (March 2002), after multiple legal battles, the Rabbitohs re-joined the competition. The response of Rabbitoh fans to their team's exclusion is an illuminating case study in fan loyalty and what can be achieved when sufficient numbers of fans are motivated to fight. Moller (2003: 217) explains the connection thus:

for supporters, following a club demands a certain kind of commitment. Being a fan entails a sense of duty and a responsibility to protect the community of which they are part. This passion is crucial to understanding Souths' struggle, because the . . . demands of supporters make little sense without their emotional commitment.

I will argue that this emotional commitment can be neatly explained by looking at fan behaviour through the emotion of loyalty. However, it must be noted that the reason Souths regained their place in the competition was due to a legal ruling that the game's management had breached the Australian Trade Practices Act. Fan outrage, while contributing heavily to the financial costs of the legal battle, had little bearing on the court decision. In fact, at one point, fans at the club were warned that their behaviour in court could be jeopardising the case (Bullock, 2000: 1).

The following cases are specific individual examples that a critic may construe as being extreme and un-representative of the majority of fans. First, in 'seeing' emotion I am using Katz's (1999) methodology that explicitly calls for evidence that borders on the sensational (see Chapter Three). Thus these examples may appear sensational and not representative at first glance. However they are not, as they represent a small snapshot of the wealth of material that the Souths' fight created for my argument. Second, the very public displays of loyalty through attendance at rallies indicates the widespread feelings of fans.

The most public displays of support for the club came on October 10 1999, just five days before the Rabbitohs were excluded from the competition. Some 40 000 people turned up for a rally and march, most bedecked in the club colours of red and green, to protest the imminent exclusion (De Brito & Hilferty, 2000: 4). It was this form of commitment that Souths managed to motivate in their fight. One banner held by fans at the rally read: 'Question: What do you get for 92 years of loyalty??? Answer: F**K All' (Rabbitoh Warren, 1999, image 26, censorship in original).

The fans took the long legal and media battle to reinstate the Rabbitohs very seriously. It was as though a member of their own family was in the dock, threatened with execution. The *Newcastle Herald* (2000: 4) described one fan known as 'Rabbit': 'Rabbit is your typical die-hard South Sydney fan – deeply loyal and unrepentant about the Rabbitohs fight'. When asked to comment on the Rabbitohs losing the appeal for re-instatement (3 November 2000) Rabbit said 'I am never going to utter the word football again . . . I have been brought up with Rugby League, four generations of us are Rugby League fanatics . . . But I didn't even watch a match last year because of my disgust with how Souths was treated' (*Newcastle Herald*, 2000:4). Rabbit's identification with the Rabbitohs forms part of his identity; he is a League supporter, but first and foremost a Souths supporter. His passion for the club is shown by his refusal to watch Rugby League for a year, despite being a self confessed fanatic. This reaction can be seen as a manifestation of loyalty. Rabbit is employing one of the few avenues of dissent that is available to him by boycotting Rugby League. This response was echoed by many other fans. For example, Wade Singleton, remarked that 'life was a case of "South Sydney first, rugby league second" ' (Courtney, 2000a: 1).

Another fan identified this exit strategy as a result of Souths exclusion. Billy Trevillian (quoted in Bullock, 2000: 3–4) claimed:

I've always said that I'm not a rugby league supporter, I'm a South Sydney supporter. And that means that I believe I represent a majority of Souths supporters, 80% or 90% that will really walk away from this game. Now I've spoken to people that don't even like sport; I had one fellow the other day, he was a Knights supporters (sic) that doesn't watch the game any more, and those people are watching very closely the outcomings (sic) of this court case. This game, without South Sydney, it's going to take a big nosedive.

One South Sydney player, Jim Serdaris, stated that 'he would never play rugby league again' (De Brito & Hilferty, 2000: 4) after the first court case was lost. Serdaris went on to explain his feelings (De Brito & Hilferty, 2000: 4):

I've had offers to go to other clubs but I've always been loyal. . . . But with this decision I'm not playing rugby league any more, I don't want to play rugby league. This used to be the No 1 game in Australia. . . . I'm going to give it up because my heart is not there without South Sydney. It's not money or anything any more, it's the right thing.

Serdaris is again echoing the 'exit' option of loyalty that Hirschman (1970) identified in his model of behaviour. According to Hirschman, actors will use the exit strategy when a continued connection to a company is no longer of any benefit and they have no reservoir of loyalty remaining. Thus, Sedaris is no longer going to engage in the sport because of the treatment of Souths, and by extension of his fan and player status, to him as well. It is noteworthy that Serdaris chooses emotive and feeling terminology in justifying his decision by saying his heart is not in it. This conjures love and commitment imagery as the heart is most often associated with love, pointing to the depth of feeling experienced by the fans in their loyalty to the club. Fans are showing that for them loyalty is emotional and motivates their actions.

This deep attachment and the sense of loss then experienced is shown by the response of another fan during a radio interview (Bullock, 2000: 4):

Myra Hagarty: My daughter Linda, she said 'Mum, there's a change in you, I can see a change. You've got nothing to talk about now, I just know it's hurting.' It is hurting me too. I miss it very much.

Interviewer: There's no way you're interested as a fan of rugby league to go and watch a game anywhere else?

Myra Hagarty: No way, no. I just stay home now. I just worry about it, like not being in it, because it was so much a part of us all the time. You've got to be a Souths' person to understand fully how it's hurt us all. A lot of my friends, they're all old and they're dying, and they're dying with a broken heart because of what they've done to Souths; they've followed them for much longer than me, like years longer than me, and mine's over 50 years.

Again the evidence shows an emotional connection and highlights the pain being felt by the fans over the treatment of the Rabbitohs. Myra Hagarty's comments offer a number of insights into loyalty. A large part of her identity and social existence is tied up in the Rabbitohs. The fact that she has less to talk about is an indication of the importance she placed on her fan status and club loyalties—it was a part of her all the time. Her daughter has pointed out that she is hurting, to which she agrees—she is feeling a loss of identity and reason for action and existence. Her particular loyalty to Souths is highlighted by her refusal to watch other teams play, despite loving the game of League.

The Burgess family offer another portrait of loyalty (Kershler, 2001: 142). Kershler (2001: 142) describes how, as a condition of marriage, Sue Burgess had to agree to follow Souths—an entirely reasonable request to David Burgess who has been a fan for 37 years. After Souths was excluded from the competition in 1999, the Burgess family made plans to move to Brisbane, only to have Souths re-instated just before the move. The family then made plans to drive the nine hours from Brisbane to Sydney to watch every game, indicating their clear commitment to their fan status. Eventually the Burgess family decided to move back to Sydney because they felt unable to be so far from their club. Dave Burgess explained it thus: 'I've just done the figures. I reckon it's cost us $20000 . . . It will be worth every cent. If I could have paid 20 grand two years ago to keep 'em in the comp, I would have done it' (Kershler, 2001: 142). The fan status and loyalty of this family provided a clear motivation for action as they structured their lives around their team. They were happy to uproot themselves and move house in order to be closer to the team and the games. According to Kershler (2001: 142), Burgess 'admits he cried when Souths were chucked out . . . and cried again when they were allowed back in'. This deep emotional attachment and commitment to the club indicates the value that the Burgess family placed upon their relationship with the club as fans. It informed their identity, gave them purpose and influenced decisions made as a family unit. As Burgess himself explained: 'I just love the Bunnies, It's the one thing we do as a family. I love 'em, absolutely' (Kershler, 2001: 142).

The committed relationship that fans have to the club is illustrated by the lengths to which they go to support their team. The *Gold Coast Bulletin* (28 November, 2002: 21) reported on one fan, Steve Lane, who lived near Brisbane but made a special trip to watch the Rabbitohs train when they visited the Gold Coast. The *Bulletin* quoted him as being 'a mad-keen South Sydney fan . . . "I've been a Souths fan since I was six. I have my own shrine at home"'. It is this religious fervour that many fans bring to their barracking. This illustrates the ritualised nature of fan loyalty, and consequently the power and influence that this has over many fans. This fan, to use Durkheimian terminology, is investing his team with the value of the sacred; 'sacred things are special things, protected, isolated, separated, prohibited, inaccessible, apart from the mundane world: they are invested with special properties' (Birrell, 1981: 357). This fan's shrine is invested with the meaning and value of his support for the Rabbitohs. The identity component of this fan's loyalty to his club is quite compelling; it is a part of who he is, as shown by the ritualised nature of his connection.

The *Gold Coast Bulletin* (29 November, 2002: 79) reported on another fan that they described as 'one of the most rabid despite the fact that he lives in Queensland'. This fan travelled from Brisbane missing a day's work just to see a training session. The *Bulletin* explained that Souths 'attract loyal fans as Garnett's [the subject of the story] phone message proves: "Please leave a message after the beep and go the Rabbitohs"'.

Another fan volunteered to work in the Rabbitohs' office, making a serious sacrifice in time and money to help the club out: 'I spend my annual leave working in the Rabbitohs' office . . . It doesn't matter that its a four-hour trip – I'm happy to do it for the club . . . My heart and soul are with the Rabbitohs', and that's where they will stay' (quoted in Guy, 2000: 141). For fans, their loyalty explains the commitment and sacrifice they will make. The loyalty they feel means that a four-hour trip is not an imposition, but almost a badge of fidelity. Once again, loyalty can be seen as a strong motive for action for some fans. These cases illustrate the myriad ways that fans operationalise, or enact, their loyalty, showing that loyalty can spur action, but that the action is determined by a host of other factors.

Fan passion is not limited to the average supporter. Mascord and Walter (2003: 25) report that Russell Crowe had taken the Rabbitohs team to dinner at a local pub in 2003. They quote Rabbitohs' captain Fletcher saying: 'I think it was just us being together, he was just like one of us . . . he just sat down and had a yarn to us, told a few stories and we enlightened him on a few of our stories'. Crowe was showing his commitment to the club by engaging with it in a family-like way. To Crowe, like many fans, this is family. The loyalty relationship provides a sense of belonging and place, giving Crowe, and fans like him, a sense of being part of something greater. While the advantages and connections of being a movie star certainly help the likes of Crowe, it is clear the he considers the Rabbitohs to be part of his history and identity, and takes his support for the club very seriously. So seriously that he, in partnership with an entrepreneur, bought the Club in 2006.

After the Rabbitohs initially lost the appeal for re-instatement, a self confessed 'mad keen' supporter Anth Courtney (2000b: 2) had this to ask of the game's management:

How, Mr Moffett, Mr Hill, Mr Murdoch, (the managers/owners of the National Rugby League, NRL) do you expect these juniors to accept such a blow and yet at the same time continue to strive towards playing in rugby league's supposed 'premier competition'? How can you place such reliant belief upon these kids, who have dreamed of playing for Souths when they grow up, suddenly and effortlessly changing their alliance (sic) and aspirations to another club? And even more incredulously, how on earth do you expect the South Sydney parents to ever allow their kids to transfer their allegiance to another club, let alone keep playing rugby league at all and not the increasingly more attractive and popular rugby union? It is this concept of the 'tribal loyalist' that the NRL, News and anyone else remotely associated with the section of the rugby league community that gloats over Souths' omission, fails to grasp.

Courtney identified some of the key components of fan loyalty through the idea of the 'tribal loyalist'. Edgar (2001) develops this idea of the 'tribal' connection of the individual to her place in the world, and the importance this has for informing her identity, particularly in the context of nationalistic identity. We are tribalistic because it is those close connections, to clan, local groups and place that give a sense of self to the actor. In Edgar's (2001: 82) words; 'we are very tribal. We have particularistic loyalties to our own home base, our football team, our neighbourhood and its local causes'. It is this team-based support that drives fans, rather than a wider affection for Rugby League. The layer of loyalty that operates for the fans is that of the club and team, rather than the code. This is relevant to my argument as it indicates that loyalty operates in layers (team versus code in this instance) and that the existence of different layers can foster conflict.

An important aspect of loyalty is that it cannot be easily switched. Once actors are loyal to something or someone it tends to be enduring. Courtney (2000b) echoed this idea by arguing that it is impossible to expect once loyal fans to switch their allegiances, especially when that switch would support the architects of the demise of the Rabbitohs. While Courtney does not use the word traitor, this charge is implicit throughout his quote. The reason that loyalties cannot be easily switched/changed is that once a commitment is made and loyal behaviour has ensued, it is emotionally and socially challenging to change it. This contention will be explored in depth in the next section on the Canterbury Bulldogs. All of the evidence from South's fans points to this contention. The identity that fans gain from being loyal supporters precludes them from abandoning the club—even though its core business, that of playing Rugby League, has been removed. Being a Souths' fan is part of who these people are.

However, this conclusion from the evidence presented needs to be qualified. There is evidence that loyalty does fade and disappear. The problem here is in accessing material that supports this. Fans who slowly give away their support do not often announce it to the world (I report on one instance shortly), which makes it very difficult for a researcher to access such examples. Consequently, it must be acknowledged that the loyalty connection can fade and disappear depending upon the circumstances. In the case of Souths, there must have been some fans who gave up after not seeing their club playing for two seasons in the competition of which they had always been part.

The requirement for loyalty to have an opposition, as I discussed in Chapter Three, or something to define loyalty against, is supported by the evidence from the Rabbitohs fight with the NRL. The NRL management, and in particular the Chairman of News Limited Rupert Murdoch (part owners of the NRL and the instigators of the split in the game in the years preceding the Souths fight), were characterised as money-hungry businessmen bent on the destruction of the 'people's game'. Some of the banners displayed during the 2000 'Save The Game' rally illustrate this point nicely. One reads: 'Heh Rupert, all I want for Christmas is my bunnies back' (Rabbitoh Warren, 2000, image 30). Another reads: 'No self respecting fish would wrap itself in a Murdoch newspaper' (Rabbitoh Warren, 2000, image 36). Others were more forthright: 'Murdoch Mob Murdered the R.L.' and 'Rupert rooted the R.L.' (Rabbitoh Warren, 2000, image 34). Another sums up the depth of feeling fans have for their club and their consequent hatred of the NRL and News Limited (South Sydney Rabbitohs, 2000, image 157):

Does anyone understand how we feel? Well imagine your closest family member has just been murdered. Murdoch is cancer & must be stopped from ruining all sport not just Rugby League.

Souths fans had a clear target that was seen as a threat to their team and they were able to attack it with boycotts, letters, talkback radio commentary and the posters and banners I quote from above.

Loyalties constructed around a sporting team and support for that team provide an explanation for some individual behaviour. In the case of Souths fans, I have shown how important their loyalty to the club was in giving them an identity as fans. This connection to the team then guided behaviour and actions, as seen in the rallies, protests and boycotts. The intensely emotional aspect of this loyalty is highlighted by many of the fans' heartfelt pleas to return their club, as well as the anger and aggression directed at those deemed responsible for Souths' exclusion from the competition. The group dynamic of fan support was shown by how fans felt a need to profess their loyalty in social ways—to 'show the colours' to use sporting terminology. What a sociological understanding of loyalty shows in the case study is that loyalty can explain how and why some people will act in certain ways. The behaviours, thoughts and feelings of the fans can be explained by applying the concepts of loyalty that I discussed in Chapter Three. This section provided further evidence supporting my argument that loyalty operates in a particular pattern.

The Canterbury Bulldogs' Crises

For loyal fans it is sometimes difficult to identify a target against which to vent their anger. This is particularly the case when the actions causing the difficulties originate from within the team or the management. Another Rugby League team, the Canterbury Bulldogs, underwent two successive crises that illustrate this difficulty.

In 2002 the Bulldogs were caught overpaying their players and it was established that the team had breached the salary cap rules placed on all teams. The salary cap system was designed to even out the competition by limiting the amount that could be spent on player contracts. Ideally, this would result in a more even competition and thus a better spectacle. The NRL stripped the Bulldogs of 37 competition points, taking them from their status as favourites to win the grand final and competition leaders to certain 'wooden spooners'. One fan summed up the feelings this aroused when he had to take three weeks stress leave from his work (Yamine & Williams, 2003: 12). This fan is quoted as saying: 'I was just shattered . . . I couldn't concentrate at work and I had a lot of sleepless nights because I couldn't stop thinking about it' (Yamine & Williams, 2003: 12).

The scandal and the response from fans spread as far as Federal Parliament. The Member for Rankin, Dr Craig Emerson (2002: 5578) said:

> I use this opportunity to speak on the plight of the Bulldogs or on 'Doggiegate', as the issue has come to be known. As a loyal supporter of the Bulldogs since 1967, I indicate that those responsible for breaching the salary cap have badly let down all Bulldogs' fans. By stripping the Bulldogs of all their competition points, other than those for the byes, the National Rugby League is punishing not only the management but also the players and the fans. I am sure the fans had nothing to do with the breaching of the salary cap . . . I note that another club has been found guilty of a technical breach of the salary cap, so it looks like there are two types of breaches: a technical breach and a Bulldogs breach. Any and all clubs found guilty of breaching the salary cap, no matter whether it is by $100,000 or $1,000,000, should be thrown out of the competition, retrospectively if need be. I leave you with this point: you cannot keep a good dog down. The Bulldogs will be back in 2003 and will win the competition.

Emerson spoke as a representative of the fans when he attacked the NRL for their handling of the breach. This attack was similar to the one mounted by Souths' fans. Emerson did take issue with the club's management, but only mildly. This is the same approach most fans took, attacking the NRL and others who dared criticise their club while avoiding blaming the club management and the players, which is perhaps where others thought the fault should lie. Ricketts (2002: 2) reports that at one game, following the announcement that Canterbury would lose the points, about a dozen spectators threw objects and insults at the television commentary box and at Phil Gould, a coach who had called for the Bulldogs' expulsion. This illustrates how loyal fans can turn their anger at any target perceived to be threatening 'their' team, or, at the very least, use team loyalty as a justification for aggressive activities. This is indicative of the blind support that loyalty often creates as the real culprits were, in-fact, the management and players of the club itself. However, this would contradict a fan's professed commitment and belonging. As McKell (2004: 3) points out; 'the Canterbury club is tribal, perhaps the last of the breed in the NRL . . . being a fan mean[s] giving a giant defiant " Up Yours" to everybody who wasn't a fan'. Thus others, peripheral to the problem, and in this case, the NRL, the media and individuals making comments, are the target of aggression. The Bulldogs and the fans also received no support from other clubs or supporters, unlike the Souths fight. Souths mustered wide and diverse support from the League community in general. The protest rallies, while being a sea of red and green (Souths' colours) also revealed jerseys from many other clubs, both current and past. The Bulldogs' lack of support from other clubs is not at all surprising as the Bulldogs' breach of the salary cap meant that it was harder for other clubs to do well—hence the lack of sympathy of other fans for the Bulldogs. It needs to be noted that the fans attacking those who were perceived to be against their club are at one extreme of the loyalty spectrum. Many fans would not have defended their club with as much vitriol as those depicted in the examples. Further, some fans did give up on the club, something I will discuss shortly.

This phenomenon of shifting blame when the object of loyalty is the cause of the problem is further highlighted by another incident involving the Canterbury Bulldogs team. During a training camp at a resort in Coffs Harbour in February 2004, allegations of sexual assault were made against a number of Bulldogs' players. Many fans responded immediately to the perceived threat of these allegations against their club and players. On *The Kennel*, the internet forum for Bulldogs' supporters, fans made a number of comments in defence of their team. 'Killer Dog' commented that Coffs Harbour is a 'hoe town ready to make the papers . . . RAPE!! Those females' legs are open 24hrs' (quoted in Devine, 2004: 15). While this is a particularly extreme example, it does illustrate the savagery that loyalty can help foster. Another view expressed by fans was that the players could not have been responsible, either the media was lying about the incidents or the alleged victim was lying. 'K E', another contributor to the forums, encapsulates this point (The Kennel, 2004):

you know frankly i dont (sic) give a rats ass if this 'woman' was hurt, look at all the lives she hurt and all the relationships she broke up because of this bulls**t. next time she should stop for two seconds and think about how serious these allegations are.

F**K THE MEDIA.

(censorship and emphasis in original)

Another fan made this appeal to supporters: 'well let me say this . . . first and foremost The Guys are INNOCENT UNTIL PROVEN GUILTY!!' (The Kennel, 2004 atomic_crimson, emphasis in original). While the woman making the allegations against the club became a clear target of fan derision early on, this thread of attack was rapidly stopped by forum administrators (obviously concerned about the tone of the attacks further tarnishing the club's image), and a different target for fan anger emerged—the media.

When fans' loyalty is questioned, anger often results, but where can fans direct their unhappiness when the cause of the crisis is the object of that loyalty? Bulldogs' fans responded by attacking others, with the media being a prime target. On *The Kennel*, 'riomach' (The Kennel, 2004a) made this comment:

> I just wanted to say that I am forever a bulldog supporter and it saddens me to see the media frenzy surrounding our boys when at the moment, we only have allegations. I hope that everyone can settle down – yes you media! – and wait until the outcome of the police investigation – whatever that may be. I really hate seeing all these damn headlines. It tears my heart apart. It's times like these when we must show our true colours – the MIGHTY BLUE AND WHITE! And I agree, I will not be turning away from the doggies. I will support them to the bitter end! (emphasis in original)

This fan's statement, of unwavering commitment, indicates that loyalty does motivate behaviour and does play a role in identity formation. This example demonstrates the emotional connection of the fan to the Club. It is also worth noting the use of emotional terminology—in particular, 'tears my heart apart', being indicative of the level of feeling this fan has for the Bulldogs.

To further illustrate these points, another fan, 'Christabella' (The Kennel, 2004) posted this message:

> There are sections of the media that will do anything to crush this club but we always keep bouncing back bigger and better than ever. There's no other club out there who I believe could fightback as well as the Doggies do and a good part of this is due to the huge amount of passion that us supporters have for the club.

For Christabella, a fan's passion and commitment is important as it helps shape identity and group connection. Further, this post echoes McKell's (2004) comment (above) that the Bulldogs are very tribal and defiant. Again the terminology used is based in feeling language, 'passion', and this fan identifies that it is the emotional connection to the club that fans experience.

In another forum thread titled *More Irresponsible reporting* (The Kennel, 2004 club_sweat, censorship and emphasis in original), the fans had this to say:

club_sweat:	As usual, the media is a joke. Fullstop. They are a disgrace. you heard it here first
PIMP:	****THE MEDIA
K E:	F**K The Media, They'd sell their mothers for a story the evil F***S
Jados:	It just shows you who is running sport in this country!!!!!! Or anything else for that matter.
Cammo:	If people stopped listening to these so called journos then they wouldn't have any power. Can't see that happening though.

While internet forums are renowned for their ersatz character, these fans are expressing a real anger and disappointment. This neatly illustrates the conflict an actor may experience when the object of loyalty is the very problem in the first place and one potential response—blame shifting. I have explored this dilemma previously through family loyalty, and it should be noted that many of the fans use the concept of family to describe their sporting loyalties. When threatened, loyal actors will often defend the object of loyalty. This is because loyalty forms part of their identity, and consequently, they are being attacked themselves. This provides motivation to defend their club and themselves. The problem when the taint is from within is that this admission makes the fans feel that their loyalties have little value, or that it is not the right thing to do. Hence the strong appeals of Canterbury fans to maintain their support and show the colours, as 'riomach's' (The Kennel, 2004b) appeal shows: 'as supporters it is up to us to show our loyalty and raise above the other fans who wish to pull us down. Lets (sic) not lower ourselves to their standard. We will gain much more respect by the way [we] all conduct ourselves in a proper manner'.

This set of comments mirrors many of the comments Souths' fans made in relation to who owns and manages the game. Bulldogs' fans are, like their South compatriots, lamenting the control the code management has and the influence of the media on the sport. Much of the critique of the media is centred on its perceived need for scandal to sell newspapers or advertising air-time. The fans, in both examples, are indicating their displeasure at what they see as a local and personal loyalty to a club being taken over by the demands of the code administration/management and the imperatives of the media. This media imperative is the increasing spectacularisation of sport for ratings gain. Fans feel as if they have been left behind, lost as passive spectators, with little real power to influence what is going on. This is an example of Rowe and Lawrence's (1998) point regarding the importance of understanding the clash of the global with the local when it comes to sport sociology. These fans are seeing, reading and hearing this clash, but conversely, as the case of Souths vividly illustrates, the fans can and do respond to the capitalist imperatives of profit and growth. What is significant is that a key avenue of dissent and resistance revolves around passions or emotions. I have identified how loyalty is used as a key emotion within these fan reactions in helping to fashion resistance, thus supporting my argument that loyalty is indeed an emotion and has a certain role within social interactions.

The comments discussed so far all use fans that are continuing to profess their loyalty to their club. However, for some fans, the scandals and misbehaviour reach a point where they cannot maintain their loyalty. One made a farewell comment to the forums (whippet_hound, The Kennel, 2004):

To be honest I am impressed by the undying support displayed by the few regulars on the forums. For me however I've had enough, after the last three years I just can't continue to be disappointed and built up only to be brought crashing back down again. I have supported the Doggies for 27 years and loved almost every minute that is except for the last three years. The scandals and wrong doings are literally killing me . . . I have made a decision to support the Nth Qld Cowboys, sure they aren't going to win the premiership but they are realistic in their expectation and I feel at least I know where I stand with them.

This fan is exercising the Hirschman (1970) strategy of exit discussed earlier in this chapter. No longer can this fan accept the conduct of the team and its management. This illustrates the point at which, for some fans, they assess their loyalty relationship as costing too much. For this fan, it was a result of being continually disappointed with off-field events. Team loyalty requires a return to the fans in terms of identity, motivation and social interaction. When the team shifts too far from the actor's perceived sense of values and morals, a re-assessment of that commitment can occur. This fan has left because the Bulldogs are no longer emotionally worthwhile. The question that arises from these cases of exit is what combination of factors lead to a fan giving up on what was once such a self-professed passion? While this is an intriguing micro-sociological question, it is beyond the scope of this work to address a factorial causal model of exit strategies. That question can only be addressed after I have established the basic premises, and understandings, of loyalty.

However, I will explore one way of understanding the reasons for fans giving up their loyalty. From a Durkheimian and Goffmanesque perspective Birrell (1981: 373–374) points out the consequences of poor character:

when character is so spectacularly lost, something else dies with it. If the moral order is to be preserved, those whose action flagrantly violate the sanctity of systematic values must be regarded as villains or weaklings, just as those who spectacularly conform to moral values must be feted as heroes.

In the case of the Bulldogs, the team had come to be regarded as villains by a proportion of the media and sporting public. They had broken the moral bonds that tie fan, player and team. 'Whippet hound' points out that the scandals are 'literally killing' him or her (though I suspect it is more metaphorical), so the moral bonds have certainly been killed for this fan. The fan's loyalty disappears when its target is morally moribund. Birrell (1981: 366) argues that one of the purposes of sport is to demonstrate respectable qualities, and 'that those demonstrations of character serve a dual purpose of establishing the character of the athlete and re-affirming the validity of the moral attributes the individual displays'. This is important to the fan because, by extension, the fan takes on some of the moral character of the player. Mewett (1999: 5) argues that this was apparent in the case of mythologising the Australian character in Gallipoli: 'by making heroes out of their troops, all Australians could claim to share the characteristics'. By making heroes out of their team's players and showing their loyalty, the fan can assume some of the heroic and athletic imagery so often associated with professional athletes. When the heroes fall, the fan also absorbs this.

The Canterbury Bulldogs' crisis serves to further illustrate and support the key contentions of my argument. Firstly, it offers a different yet equalling compelling example of fan loyalty to complement and extend the South Sydney case. Secondly, the examples further support the proposition that loyalty is an emotion and that it helps to furnish identity and motivation for action. The Bulldogs' examples also further illustrate how familial and passionate language is used in the context of sport and fan interactions. This adds evidentiary weight to my contention that loyalty operates in a similar manner irrespective of the layer being analysed, meaning that loyalty is a distinct phenomenon that exists within a range of social interaction.

Conclusion

This chapter has used several case studies and examples to show how fans connect, belong and identify with their teams. I have shown how loyalty provides fans with an identity and reason for action. This is particularly the case with Souths' battle to return to the Rugby League competition. Many of the fans professed an attachment to their club as if it was family—pointing to the deep emotional bonds that fan loyalty creates. In the case of Canterbury, the inner conflict that occurs when the fan feels that they have been let down is highlighted. Fans made a choice; some continued to value their connection to the club over and above the anguish it caused, while others decided that it was no longer of emotional value. While I lack the evidence to conclusively say why some fans would choose the exit strategy over others, I would posit that this depends on their loyalties to other social structures and forces.

This chapter has helped to bridge the gap between the layer of family loyalty in Chapter Five and national loyalty discussed in Chapter Six. What I have shown is that sport also makes use of loyalty in a very similar way to the other layers already discussed. This accumulation of evidence across a wide range of social levels and from diverse sources helps form a more coherent picture of the function of loyalty and the way it is invoked in modern society. The last area that I want to survey for evidence is what I have termed cultural loyalties, that is the use of loyalty in entertainment forms, marketing schemes and in the workplace.

Chapter Seven
Cultural Loyalty

'Her loyalties are uncertain'
        Professor Walsh commenting on Buffy the Vampire Slayer in *A New Man*.

Introduction

Thus far I have dealt with loyalty in a range of social settings; the family, the nation and, sporting organisations. Many of the case studies have used popular culture sources as the evidentiary base with which to explore that particular layer of loyalty. In the first part of this chapter I will be turning to popular culture itself to examine the way it represents loyalty. I will do this by focussing on a successful and widely academically studied television program—*Buffy the Vampire Slayer*. The purpose of this case study is to investigate if the representation of emotion in popular culture fits within my loyalty framework. Thus, in assessing the representation of emotion by television I will be scrutinising more evidence on the various aspects of loyalty that I have identified thus far.

This chapter will further justify the use of cultural sources as evidence in this book. By directly engaging with the material and showing how representations of loyalty in popular culture support my case, I can question if loyalty as represented is an accurate reflection of lived experience. This chapter then is essential in accumulating sufficient evidence to claim that loyalty is indeed an emotion.

Loyalty and Buffy the Vampire Slayer

In this section I draw out a number of examples of how loyalty is used in a popular television drama—*Buffy the Vampire Slayer* (*BtVS*). In Chapter Three I established the methodological rationale for using popular culture sources such as television shows as evidence to inform my argument, primarily by drawing on Docker's (1994) work. The key rationale is that television drama must reflect to some degree the lived reality of emotions or the audience would not watch. *BtVS* provides excellent material because loyalty has been a central emotional theme of the series. It is also an internationally popular show with a well developed cult following and internet fan community. *BtVS* has also been the subject of extensive academic scrutiny with an international journal dedicated to its study (*Slayage*), and many published books (see Badman, 2002, for an academic bibliography).

Before turning to the analysis, it is important to establish how important television is in contemporary life and the extent of the medium's impact. Williams (1990: 23) identifies television as central to the control and influence of the population in modern society. Firth (2000: 33) goes even further, arguing that:

> ... television has been the dominant medium of the second half of the twentieth century. It has transformed political communication and the process of democracy .... It is a source of new forms of cultural identity. It dominates the household world and has reshaped domesticity. It is the centre of what is now meant by commercialism, advertising and selling.

The consumption of television programming in Australia averaged 114 minutes per day in 1997 and is a central leisure pursuit for many people. The other most popular passive leisure activities were 'general reading' at 25 minutes and 'doing nothing' at 13 minutes (ABS, 1998). Americans, on average, watched 156 minutes per day of television in 2005, which made it the most popular leisure activity in the United States (BLS, 2006). Given that Kellner (2004) posits that *BtVS* 'functions as an allegorical spectacle about contemporary life', it is relevant to use an acclaimed show on the most popular leisure activity as evidence for the way loyalty is construed in society.

In analysing the representation of emotion on television (or in other words, its construction) it is clear that the producers, writers and directors influence how the emotions are used and shown. As Josh Whedon (creator of *BtVS*) states himself: 'The two things that matter the most to me: *emotional resonance* and rocket launchers. 'Party of Five', a brilliant show, often made me cry uncontrollably, suffered ultimately from a lack of rocket launchers' (emphasis added, audio commentary for *Innocence*). Whedon views emotional resonance with the audience as a central aim of good television. A review of the episode *Innocence* argues that 'Whedon's script, which ruminates on friendship, loyalty, trust and betrayal, has beautifully honed dialogue, and exhibits his customary command of the dynamic relationships between the lead characters' (*bbc.co reviews*, 2004). Creators of television programming must make the emotions appear real in their representations and effects on television, otherwise there is no resonance with the audience, who consequently, will not relate to the show. This is particularly the case with shows like *BtVS* that ask the audience to suspend their disbelief in relation to the core story drivers: super-powers, magic, demons and vampires. Emotional reality allows the viewer to more readily bridge the gap between an unreal world and their own existence. It is the emotional response that matters here, rather than the eliciting events, as the audience merely has to feel that they would act, think and emote in the same way that the characters do.

Furedi (2004: 57), commenting on the rise of emotional manipulation in the political sphere, reports that:

in Britain, politicians have even consulted Peter Bazalgette, the creator of the successful reality television programme, *Big Brother*, to advise them how to connect with the voters, particularly young people. Bazalgate claims that the reason why young people were more likely to vote for a contestant on *Big Brother* than for a political candidate is because 'they are emotionally engaged by the program'.

Here we have two very successful TV writers/producers commenting that the most important thing within the medium is emotion, and that it is creating an emotional connection between the audience and the show that fosters emotionality.

This accords with Docker's (1994: 276) position on programming when he argues that 'if networks . . . didn't put on programs that answered to such popularity and popular traditions, they would financially ail and die'. Audience Development Australia, a media ratings and survey company, reports that the television audience wants 'to support Australian writers and actors, seeing television drama as playing an essential role in portraying modern day Australia, promoting the physical and emotional identity which characterises this country' (ADA, 2003). Again, emotional resonance is viewed as important by the producers of content. This means that television programs must accord with emotions as they are in society by drawing on the common understanding and experience of the emotions by the audience. This emotional representation draws on the history of emotions and popular culture.

The preceding discussion provides the rationale for analysing loyalty in television generally and in *BtVS* specifically. The emotions as shown in television are a representation of the reality of the experienced emotion. The only caveat that must be acknowledged is that television drama has a tendency to overdramatise emotions and their influence on people's actions—with the soap opera genre being the prime example (Modleski, 1990). This is a required aspect of the medium—subtlety has a tendency to merely confuse the audience and be lost with only an hour (or in reality about 40 minutes of the hour) of broadcast time for each episode. This is more a function of the medium's restricted formats than an inability to relate on the part of the audience. Television also has 'license to explore the bizarre and singular forms that emotions can take, both insofar as they describe specific characters and as they play out in dramatic circumstances' (Korsmeyer, 2003: 162). This allows the researcher access to a range of emotions in circumstances that would otherwise be impossible to analyse. Emotions in television can be seen as distilled and concentrated versions of the emotion in reality. This makes it easier to identify the emotional themes and motivations and hence easier to engage with critically.

Buffyverse Loyalty

In this section I will draw out examples from *BtVS* to illustrate the five aspects of loyalty that I argue constitute the emotion. While I choose to focus on *BtVS*, this analysis could apply equally well to any other genre of television drama, from police or medical dramas to soap opera. It can also apply to movies. However, long running dramas like *BtVS* (seven seasons) provide ample dramatic space for the exploration and development of loyalty—hence its usefulness in this analysis.

Loyalty is one of many emotions that we feel. Consequently it is often mixed with, for example, love, jealousy and anger. The examples that I use to illustrate loyalty necessarily have aspects of other emotions tied in with them. This does not diminish the expression or feeling of loyalty, as all the emotions are intimately tied together. What I am acknowledging here is that emotional life is inherently complex, this is one area in which television drama mirrors reality. I have chosen to divide the analysis of *BtVS* into the aspects of loyalty discussed in Chapter Three for ease of discussion.

Loyalty Is Socially Constructed

As discussed previously, loyalty is a social emotion, both in its expression and formation. The following examples serve to highlight how social interaction fosters loyalty and how dominant societal views on loyalty are reflected by television. In effect we see two social constructions here, the socialisation with others fostering loyalty over time (due to shared ideals and friendship) and the societal construction of loyalty focusing on the maintenance of social bonds.

The 'Scooby-gang', as Buffy's friends and supporters come to be known, is partly bound together by their shared experiences and knowledge of the underworld—vampires, demons and the dark. Conflict within the group often occurs because one of the members is not included in the current information and gossip. For example in *The I In Team* Giles (Buffy's watcher or trainer/handler) becomes agitated that no-one in the group has informed him that Buffy's new boyfriend is actually a member of the Initiative (a competing anti-vampire government organisation).

The ritualised nature of loyalty is illustrated by how the Scooby-gang congregates in the school library during the first three seasons. The secrecy of their role in the world is a repeated theme that helps bind them together. They engage in a range of specific activities in the library and while they often complain about it, the ritual of 'researching' the current threat is a strongly binding force.

The 'natural' loyalty to family can be seen in Buffy's attachment to her mother and, when she arrives (in season five), her sister Dawn. Buffy's loyalty and love for Dawn is so strong, despite Dawn not being her 'sister', that Buffy sacrifices herself instead of Dawn to save the world (*The Gift*). Dawn was the human form of a mystical key that could open portals between worlds. The monks who were in charge of safe keeping the key fashioned it into Dawn to take advantage of the familial loyalty bonds that exist between sisters, thus ensuring the best possible protection for the key. Familial loyalty is a strong and enduring theme of *BtVS* (Kaveney, 2001: 5–6). The various nemeses that Buffy face often attempt to subvert or use this connection for their evil ends. In *Conversations With Dead People* Dawn is confronted by the returning ghost of her mother, sowing dissent by given warnings that Buffy 'won't choose' her. Dawn is troubled by these predictions that she will come second in Buffy's decisions. It is only when Dawn is convinced that the ghost is not her mother that her fears around Buffy's loyalty lessen.

Buffy also has a strong commitment to her mother and will often prioritise her safety. When Buffy's mother (Joyce) is threatened by Faith in *This Year's Girl* there is never any question in Joyce's mind that Buffy will save her—she knows that family loyalty is strong. Conversely, Faith (who has not had this familial experience) does not understand the strong pull of family. What the examples from *BtVS* show is that familial loyalty in this television program is similar to the examples of familial loyalty that I explored in Chapter Four. Further, the appeals to familial loyalty made during wartime (as discussed in Chapter Five) also share a certain resonance with the show. Consequently, these representations add further weight to my contention that loyalty is central to familial emotional reciprocity.

Some loyalties can be assumed by one party but not the other, and this particular construction of loyalty inevitably leads to conflict. When Giles arrives to 'watch' Buffy on behalf of the Watchers' Council, he assumes that as the Council is tasked to watch and support their slayers, so should Buffy be loyal and obedient to the Council's demands. This relationship between the Council and Slayer is riven with conflict throughout *BtVS*. Buffy feels that if she works within the Council's decrees the Council should return this loyalty by helping her. The Council, however, refuses to aid Buffy when Angel is poisoned and this, among many other examples, ultimately leads to Buffy turning her back on the Council (*Graduation Day, part one and two*). Loyalty requires reciprocity (or at least the promise of) and when it becomes plain that there is no return, loyalty can rapidly lapse, or worse, convert to anger, distrust and disappointment on the part of the aggrieved actor. This may invoke treason, betrayal and disloyalty.

Loyalty as Motivation

The motivation that loyalty provides has been a key concern. If loyalty is invoked to justify action in *BtVS*, then the evidence that loyalty helps to drive action strengthens. Giles has a constant and enduring loyalty to Buffy and slaying. He turns away from the Watcher's Council to support Buffy—despite the Council being his work, life and history. Giles has chosen between layers of loyalty. The Scooby-gang's enduring commitment to Buffy and slaying constantly places them in danger, but they will never let Buffy down.

Xander is a character who has a constant protective loyalty towards Buffy. Despite demon research being deadly boring for Xander, he cheerfully engages in it. Xander is committed to Buffy, as he himself comments in *The Zeppo:* 'well you know I'm here for you . . . just tell me what I can do'. This is representative of Xander's loyalties to Buffy, Willow and the Scooby-gang. It is this connection that gives Xander his identity and explains his reason for being. As Xander notes from time to time, he has nothing special going for him, he is not an ex-demon, or witch, or werewolf. He is just an average 'Joe'.

In *End of Days* Buffy conspires with Xander to have him kidnap Dawn and leave town before the final showdown of the series in an attempt to save her as the Scoobies do not expect to survive. Xander, despite or perhaps because he also sees Dawn as a little sister, complies with Buffy's request. He knows that Dawn will be extremely unhappy with him (as borne out when she stun-guns Xander in order to be able to return to Sunnydale) but he does it anyway—primarily because Buffy asked. The interchange between Buffy and Xander, when planning the kidnap, highlights these themes:

> **BUFFY:** I know. That's why I need you to do this. Xander, I need someone that I can count on no matter what happens.
>
> **XANDER:** (shakes his head) I just always thought that I would . . . I would be there with you . . . ou know, for the end.
>
> **BUFFY:** (indignant) Hey.
>
> **XANDER:** (quickly) Well, not that this is the end.
>
> **BUFFY:** Thanks a lot.
>
> **XANDER:** No, no, no. By the end, I meant, uh . . . a heroic, uplifting way. See, I'm still optimistic. You're just thrown off a little by this gritty-looking eye patch.
>
> **BUFFY:** (smiles) I know what you meant.
>
> **XANDER:** I should be at your side. That's all I'm saying.
>
> **BUFFY:** You will be. You're my strength, Xander. You're the reason I made it this far. I trust you with my life. That's why I need you to do this for me.

The theme of loyalty and love is strong here, and sticking 'till the end' is a common theme of loyalty type interactions. Buffy knows Xander is loyal, hence her opening gambit of proclaiming that she needs someone that she can count on. The loyalty connections exhibited by the characters are very similar to the connections discussed in previous chapters. This further shows that loyalty can motivate behaviours, actions and beliefs. Loyalties are used to maintain social connections and as a way of governing reciprocity in relationships. The interchange above highlights this idea of favours returned on the basis of prior loyalty.

Loyalty and Identity

Loyalty plays a role in furnishing identity. The identities of the Scooby-gang are inextricably intertwined with Buffy and slaying—they are who they are because of that loyalty. As discussed above, Xander's identity becomes linked with his role as Buffy's friend. Similarly, slaying creates a space and identity for Willow beyond computer-nerd, as her identity grows and flourishes through her connection with Buffy.

A lack of loyalties to help define an individual's identity can affect who they are and how they act. Spike, a problematic character who is significantly transformed over the course of *BtVS*, goes through a stage when he lacks loyalty to anyone but himself. He loses the ability to actualise his vampire nature when he is 'de-fanged' by the Initiative (*The Initiative*). Spike goes through a process of being lost, no longer is he a 'true' vampire—his identity is challenged. As Kaveney (2001: 21) argues: 'Spike at this point is incapable of loyalty, sometimes supporting the Scoobies out of self-interest . . . and sometimes betraying them'. He is lost until he develops a true attachment to the Scoobies through his developing affections for Buffy (season five). Not only does this new connection provide Spike with purpose and reason for action, it also spurs him to try and become more human during season six, culminating in his re-ensoulment in *Grave*. The state of flux that Spike experiences also affects how others see him. The Scoobies are no longer sure of Spike's loyalties as he appears to be part of the gang and on Buffy's side, yet their historical knowledge of him is as a blood-sucking fiend. This gives him back his conscience and makes him more human, and he hopes, more desirable to Buffy.

The progression of this particular *BtVS* character, Spike, reiterates how loyalty and identity interact. As I have shown in the previous chapters, loyalties help the actor assess with whom they have a social connection. Loyalties also allow people to claim an identity position—by affirming their connection to others, be they close (such as family) or more distant (like the nation). This example further supports the case studies of previous chapters. Further, this popular culture representation not only reflects but must also propagate a particular view of loyalty. The perspective that is being created and reflected is that the connections the actor has to others, as mediated through loyalty relationships, is a determinant of identity. This includes not only the identity of the actor that is self perceived, but also the identity position that others perceive that actor to have.

Loyalty Operates at a Number of Layers

Buffy has a number of competing layers of loyalty to contend with. She has family loyalty, loyalty to friends, loyalty to lovers, school loyalty and loyalty to her calling—slaying. These layers of loyalty often come into conflict. For Buffy the strongest layer becomes slaying—she has been 'chosen' for this role in the world and after an initial period of resistance comes to revel in the role. Buffy's various layers of loyalty are called upon in different episodes. For example, in *Choices* she needs to save her friend Willow—despite being begged not to by her then watcher Wesley—and in *This Year's Girl*, her family. In the final few episodes of season three, *The Prom*, and *Graduation Day Part One* and *Part Two*, Buffy is recognised by her fellow students as the 'class protector' and proceeds to save the students from the evil Mayor during graduation. Buffy chooses slaying over her other loyalties in *Lies My Parents Told Me*, commenting that 'the mission is what matters'. Negotiating these loyalties and obligations is a recurrent theme in *BtVS*.

In *The Gift*, Buffy is offered the stark choice of killing her sister, Dawn, or letting her live and having the world overrun by demons from hell, with the probable result of death. Buffy responds to this choice by saying that if Dawn will die anyway, should the world be overrun, 'then the last thing she'll see is me protecting her'. She then realises that she has chosen family over not only her friends but all of humanity. Her last response to the gathered Scoobies, shaking her head is 'I'm sorry . . . I love you all'. Buffy's family loyalty is first here—and the internal anguish is obvious.

These conflicts illustrate how actors can be forced to choose between competing layers. The options that Buffy is presented with, while supernatural at times, echo the same choices offered to social actors, such as between family, friends and job. The theme that family loyalty is the strongest incarnation of loyalty is echoed in this chapter, adding further weight to my argument that familial loyalty operates as the primary site of loyalty interaction.

Buffy never comes easily to the decision of which loyalty to favour. Much of the time in the episodes is devoted to her consideration of the choices offered. It is this often angst-ridden contemplation that illuminates the layered nature of loyalty. The choice of which layer to follow is never easy (it cannot be easy for Buffy, otherwise the purpose of television is lost—to entertain) and forms the basis for much conflict.

Loyalty Is Contested

The conflict that loyalties create is another constant theme in *BtVS*. In the final episode of Season Two, *Becoming, Part Two* Buffy is forced to kill her lover Angel as he is a vampire who has lost his soul and consequently becomes evil again. The anguish this causes for Buffy is obvious. Buffy has a loyalty to protecting humanity and slaying the evil in the world, yet the deep affection and attachment that she feels for Angel is in direct conflict with her role as slayer, necessitating a difficult choice.

Season four provides rich illustrations of the contested nature of loyalty. Buffy is drawn into the government's Initiative program, a program designed to study and control demons and vampires. This creates conflict between Buffy and the Scoobies when she begins to patrol with the Initiative rather than with them. This conflict comes to the fore in *The Yoko Factor,* when a number of simmering conflicts in loyalties are debated. Each of the major protagonists—Giles, Buffy, Xander and Willow—feel that they have been excluded from the group. This is because of a distance forming between the characters due to their lack of shared activity and their own new relationships, which is largely a result of Buffy working with the Initiative. Each is hurt, as each feels excluded and left out—something that should not occur between doggedly loyal friends. What this illustrates is an avenue for developing and maintaining loyalty ties in friendship—shared activities and purpose. While this is hardly a profound revelation, the fact that this form of loyalty building and maintenance is depicted in popular culture indicates that this is a real means of interaction.

Riley, a member of the Initiative and Buffy's love interest for season four has a continuing loyalty conflict. He is a soldier but also Buffy's lover, which creates conflicts between loyalty layers that are similar to the examples I explored in Chapter Four. When the commander of the Initiative tries to kill Buffy in *The I in Team* he is torn between the two. Riley is forced to choose where his loyalties lie in the following episode, *Goodbye Iowa*. This conflict that Riley experiences is intense and emotionally draining. His previous belief in the Initiative project is destroyed—and consequently he flees from the military when they turn on him. This deprives him of identity and motivation. No longer is it easy for him to do good when he knows that the Initiative does not act for the benefit of humanity. Ultimately he joins with Buffy to defeat the season nemesis Adam and the remnants of the Initiative. But his loyalty to the military is strong and he leaves Sunnydale and returns to them in *Into the Woods* in season five, but only when his belief in Buffy's love and loyalty begins to wane. This story arc illustrates how loyalties can change and be overtaken by other competing loyalties. Riley's inner conflict is over a choice of loyalties and he ultimately chooses the loyalty that has been longest and most encompassing. This shift in loyalty, and the effects that it has on others, is where the conflict arises.

When loyalties come into conflict, the damage that follows can be difficult for the actors involved. In season seven we see an earlier slayer, Nikki, repeatedly explaining to her son that slaying comes first—it is the 'calling'. We discover that this son (Robin) is now the grown up Principal of the local high school, bent on the destruction of vampires, demons and evil. He works well with Buffy until he realises that it is Spike who killed his slayer mother. This leads to a confrontation where Giles and Robin conspire to kill Spike—even though Spike is on the good side. Spike, despite besting Robin, refuses to kill him. His loyalty to Buffy and the cause is stronger than his rage at the attack. Buffy eventually stops the fight and confronts the protagonists—reminding them firmly that the first loyalty must be to defeating the evil that is on the way, rather than petty revenge among each other (*Lies My Parents Told Me*). Again we see loyalty invoked as justification for action. The way loyalty is used in this encounter shows that it must be considered absolute commitment; you are either loyal to the cause or part of the problem. This also furthers the case that loyalty is often considered a singular commitment, and that if deemed strong enough, should overwhelm competing commitments. What is of interest sociologically is the process by which one loyalty overwhelms another. In this example, it is the ascribed social value of the activity (saving humanity) that comes first. There is a similarity in the appeals to national loyalty in times of war to the appeals that Buffy makes in this episode (and season).

In the lead up to the series finale, the Scooby-gang and potential slayers decide that their first loyalty is to the mission—saving the world. They confront Buffy over her approach to the threat and in a heart-wrenching interplay Dawn proclaims her love for Buffy as a sister but her inability to follow Buffy's leadership anymore (*Empty Places*). This highlights the intense anguish and conflict the individual can feel when competing layers of loyalty come into conflict. Dawn is quite explicit in separating her feelings for Buffy, her sister, versus her feelings for Buffy, the slayer and leader. In effect, Dawn chooses between layers of loyalty, a choice that Buffy has also had to make twice about Dawn. Buffy, however, chooses Dawn each time. What is of particular note is the conflict in this episode—it revolves around making choices between different courses of action that have intense emotional energy invested in them. Dawn's anguish reflects the type of feelings explored in previous case studies when actors are forced to make a difficult choice (such as the decision to turn a family member over to law-enforcement officials). Non-requited loyalty is one source of conflict. Those affected by the choice are hurt because they were not chosen. This conflict is wrapped in complex social interactions and reciprocities, which loyalty appears to help govern. The second site of conflict, the internal anguish, can also deeply trouble the actors. This is because of an awareness of the reciprocities that loyalty denotes, even though they are forced to choose one over the other.

Television, Loyalty and the Buffyverse

The representations of loyalty in *BtVS* accord with the previous case studies I have explored, providing more evidence for Docker's (1994) view of popular culture and its reflection of real experience. What is significant is that cultural representations of loyalty corroborate the findings in my case studies. Of particular convergence has been *BtVS* and family loyalty. For example, the behaviour of Buffy towards her family is similar to the examples drawn out in Chapter Four. The small group cohesion of the Scooby-gang is similar to small unit military cohesion, not surprising given that one could characterise them as an informal military force fighting demons and vampires.

This allows me to claim that television drama shows emotions in a way that is similar to the other manifestations of the emotion that I have explored. The characters' actions are informed and justified by their emotional states. Consequently this offers more support for my central argument, that loyalty is an emotion that helps guide social action.

Mediated Loyalties—Conclusions

In this chapter I have explored television and the way loyalty is used in a particular show. *BtVS* is an example of the attempt by television programs to reflect a real emotional experience that resonates with the audience. This also extends to all forms of media entertainment—such as books, films and stage productions. The depiction of loyalty relationships within *BtVS* accords with the real life case studies and examples I have outlined to date, offering strong evidence in support of one of the main arguments of this book, namely that loyalty is a socially mediated emotion that occurs through interactions between the actor and other actors and social institutions. It is also closely linked to social action. The effects of loyalty can be inferred from the behaviours, cognitions and feelings of the actor. Television thus provides a unique lens with which to explore emotion.

My use of *BtVS* also serves as a check on the mediated loyalty experiences that I use as my primary source material in my previous case study chapters. In effect, I am testing the sources I use by analysing one of the media itself—television—for its validity. I have taken the nature of the sources I use in the case studies for granted—the newspapers, books, television shows and academic discussions. By questioning how television (perhaps the most influential popular cultural medium) represents loyalty I can claim that all my sources share a similar conception of loyalty. Further, by also showing how narrative, by drawing on Docker, is central to mediating social understandings, I have demonstrated one of the key avenues by which loyalty is maintained, reinforced and propagated in society. This answers the question of how loyalty evolves, while retaining its underlying aspects (as the historical reports show)—it is part of the emotional fabric of society.

Television is the medium and the message, it reflects, yet creates and propagates. This is the case with all social intercourse. It is part unique, part reflection of what has gone before and part expectation of the future. Loyalty fits into this by bringing previous connections, obligations and reciprocities into the present with a view to predicting and managing the future. This is why loyalty, and emotions generally, continue spiralling through interactions—governing and guiding the behaviours, thoughts and feelings of the actor through time.

Chapter Eight
Conclusion

Loyalty cannot be blueprinted. It cannot be produced on an assembly line. In fact, it cannot be manufactured at all, for its origin is the human heart—the center of self-respect and human dignity.

Maurice R. Franks

This book has examined the influence of loyalty on the cognitions, feelings, behaviours and actions of the actor. In the preceding seven chapters I have sought to explain the social processes that underlie the use and meaning of loyalty in Western Civilisation. It is indeed curious that so little academic thought has been devoted to elucidating a concept that has been part of social interaction since time immemorial. Perhaps this is due to the broad nature of the concept, including micro-sociological interaction (the decision to stay loyal to a friend) and macro-sociological forces (how to mobilise a nation to war) which makes it difficult to theorise. This is why I formulated the central question of this book as: *what is loyalty?*

As befits the concluding chapter I will begin by drawing together my arguments and case studies and thus illustrate what loyalty is. I shall follow the same structure as Chapter Three and revisit the aspects of loyalty that I postulated as being central to the concept—identity, motivation to action and layering. This thematic approach will allow me to argue for an overarching definition and understanding of loyalty across social sites.

Throughout the book I have taken the view that loyalty is indeed an emotion and consequently, I have used sociological tools for studying emotion in exploring loyalty. This use of emotions theory to elucidate loyalty allows me to make two claims. The first claim is that even if loyalty is not an emotion, what I have demonstrated is that when the tools of sociologically-inspired emotions theory are applied to the concept we gain an understanding and insight into the phenomenon of loyalty that is beyond any previous understanding. The second, more controversial, claim is that loyalty is an emotion. In this conclusion, I will support my contention that loyalty is an emotion by testing my understanding of loyalty against a range of definitions of emotion offered in the literature. If the picture of loyalty that I have tested and sketched broadly matches the definitions offered then I can confidently assert that loyalty is an emotion.

I conclude the chapter by placing my argument in the context of emotions theory and sociology more generally. I see the arguments of this books as the start, not the end of sociologically-inspired investigations into loyalty. Consequently, I postulate how to further advance our understanding of loyalty.

Layered Loyalty

The concept of layering can be considered a useful heuristic device with which to explore how an actor negotiates the range of competing loyalties that they will inevitably experience by being part of a social structure. Layering also highlights how loyalty operates across a range of social sites, spanning micro- and macro-sociological interactions. I defined layering as referring to the multiple types of loyalty that operate on the individual, spanning the micro to the macro levels of social structure. The concept of layering also gives an insight into how and why conflict ensues when multiple loyalties are called upon.

The loyalty an actor expresses is significantly influenced by previous interactions. For example, this proposition was supported by the actions of the South Sydney Rabbitohs fans in response to their club's exclusion from the competition. A recurring and consistent theme in the reactions from the fans was the level of commitment that they previously held. Those who identified strongly with the team over an extended period couched their feelings of loss through emphasising how loyal they had been to their team. This observation is not particularly profound. It makes intuitive sense that our previous commitments will influence the strength of our loyalties. However, what is interesting and novel is that this longevity of emotion is a key determining factor of loyalty return—along with the perception of reciprocity. Additionally, this argument directly challenges the biological models of emotion—at least in terms of causing emotional behaviour. It is undeniable that the body mediates emotion through biological mediums—but the meanings attached are social.

Thus, an actor needs to be socialised into their loyalties. Learning what was an appropriate target for loyalty was a key component of exhibiting it properly and that an actor could not be loyal to an object, event or idea that was not socially acceptable (to at least some). The key evidence that I examined with a view to testing this proposition were the experiences of migrants trying to develop a loyalty to their adopted home, and the popular cultural representations of loyalty. My case studies demonstrated that some migrants are excluded from the layer of loyalty focused on nationalism. This was shown through the examples of migrants identifying themselves as feeling excluded and disconnected and also shown by the response of the wider community. In particular, the reactions to people of enemy ancestry during the two World Wars illustrates how loyalty can mediate social exclusion.

Further, this explains why it is difficult for an actor to have a loyalty to concepts that are not generally accepted as appropriate loyalty targets, such as humanity, because there is a lack of an 'other'. The proof of this is in the very representations of when actors can attach loyalty to humanity, such as in many science fiction stories where it becomes humanity versus the alien other. My central case study of represented loyalty, *BtVS,* further supports this case as the characters on occasion do have a greater loyalty to humanity (usually couched in terms of 'saving the world' in episodes). They have this loyalty because there is the threat from the other and it is acceptable within that social context to attach loyalty to humanity. The reliance of Buffy on the mantra that 'it is the mission that matters' most exemplifies this loyalty layer. In terms of loyalty targets and 'others', it will be intriguing to see if concepts such as 'climate change' or 'globalisation' can manifest a loyalty response in the future.

Conflict is an enduring theme of loyalty-based interactions. One avenue of explanation for this is offered by the concept of layering as this acknowledges that inevitably actors will have competing demands made on their loyalties. My case studies illustrated the conflict that repeatedly ensues between layers. Family loyalty is a very common area of conflict and my studies of step families and blended families illustrated the role that loyalty plays in conflict. Family is often an intense site of emotional conflict as loyalty betrayed in that context often has very real and immediate consequences. This was exemplified by the anguish experienced when one family member turns against another, such as with the Unabomber's brother or with the sister who opposed the death penalty for her brother's killer. The McCarthy period in the USA exemplifies how differing layers of loyalty can be perceived of as a threat.

The case studies into familial-like loyalty that was not family (the military, gangs and, to a small extent, religion) demonstrate that many social institutions have mechanisms that are designed to manage competing loyalty layers. This management of loyalty layers is intended to reduce the internal conflict that an actor may feel if their loyalty is challenged. This would go part way to explaining why gangs and military forces try and reduce the power of previous familial ties through subsuming family ties into the gang and unit. The experience of migrants in a new country also points to how the imagined community of a nation state is construed to limit potential conflict within layers. The repetitive questioning of a migrants allegiance by the 'local' gate-keepers can be seen as part of a strategy to affirm a singular loyalty. Conversely, for the migrant this can be felt as exclusionary behaviour. This insight, that social forces are brought to bear to constrain loyalty, indicates the effect loyalty can have in social relationships. If this observation was not true, at least to some extent, then the quite intricate loyalty layer management that occurs would not be needed.

As part of conflict and layering I postulated that actors would have a set hierarchy of loyalty. Drawing on the problematic postulations of an intelligence interrogator, I sought to explore which layer of loyalty is strongest and why. The answer, albeit tentative and requiring more empirical study, is that the family is the strongest layer of loyalty with the social distance of the subsequent layers determining the strength. What I mean by this is that actors tend to be most loyal to what is closest to them, both emotionally and physically. In other words, the stronger and tighter their immersion in a particular social milieu the more likely that loyalty will surface. Thus family is strongest, followed by friends, intermediate personal commitments/belief systems (like religion, sport and politics) and finally wider social structures such as the nation. The evidence of the case studies supports this conclusion as actors repeatedly acknowledged a hierarchy of loyalty that matches this. However, it must be noted that social immersion certainly plays an important part in which layer is most salient at the time. My case study on small military unit cohesion demonstrated the strength of that loyalty over and above any competing loyalties. Further, in particular historical moments another layer may become more salient to the actor. The reactions of people during war and conflict illustrate how a wider loyalty, that to the nation, can become the most dominant loyalty layer. This observation helps explain how particular macro-social processes can draw on latent loyalties and why these appeals can be so motivating. The conscription debates illustrate this point by demonstrating that at particular times, the social milieu can over-ride competing loyalty layers and draw upon specific loyalties for the furtherance of social goals. In this example it was the defence of Empire and country. It also helps explicate why the loyalty conflict during these particular moments can be so intense, as shown by the viciousness of the attacks based on actors' perceived competing loyalties.

Loyalty and Identity

It is a given that we all have an identity. The purpose of placing loyalty and identity together was to ascertain whether loyalty plays a role in furnishing individual and group identities. Broadly, I characterised this by suggesting that loyalty operates to mediate an actor's connection with other people and institutions, which in turn helps to construct an actor's identity position. As a component of this, loyalties also offer belonging and identification with particular people, causes, places and institutions.

Role theory is one means of conceptualising identity formation (Gerth and Mills, 1964). Drawing on this theory, I postulated that loyalty may act as an emotional marker to indicate which role, and hence identity, an actor should be performing. My exploration of roles within the case studies allowed me to conclude that loyalty does help the actor perform appropriate roles. It does this by orienting the actor to their current social circumstances based on previous interactions. Hence, when an actor comes to the defence of their object of loyalty, they are performing a particular role. The case studies repeatedly demonstrated this, and one key example was the role of gang loyalty in maintaining identity. Gang members identified how central their gang affiliation is to who they are, and crucially that connection was often based on loyalty or loyalty like terminology and commitments.

Loyalty denotes belonging. The belonging aspect of loyalty then illustrates for the actor their identity position, role in an interaction and possible actions. The examples of fan loyalty demonstrated how feelings of belonging and being connected to a greater entity partially informed the identity of fans. Being loyal to a sports team can indicate a connection that subsequently denotes an actors' actions—such as boycotting the very sport the fan's team can no longer play. An actor can have belonging without loyalty. However, when the emotional investment that loyalty implies is part of the belonging, the actor will be encouraged to greater levels of identification, feeling and outright passion with regards to that loyalty. This is why those who are loyal to a concept may passionately defend it—they belong to it and it consequently forms part of their being. This is qualitatively different from, and beyond, any sort of contractual belonging an actor may have—the key difference is the attachment of feeling, mediated through loyalty.

In Chapter Three I argued that emotion generally has a curious absence from the literature on identity. I postulated that this absence occurs because of the under-theorising and testing of emotion and identity in the literature. Feelings of loyalty certainly do help construct an actor's identity. The evidence suggests that emotion is an important component of identity formation as it mediates between the actor and the social world. Emotions guide the actor to aspects of their existence that are relevant and therefore part of their identity.

Loyalty and Action

Barbalet (2002) argues that emotion is central to sociology as no action can occur in a society without emotional involvement. Consequently, how those emotions guide, direct and motivate the actor should be a key concern of sociology. I have sought to demonstrate how loyalty is involved in these processes.

When an actor engages in an activity they are making a prediction about what may happen as a consequence of those activities (whether it is consciously reflected upon or not). Feelings can help guide that process and, consequently, I postulated that the presence of a loyalty allows an actor to predict what may happen in the future and thus act accordingly. This was borne out through the case studies which showed that a past loyalty helped predict a future loyalty and therefore helps guide action. Many of the conflicts over loyalty occurred because loyalty was not reciprocated. This negative case showed that actors expect a future return on loyalty and use this as a base for their own action. Familial loyalty clearly exemplified this. This 'dis-loyal' test of action showed that loyalty helps guide action.

Given that loyalty does help guide action, the next task was to ask whether this held across all layers of loyalty and whether that motivation operated in a similar manner. The case studies, spanning multiple loyalty layers, indicated that loyalty has motivational qualities. The actions predicated, through the actor's commitment to a cause or person, are similar across layers. The actions that follow are necessarily different—but that is because the targets of loyalty are different and the manner of showing that commitment is predicated on the object of commitment.

A weakness in my argument is the *post-hoc* justifications that I use to explore justification for action. Perhaps it is easier for an actor to blame loyalty after an event then to actually experience it during the event. This is a weakness in all research that uses this methodology. However, I do not consider this a serious flaw in my evidence for two reasons. First, *post-hoc* justifications are a perfectly valid way of 'seeing' emotion, and further, if an actor cites loyalty as the justification then to them, it is. Second, my case study on *BtVS* allowed an analysis of loyalty across seven seasons (and multiple story arcs), clearly demonstrating that loyalty does operate before, during and after an activity.

The role of emotion in guiding action is a central proposition of the sociological literature. I have added more weight to this explanation for social action through my exploration of loyalty. However, before I can state with confidence that loyalty helps guide action through an emotions framework, I need to establish that loyalty is indeed an emotion.

Definitions of Emotion

The term *emotion* has a variety of definitions in the various intellectual schools of thought dedicated to its explanation and exploration. These range from biological definitions focusing on measurable change within the body to 'lay' definitions that argue if society calls it an emotion then it *is* an emotion. I will take a small sample of a range of theories (mainly from sociologically-informed perspectives) in this section that attempt to provide definitions of emotion. While this is by no means an exhaustive review, which would be far beyond the scope of the book, I will discuss a representative number of theoretical positions and argue why and how loyalty can fit within the definitions. This discussion is important for my argument as it validates the use of emotions theory to explore loyalty. It also allows me to show that my definition of emotion and loyalty can fit the definitions of emotion offered in the literature.

Emotion, as I take the term to mean in the context of this work, is a socially negotiated feeling, behaviour and cognitive state that an individual experiences as a consequence of interactions within the world. These emotions are defined by the actor's particular social and historical milieu and serve to orient the actor to events, people and interactions that are relevant to them. Emotion does not have to be recognised. It can simmer below conscious reflection. Emotion is also embodied, the actor must use bodily senses to understand and participate in the world. This does not mean that emotions are hereditary in an evolutionary manner—physical sensations are, the labels and social relationships attached to them are not. Emotion can also be self-generated, but this generation (such as contemplation) occurs within the actor's perceived social milieu.

I contend that loyalty is an emotion that reflects attachment to something or someone the actor cares about. The attachment is stable and deep because of the social functions loyalty serves. It links the actor to social groups, it helps to define identity and motivates action. Loyalty operates at different layers and these layers are always simmering as part of an actor's emotional existence. Which layer is most salient is a product of social interactions. The simultaneous loyalties of an actor to different people, places, institutions, concepts and ideas is often a cause of conflict.

In the following discussion I may be accused of only selecting examples that are either supportive of my argument or that are easily dismissed. This is certainly the case—I have chosen a range of definitions to support my argument. However, what I am constructing is an argument for loyalty to be considered an emotion and, consequently, when theory-building it is acceptable to choose argument(s). The real test of these various viewpoints on emotion is the evidence of my case study chapters and the support I garner for the proposition that loyalty is an emotion. At the very least, this allows me to make a plausible case.

According to Barbalet (1992: 150), emotions are 'psychophysiological phenomena of micro-sociological or social psychological concern'. This means that emotion, for the actor, is an artifact that registers in their dispositional being by changing their body's feelings, reactions and interpretations. This physiological aspect manifests in fluttering stomachs, dry mouths and flight to name just a few physical responses. But it is also a mental response, as emotion can change the disposition of the actor. Barbalet (2003: 1) explains this idea at length:

[a] person may be negatively or positively involved with something, profoundly involved or only slightly involved, but however or to what degree they are involved with an event, condition or person it necessarily matters to them, proportionately. That it matters, that a person cares about something, registers in their physical and dispositional being.

This dispositional shift can change the way an actor thinks, expresses and articulates the story of, and ideas about, a given event. Thus, emotion is central to all social processes as it guides action. My case studies have demonstrated the centrality of loyalty to action. Barbalet (1992: 151) summarises this point neatly: 'emotion is central to social processes not only in being central to identity and affiliation but also in being the necessary basis of social action and the form it takes'.

Loyalty fits into Barbalet's emotion typology. Loyalty is a psychophysiological phenomenon in that it has attendant physical manifestations when it is called upon. Consider the physical responses that can be felt when loyalty is called into question. Depending upon the power differential, the actor may feel all the manifestations normally attributed to fear and flight or fight responses. These responses, while on the surface appear to be fear, are much more complex in the origin of the physical manifestation. It is the loyalty relationship—the rights, responsibilities and obligations that are being called into question when the issue of disloyalty is raised that triggers the physical manifestations. Dispositionally, the actor cares about the event. It matters on both the individual micro-sociological level and the macro-social level. The case studies showed that the actor can be worried about their own continued health, in the extreme cases of disloyalty, and the social impact that this event may have. Barbelet (1992:160) acknowledges this dual aspect to emotion by stating that emotion 'is always situated and therefore has a context . . . . Each of these elements of emotion – the contextual and the experiential – is necessary in any adequate conceptualisation of emotion'. One of the key strengths of this definition is that it incorporates the body (the experiential), but still posits emotion within the social. Barbalet's general definition of emotion also accords with Shklar's (1993) specific definition of loyalty discussed in Chapter Two—adding weight to both their arguments and, consequently, mine.

In an attempt to draw out the use of emotion in film (and by extension all visual entertainment) Carroll (1999: 22) posits a definition of emotions that identifies its base in everyday language and conceptions of emotion. Carroll (1999: 22) argues that:

> Certain phenomena, such as fear, anger, patriotism, horror, admiration, sorrow, indignation, pity, envy, jealousy, reverence, awe, hatred, love, anxiety, shame, embarrassment, humiliation, comic amusement, and so on, are paradigms of what counts as emotion in ordinary language, even if sometimes ordinary language also stretches farther afield.

I do not think I am doing an injustice to Carroll's typology by adding loyalty to the list of emotions he cites as ordinary, common use emotions and emotive terms. Carroll (1999: 22) goes on to defend this definition of emotion by arguing that 'these garden-variety emotions are not only paradigmatic but also exhibit common structural features'. These features point to them being a core class of like phenomena, or to simplify Carroll's point—the ordinary usage sees these things as being emotion as they share key aspects. Hence, Carroll argues that his analysis is 'a rational reconstruction of some already existing intuitions rather than as the invention of a new concept' (1999: 22).

It is therefore the everyday common usage of terminology that most people classify as emotion or emotive terms that are our actual emotions. It does not require 'scientific' measurement of bodily arousal or changes in the endocrine system but, instead, an analysis of the social representations and actions of emotion in general parlance and thought. Fehr and Russell (1984: 469) found that when subjects were asked to list the emotions, they came up with a wide and varied list of terms. Loyalty was included in the list and was named by subjects as often as awe, shame and exhilaration—these three are often cited as emotion in the general literature. What this points to is that if the general populace use terms like these to denote their emotional life, the researcher would be amiss in not taking this into account in their definition of emotion. Much of the material I use in the case studies was selected on the basis that loyalty was mentioned in the materials—as suggested by Carroll's (1999) argument.

Another means of conceptualising emotion is to define it functionally. Planalp (1999: 161) offers the view that 'emotion orients us to the *good* and to the *should*: to things that we value and to things that we feel we ought to do' (emphasis in original). Thus, emotion orients us to what is going on in the world and alerts us to act or not act depending upon the stimuli and the emotional response it engenders. In Planalp's typology, loyalty would appear like this: loyalty orients the response and/or perception of an event, action or interaction and encourages a specific behaviour (which can be non-reaction). Conflict is the best example of loyalty orienting us to the good and the should. Loyalties indicate which side an actor should support in conflict—which is inevitably the 'right', 'good', 'just' and 'correct' side. It also suggests a course of action. My case study on national loyalty fits Planalp's definition of an emotion. In nation-state conflict an actor can join up or support the war effort in other ways. The actor is orientated to the good and should—supporting their country, or in the case of dissenters, justifying that perceived dis-loyalty with a different loyalty. In the examples explored in Chapter Five, those different loyalties included the family, religion and ethnicity. The conflicts over conscription in the World Wars and Vietnam conflict illustrate this process.

Frijda (1988/1998: 273) offers another conception of emotion, after decrying the difficulty and inherent conflict in attempting to define an emotion. He argues that '[e]motions, quite generally, arise in response to events that are important to the individual, and which importance he or she appraises in some way' (1998: 271) and 'what we loosely call 'emotions' are responses to events that are important to the individual'(1998: 273). Frijda goes on to provide a set of laws governing the elicitation, response and continuation of emotion. It is a stimulus, either internal or external, that the individual appraises as significant and thus manifests an emotional response. Loyalty fits this conception of emotion as it is a stimulus that registers as important to the individual. This definition is, however, slightly limiting. As several other theorists have argued (Barbalet 1992: 160, Carroll, 1999: 23), we do not have to register emotion, or in Frijda's terms, appraise it, for the emotion to occur and or affect our disposition.

Solomon (2002) provides yet another means of conceptualising the slippery concept of emotion. He points out that 'every emotion can be viewed from a different perspectives and has different *aspects*' (2002: 131, emphasis in original). Solomon points out that every emotion has five aspects:

(1) behavioural expressions (including elaborate plans for action and verbal behaviour), (2) physiological (hormonal, neurological, neuro-muscular), (3) phenomenological (sensations, ways of construing the objects of emotion), (4) cognitive (appraisals, perceptions, thoughts, and reflections *about* one's emotions), and (5) the social context (the immediacy of interpersonal inter-actions, pervasive cultural considerations). (2002: 131–2, emphasis in original)

These should not be considered as a component, or combination theory of emotion. As Solomon (2002: 132) points out in his defence: '[t]hese aspects are often interwoven and they should not be construed (as they often are) as competing conceptions of emotion'. Thus Solomon is proposing a holistic theory of emotion.

Like so many of the emotion theorists, Solomon does not mention loyalty. However, his holistic approach can be applied to loyalty. Taking Solomon's theory and applying it to loyalty we gain a picture of loyalty as an emotion in the following terms:

1. Behavioural expressions: loyalty has many and varied display patterns and verbal expressions. National loyalty requires the actor to show loyalty through acts such as wearing the appropriate colours to sporting events and national holidays. A loyal football fan often wears their loyalty on their back with the team jersey. Loyalty needs verbal reinforcement; actors profess their attachment, support and connection to people, organisations and institutions. This emotion also provides direction and plans for action in different contexts.

Loyalty provides an understanding of the appropriate action when the actor's country is threatened, as the volunteers in times of war attest.
2. Physiology: this is perhaps the weakest aspect of loyalty as an emotion, primarily because of the dearth of literature, especially from psychology but also neurological and biological researchers (and of course my own methodology). I can only speculate on these responses by referring to how people report their internal physiological responses/changes when loyalty (and its converse disloyalty) are evident. However, Chapter Four, in dealing with family loyalty provided a number of examples where people stated how physically difficult it is to be disloyal and that they manifested various physical responses to loyalty events.
3. Phenomenological: loyalty has specific ways of construing the environment and the objects of loyalty. This subjectivist approach is concerned with the experience of the emotion by the actor. Thus, it is the emotion as felt by the actor and not tainted by experimentation or questioning that is required in order to build a picture of the emotion. This is best at a non-conscious level with the actor merely relating current and past emotional experiences without cognitive appraisal clouding the judgement.
4. Cognitive: actors appraise and reflect on their loyalties often. Indeed it is the stock of stories, art and literature about loyalty that helps construe the meaning and expression of the emotion. This cognitive aspect is particularly relevant when loyalty is not reciprocated and becomes disloyalty. Often the refrain from an actor is couched in terms of 'how could you do this to me' or 'but you owed me your loyalty' or 'I expected loyalty'. The case studies provided significant evidence in support of this aspect.
5. Social context: or what Harre (1986) would call the moral order. Loyalty has a clear social context and existence. It manifests itself by and through social interaction. It is quintessentially a social emotion as it would not exist without a social structure. The cultural considerations of loyalty are also present and were demonstrated in this book by analysing how loyalty operates in different cultural times and contexts. The most powerful example of cultural and social relativity and specificity is the way loyalty has changed in western society since feudal times, through the rise of nation states and onto diverse and diffuse targets now, mirroring social complexities and structures.

Loyalty therefore fits within Solomon's definition of an emotion. Perhaps of more relevance to my argument, is that this typology also proposes a means of studying emotions. Thus, not only can I argue that loyalty is an emotion, but that this acceptance of loyalty as an emotion provides a range of explanatory methods for understanding and communicating the meaning of the emotion.

Building on Solomon's work, Kristjánsson (2003:353) offers a three-pronged definitional test: emotions must have intentional objects; they are propositional; and they have reasons. It is also possible to place loyalty into Kristjánsson's definition. Loyalty has a clear intentional object; that is the person or cause to which one is loyal. Loyalty is propositional in that it can be articulated in a declarative sentence: I am loyal to my country. The reason we are loyal is also easily articulated: one is loyal to their country because they were born there and grew up in the social milieu of nationhood, or I am loyal to my family because family bonds are strong. The case studies demonstrated repeatedly how loyalty fits this definitional test.

Yet another approach to the definition of emotion is taken by Royzman and Sabini (2001) in their argument for not including disgust in the category of an emotion. Royzman and Sabini (2001: 33) posit that 'emotions must have abstract elicitors and flexible responses and that drives which fail to meet these criteria remain drives'. By abstract elicitors they mean that the stimuli must generate the response of an emotion because 'they convey the abstract, formal properties' of the emotion each time (2001: 31). Thus, in the examples they use, danger is an emotion, as the elicitors for danger, while being varied, generate the same abstract response. Conversely, in Royzman and Sabini's typology a surge of appetite is not an emotional response but a drive because it is the food that is creating the response – it does not elicit an abstract emotional reaction (2001: 31). What Royzman and Sabini are suggesting is that emotions require a different type of processing than drives as well as an understanding of the social implications and relations attached to a particular emotional response. Royzman and Sabini then defend the idea that processing does not need to have occurred in every episode of emotions, but that it did at some point:

there must be *a personal history* of having processed the connection between the cue and the relevant abstract concept if the ensuing episode is to count as emotion. Our position insists that this history be personal or within the life-span of the individual rather than within the life-span of the species. Thus while we accept that a history of appraisal followed by a life of habit is consistent with the experience of emotion, we do not accept that evolution can take the place of habit. (2001: 32–3, emphasis in original)

This is a highly social definition of emotion—and does not allow for evolution or biological definitions of emotions. Royzman and Sabini can hold this position as they have effectively defined away some aspects of existence that are evolutionary (in some emotion typologies) as 'drives' and not 'emotions'. The primary example, and the crux of their argument, is that disgust is a drive, rather than an emotion. This position is in opposition to Ekman's (1992) argument that you can have both individual and species learning (see Chapter Two for a full elucidation of Ekman's position).

The second aspect of Royzman and Sabini's (2001) definition is that an emotion also has to have flexible responses. That is, a range of (in)actions are available to the individual in response to the elicitation of an emotion. The example they cite is anger. While anger is relatively uniform in its elicitation, that of a transgression against the self or society that is damaging or disruptive, the response is varied. In Rozyman and Sabini's view, you can write a scathing epigram or draw a caricature which are 'as abstract a version of the primordial hissing-and-biting attack behaviour as one can conceive' (2001: 31). They contrast anger with thirst, lust and appetite and contend that the latter each have an obvious and singular response (drinking, sex and eating respectively), rather than a flexible one (2001: 31).

This brings us to loyalty—does it have 'reasonably *flexible* responses to relatively *abstract, generative* classes of eliciting events' (Royzman and Sabini, 2001: 54 emphasis in original)? As I have demonstrated through the case studies, there are a very wide range of events that generate loyalty. The identification of loyalty layers shows different eliciting avenues, be it family, friends or nation states. To be an emotion in this definition, the events must be abstract and not concrete. Many of the elicitors of loyalty are abstract. One does not automatically receive a loyalty response, and there must be appropriate antecedents to generate loyalty (unlike a glass of cool water and thirst). The class of eliciting event is a challenge to one's connection with an other, be it an individual, organisation or structure. It is therefore a very wide generative class. The response, according to this perspective, must also be flexible, one that is not a fixed behaviour each time the elicitor occurs (again, when confronted with a glass of cool water and thirst the response is consume it). Loyalty can be responded to in a wide range of ways. It depends on who calls upon loyalty and how and why. The actor can respond by rushing to the defence of the loyalty target, with as many varied 'defences' as there can be in an anger situation. The actor may refuse to return loyalty, or switch loyalties. Loyalty can mean the actor chooses one product, brand or team over another despite any other considerations, such as price or prospects of winning. Loyalty has a wide range of behaviours, cognitions and actions that are associated with it action. Thus, loyalty fits neatly within Royzman and Sabini's (2001) emotion definition.

In an earlier article, Sabini and a colleague (Sabini & Silver, 1998) made the case that genuine emotion must be involuntary and beyond mental control—almost like an un-controlled 'outburst'. They argue that 'at least some element of every genuine emotional experience must be beyond the will . . . only those judgements able to overpower the will are capable of being part of emotions' (Sabini & Silver, 1998: 231). This is a profound argument in that it posits a claim to universal knowledge about 'real' and 'perceived'. While I do not have the space to delve into the deeper philosophical question of 'will', what I can do is expand this argument to its logical conclusion. Sabini and Silver (1998: 232) argue that '[n]atural expressions of emotion are more powerful than verbal glosses because they are taken to be involuntary and for that reason taken to be authentic and sincere'. This is a biological reductionist argument. If the only real emotions are beyond the will and if the best way to exhibit the emotion is natural expression, than this comes very close to the position that emotions are not only irrational but uncontrollable or, from the perspective of Lutz (1996), Furedi (2004) and Barbalet (2002), we are pathologising emotion as an 'other' that may require management. The second problem with the assertion of Sabini and Silver is that it does not allow for the creation of emotional states, either through social interaction or through drugs (see Chapter Two for another aspect of drugs and emotion within the existentialist position). Are the emotional feelings and expressions created through this not real? It is also conceivable that emotions can come out of behaviour. This is why there are expressions like 'she worked her way into a rage over x'—clearly the rage is real but its origin may be a conscious creation of the actor. Popular culture is very adept at eliciting emotional responses, be it movies, TV or books. Do tears at the plight of a movie character reflect a real emotion? Ultimately this is a fine distinction that cannot survive analysis. Further, W.I. Thomas offers a different perspective on the 'real' and 'perceived' when he states that: 'If men define situations as real, they are real in their consequences' (quoted in Merton, 1980: 29). Thus, while the emotion may be generated from the unreal or outside the individual actor, they are still true in their consequences.

Sabini and Silver are also only seeing one part of the emotion process. We can have emotion, cognition then behaviour, or behaviour, emotion then cognition. This raises the problem of when something actually is an emotion. In Sabini and Silver's (1998) typology, something can be defined only as an emotion when it is beyond the will. However, as I have discussed, this does not provide an answer for emotional occurrences which do not neatly fit their outburst model. Putting aside this critique of their position for a moment, can loyalty have an unwilled aspect that would point to its emotional nature? As the case studies show, when loyalty is challenged or called upon, the actor often manifests a deep and immediate emotional response. This 'call to arms' inspires the actor to engage in a myriad of behaviours designed to defend or enhance the object of loyalty. A further issue is the contention that many of our emotions simmer below the surface of conscious reflection (see above). Thus, in this model of emotions they cannot break free and 'overpower the will' as they are not acknowledged as being in existence. Thus, the Sabini and Silver 'will' model works well in some situations but falls short of offering a broad definition of emotion. However, notwithstanding these limitations, loyalty can still be considered an emotion within their model.

Averill offers yet another definition of emotion: 'emotions are responses that have been institutionalized by society as a means of resolving conflicts which exist within the social system' and ' . . . emotions are social constructions. That is, they are fashioned, organized, brought about – in short, *constructed* – according to rules of culture' (Averill, 1980: 35, 43, emphasis in original). This is more a call to arms—for sociology to engage in emotion and acknowledge the role of social structures—than an actual definition in that Averill is defending his broad approach to the study of emotions in general. The case studies have demonstrated how and why loyalty is fashioned through social action to regulate and direct conflict, although 'resolving conflict' in the stricter definitional sense is not often construed as one of loyalty's virtues. Loyalty is cultural in its creation and expression, as shown by the existence of appropriate and inappropriate targets for loyalty, as well as the means by which an actor may express different loyalties (consider the absurdity of wearing a picture of a family member on your jersey to signify your support of them versus wearing the image of the star player for a sporting team).

Loyalty therefore fits within the emotions definitions offered by many of the leading theorists. It is an emotion because our loyalties conjure affect-laden responses. Some of these responses are intermingled with other emotional states such as pride, joy, anger and even sadness. But this intermingling does not diminish loyalty as an emotional state, as it is rare to only experience a single emotive state, and most emotions that we feel occur in combination. Loyalty can be understood as an emotion because of its similarity to many other emotional states in the way we feel and interpret it. It is conjured through social contacts, with both people and institutions, like other emotions. Loyalty can motivate us to do things we would not otherwise consider, such as going to war for our country, or lying to protect a loved one. It can be used to justify many behaviours and reactions, both good and bad, in the same way that other emotions are used to justify some behaviour (for example, she was so sad that it is not surprising she refused to speak, or so angry that yelling was understandable).

I can therefore claim that loyalty is indeed an emotion. This insight offers a significant advancement to the sociological literature on emotions. What this allows is further research into loyalty employing an emotions framework that can only advance the field, and I hope, contribute to strengthening the emotions research agenda.

Epilogue

I have chosen to finish the arguments of this book with an epilogue (see Barbalet 2002) as I consider this work a beginning in elucidating how loyalty functions. Further, sociologically-inspired explorations into emotions are still in their infancy, despite a very long history. Consequently, this is just a small step towards extending the field.

A number of research avenues have become apparent out of my work on loyalty. This book only explored loyalty in a few contexts, albeit of a sufficiently wide scale to draw conclusions from. Thus, there are several areas that require more exploration. The first is religious-based loyalties. Does religion serve as a focal point for loyalty and does it match the parameters for loyalty that I have shown? Second, loyalty has been invoked with regularity in the fields of marketing and human resources. These social sites raise further questions regarding loyalty. Does the explicit financial component of these interactions modify the way loyalty is used? Can loyalty be construed by the promoters of capitalism to further sales?

A question that I was unable to grapple with adequately was the idea of age based loyalties. This issue arises because it appears that some loyalties diminish over the life course and others strengthen. Are the passionate political loyalties of youth replaced with quieter loyalties to clan and family as we age? This is a commonly expressed view—but it does require sociological unpacking. It is unfortunate that my methodology (excluding the use of *BtVS*) did not allow for the exploration of loyalty across time within the same subject. Research that engages with subjects' loyalties across longer time-frames could address the age based hypothesis and also start to answer how and why loyalty waxes and wanes.

This book represents a contribution to ways of 'seeing' emotion. The problem of engaging with emotional states is a serious methodological flaw of some literature. For example, one of these flaws is relying on experimental manipulation to investigate loyalty. Based on my analysis of loyalty—how it is created, re-enforced and expressed—it is not feasible to manipulate an actor for a loyalty response in the time-frames involved with laboratory experiments. Further, emotions are rarely expressed in a pure form, emotions are felt and expressed together and constantly evolve. However, using the sources I have allowed me to side-step much of this methodological angst. The way I have employed popular cultural sources needs further testing and replication, not only with loyalty, but with all emotions. If this means of knowing emotion can work for other emotions and, critically, if it can extend our understanding, then my work has been justified.

My examination of how loyalty has been used in larger social contexts has helped illuminate the macro-sociological processes involved in the emotion of loyalty. In particular, my use of wartime loyalty has illustrated the role emotion plays at the level beyond the actor. My work has made a contribution towards answering Barbalet's (1998) call for the exploration of emotion and its role in macro-historical processes. However, it has merely touched upon the role loyalty may play in such processes. It is imperative that further research is done in this field. I echo Barbalet's call not only for more on loyalty, but more research generally on the macro-sociological role of emotions in guiding action.

The discipline also requires more micro-sociological research into the minutiae of how the individual actor experiences emotion, the role it plays in agency and how this meshes with social structures. Katz's (1999) work offers a very useful method to engage the actor and see their emotional state. This requires replication across the gamut of emotions.

Once sociology has explored more emotions, from both a macro and micro perspective we will be in a considerably stronger position to develop a coherent 'general theory' of emotion that can offer an explanation of this phenomenon that is central to social action and society. Further, and perhaps critically for the discipline, we can then challenge the biologically reductionist perspectives that also continue to be the 'common sense' view.

I feel that I can confidently claim at the end of this journey, supported by my case studies and analysis, that loyalty is indeed an emotion. Loyalty denotes social relationships, reciprocities and connections and when we speak of loyalty we a referring to a specific social interaction that has, at its core, a commonality across social spaces and serves a set of specific purposes. Loyalties help to guide action and construct identity, and consequently it is a central emotion in social processes. It is not merely a behaviour, cognition, contractual relationship or subset of another emotion—but rather an emotion in its own right.

Bibliography

ADA. (2003) 'Dramatic Tension', smh.com.au, http://www.smh.com.au/articles/2003/10/30/1067233324474.html Accessed 31/10/2003.
Adams, Phillip. (2002), 'Yes, Yes, Mr President', *The Australian*, 22 June 2002.
Ahmed, Sara (2004), *The Cultural Politics of Emotion*, Edinburgh: Edinburgh University Press.
Ambrose, Stephen E. (1992), *Band of Brothers*, London: Simon & Schuster.
Anderson, Benedict. (1991), *Imagined Communities: Reflections on the Origin and Spread of Nationalism*, London: Verso, revised edition.
Anderson, Benedict. (1992), 'The New World Disorder', *New Left Review*, no 193, pp. 3–13.
Ang, Ien. (1998) 'Migrations of Chineseness: Ethnicity in the Postmodern World', Mots Pluriels, 7.
Aristotle. (1951), *The Politics*, T.A. Sinclair (trans.), Hamondsworth: Penguin.
Arkinstall, Jack. (1999), 'Through Thick and Thin – Letter', *The Times*, 24 June 1999, p. 23.
Armstrong, Este. (1999), 'Making symbols meaningful: Human emotions and the limbic system', in: Alexander Laban Hinton (ed.), *Biocultural Approaches to the Emotions*, Cambridge: Cambridge University Press.
Australian Bureau of Statistics (ABS). (1998), *How Australians use their time*, Cat. no. 4153, Canberra: ABS.
Australian Bureau of Statistics (ABS). (2004), *Australian Historical Population Statistics*, Cat. no. 3105.0.65.001, table 73.
Averill, James R. (1980), 'Emotion and anxiety: Sociocultural, biological, and psychological determinants', in: Amélie Oksenberg Rorty (ed.), *Explaining Emotions*, Berkeley: UCLA Press.
Baca, Stacey. (1996), 'Is Loyalty Dead? Family Allegiance Survives in a World Devoid of Ties', *Denver Post*, 21 March 1996, p. A–01.
Badman, Derik A. (2002), 'Academic Buffy Bibliography', *Slayage*, 7, pp. 1–8.
Baines, G. (1998), The Rainbow nation? Identity and nation building in post-apartheid South-Africa'. *Mots Pluriels*, 7, http://www.arts.uwa.edu.au/MotsPluriels/MP798gb.html.
Banfield, Edward C. (1958), *The Moral Basis of a Backward Society*, New York: The Free Press.
Banks, Amanda. (2004), 'Call for reform after SAS plot', *News.com.au*, http://www.news.com.au/common/printpage/0,6093,10406965,00.html, Accessed 11/8/2004.
Barbalet, J. (1992), 'A Macro Sociology of Emotion: Class Resentment', *Sociological Theory*, 10, 2, pp. 150–163.

Barbalet, J. (1998) Emotion, Social Theory, and Social Structure: A Macrosociological Approach, Cambridge: Cambridge University Press.

Barbalet, J. (2002), Introduction: Why emotions are crucial, in: J. Barbalet (ed.), *Emotions and Sociology*, Oxford: Blackwell.

Barth, Alan. (1951), *The Loyalty of Free Men*, London: Victor Gollancz.

Basham, Richard. (1996), 'The Roots of Asian Organized Crime', *IPA Review*, 48, 4, pp. 11–17.

bbc.co reviews. (2004), 'Episode Guide: Innocence', http://www.bbc.co.uk/cult/buffy/indetail/innocence/reviews.shtml accessed 7/12/2004.

Beaumont, Joan. (1995), 'The politics of a divided society', in: Joan Beaumont (ed.), *Australia's War 1914–18*, St Leonards: Allen & Unwin.

Benedict, Ruth. (1991), *The Chrysanthemum and the Sword*, Rutland: Tuttle.

Birmingham Post. (2003), 'Alleged Killer's relatives 'gave alibi out of misguided family loyalty'', 19 November 2003, p. 3.

Birrell, Susan. (1981), 'Sport as Ritual: Interpretations from Durkheim and Goffman', *Social Forces*, Vol 60, 2, pp. 354–376.

Bloch, Herbert A. (1934), The Concept of our Changing Loyalties, New York: Colombia University Press.

BLS. (2006), 'American Time Use Survey Summary', Bureau of Labour Statistics, http://www.bls.gov/news.release/atus.nr0.htm accessed 10/9/2006.

Born, Georgina. (2000), 'Inside Television: Television Studies and the Sociology of Culture', *Screen*, 41:4, Winter, pp. 404–24.

Boszormenyi-Nagy, Ivan, and Spark, Geraldine. (1984), *Invisible Loyalties: Reciprocity In Intergenerational Family Therapy*, New York: Brunner/Mazel.

Bowden, Mark. (2003), 'The Dark Art of interrogation', *The Atlantic Monthly*, October, online version.

Braithwaite, John. (1989), *Crime, Shame and Reintegration*, Sydney: Cambridge University Press.

Bullock, Chris. (2000), 'South Sydney vs. the National Rugby League', ABC Radio National, Background Briefing, no 26. http://www.abc.net.au/rn/talks/bbing/s159144.htm

Byrne, Jennifer. (2004), 'Lunch with Jennifer Byrne', *The Bulletin*, http://bulletin.ninemsn.com.au/bulletin/EdDesk.nsf/printing/14FE077020392974CA25 6E5C00160035. Accessed 29/4/04.

Byron, Brian. (1972), *Loyalty in the Spirituality of St. Thomas Moore*, Nieuwkoop: B. De Graff.

Cahill, S. (1999), 'Emotional Capital and Professional Socialization: The Case of Mortuary Science Student (and Me)', *Social Psychology Quarterly*, 62, 2, pp. 101–117.

Cancian, Francesca M. (1987), *Love in America: Gender and Self-development*, Cambridge: Cambridge University Press.

Carpenter, David A. (2000), 'The Second Century of English Feudalism', *Past and Present*, 168, pp. 30–71.

Carroll, N. (1999), 'Film, Emotion, and Genre', in: C. Plantinga and G. Smith (eds.), *Passionate Views: Film, Cognition, and Emotion*, Baltimore: John Hopkins University Press.

Charlesworth, Max. (1968), 'Australian catholics and conscription', in: Roy Forward and Bob Reece (eds.), *Conscription in Australia*, St. Lucia: University of Queensland Press.

Clarence, E. (1999), 'Citizenship and identity: the case of Australia', in: S. Roseneil and J. Seymour (eds.), *Practising Identities: Power and Resistance*, London: MacMillan Press.

Clark, Candice. (1997), *Misery and Company: Sympathy in Everyday Life*, Chicago: University of Chicago Press.
Clarke, Simon. (2003), 'Psychoanalytic Sociology and the Interpretation of Emotion', *Journal for the Theory of Social Behaviour*, 33, 2, pp. 145–163.
Collins, Randall. (1984), 'The Role of Emotion in Social Structure', in: Klaus Scherer and Paul Ekman (eds.), *Approaches to Emotion*, New Jersey: Lawrence Erlbaum.
Collins, Randall. (2004) Interaction Ritual Chains, Princeton University Press: Princeton.
Cooper, Tracy E. (1996), '*Mecenatismo* or *Clientelismo*? The Character of Renaissance Patronage', in: David G. Wilkins and Rebecca L. Wilkins (eds.), *The Search for a Patron in the Middle Ages and the Renaissance*, Lewiston: Edwin Mellen Press.
Courtney, Anth. (2000a), 'A message to South Sydney fans, with pride', www.rabbitohs.com/burrows/opinions/2000/10-courtney.shtml. Accessed 5/4/04.
Courtney, Anth. (2000b), 'George & Orwell', www.rabbitohs.com/burrows/opinions/2000/11-courtney1.shtml. Accessed 5/4/04.
Craib, Ian. (1998), *Experiencing Identity*, London: Sage.
Crossley, Nick. (1998), 'Emotion and communicative action: Habermas, linquistic philosophy and existenstialism', in: Gillian Bendelow and Simon J. Williams (eds.), *Emotions in Social Life: Critical Themes and Contemporary Issues*, London: Routledge.
Darwin, Charles. (1872/1998), *The Expression of the Emotions in Man and Animals*, London: HarperCollins.
De Brito, Kate. and Hilferty, Tim. (2000), 'Silence then the Tears of Despair – Heartache as Club's Hopes Crash in Court – Souths-the Verdict', *The Daily Telegraph*, 4 November 2000, p. 4.
De Ruyter, K.O. and Wetzels, Martin. (2004), 'With a Little help from My Fans – Extending Models of Pro-social Behaviour to explain Supporters' Intentions to buy Soccer Club Shares', *Journal of Economic Psychology*, 21, pp. 387–409.
Devine, Miranda. (2004), 'Crying Wolf Belittles Plight of Real Victims', *Sun Herald*, 29 February 2004, p. 15.
Dizard, Jan E. and Gadlin, Howard. (1990), *The Minimal Family*, Amherst: University of Massachusetts Press.
Docker, John. (1994), *Postmodernism and Popular Culture*, Cambridge: Cambridge University Press.
Doherty, William J. (1999), 'Divided Loyalties: The Challenge of Stepfamily Life', *Family Therapy Networker*, May/June, 54, pp. 32–38. [My page numbers refer to Prof. Doherty's word document of this article as this was the only way to source it]
Donaldson, Amy. (1995a), 'Deadly Dominoes', *Deseret News*, 23 February 1995, p. A21.
Donaldson, Amy. (1995b), 'Even 'Loyal' Have Limits in World of Gang-Banging', *Deseret News*, 23 February 1995, p. A22
Donaldson, Amy. (1996), 'Bonds of Loyalty Make Gangs a Powerful Force', *Deseret News*, 22 June 1996, p. B1.
Dunn, John. (1988), 'Trust and Political Agency', in: Diego Gambetta (ed.), *Trust: Making and Breaking Cooperative Relations*, New York: Basil Blackwell.
Edgar, D. (2001), *The Patchwork Nation*, Melbourne: HarperCollins.
Edwards, Lindy. (2002), *How to Argue with an Economist: Reopening Political Debate in Australia*, Cambridge: Cambridge University Press.
Ekman, Paul. (1984), 'Expression and the Nature of Emotion', in: Klaus Scherer and Paul Ekman (eds.), *Approaches to Emotion*, New Jersey: Lawrence Erlbaum.
Ekman, Paul. (1992), 'An Argument for Basic Emotions', *Cognition and Emotion*, 6, pp. 169–200.

Ekman, Paul. (1999), 'Introduction to the third edition', in: Charles Darwin (ed.), *The Expression of the Emotions in Man and Animals*, 3rd Edition, London: Fontana.
Elias, Norbet. (1994), *The Civilizing Process*, Vols. 1 and 2, Oxford: Blackwell.
Emerson, Craig. (2002), 'Bulldogs: Salary Cap', Australia, House of Representatives 2002, Debates, Volume 11, HR 5578.
Evans, Dylan. (2001), *Emotion: The Science of Sentiment*, Oxford: Oxford University Press.
Evening Herald. (2003), 'Time for us to get Real', 12 April 2003, p. 61.
Fehr, Beverly and Russell, James A. (1984), 'Concept of Emotion Viewed from a Prototype Perspective', *Journal of Experimental Psychology*, 113, 3, pp. 464–486.
Firth, Simon. (2000), 'The Black Box: The Value of Television and the Future of Television Research', *Screen*, 41, 1, Spring, pp. 33–50.
Fisher, Gene A. and Chon, Kyum Koo. (1989), 'Durkheim and the Social Construction of Emotions', *Social Psychology Quarterly*, 52, 1, pp. 1–9.
Fitzpatrick, Sheila. (2004), 'Happiness and *Toska*: An Essay in the History of Emotions in Pre-war Soviet Russia', *Australian Journal of Politics and History*, 50, 3, pp. 357–371.
Fletcher, George P. (1993), *Loyalty: An Essay on the Morality of Relationships*, New York: Oxford University Press.
Foley, A. (2000) Deck to Deck, Sabina, Assunta & John Buonaccorsi. http://svc018.wic010p.server-web.com/deck_to_deck/01_stories/sabina.htm accessed 28/5/2004.
Forward, Roy. (1968), 'Conscription, 1964–68', in: Roy Forward and Bob Reece (eds.), *Conscription in Australia*, St. Lucia: University of Queensland Press.
Fried, Richard M. (1990), *Nightmare in Red: The McCarthy Era in Perspective*, Oxford: Oxford University Press.
Fried, Albert. (1997), *McCarthyism: The Great American Red Scare*, Oxford: Oxford University Press, edited documentary history.
Frijda, N.H. (1998), 'The Laws of Emotion', in: *Human Emotions: A Reader*, J. Jenkins, K. Oatley and N. Steins (eds.), Malden: Blackwell.
Frijda, N., Markam, S., Sato, K. and Wiers, R. (1995), 'Emotions and emotion words', in: J. Russel, J. Fernández-Dols, A. Manstead and J. Wellenkamp (eds.), *Everyday Conceptions of Emotions: An introduction to the Psychology, Anthropology and Linguistics of Emotion*, Dordrecht: Kluwer Academic Publishers.
Fukuyama, Francis. (2004), 'State-Building: Governance and World Order in the Twenty-First Century', New York: Cornell University Press.
Furedi, Frank. (2004), *Therapy Culture: Cultivating Vulnerability in an Uncertain Age*, London: Routledge.
Gerth, Hans and C. Wright Mills (1964), *Character and Social Structure: The Psychology of Social Institutions*, New York: Harbringer.
Gloucestershire Echo, (2002), 'Teenager tried to stop arrest', 11 March 2002.
Goffman, Irving. (1991), 'Total Institutions', in: P. Worsley (ed.), *The New Modern Sociology Readings*, London: Penquin, pp. 369–373.
Gold Coast Bulletin. (2002), 'Sadness and Joy', 28 November, p. 21.
Gold Coast Bulletin. (2002), 'Rabbitoh faithful hop it to training', 29 November, p. 79.
Grodzins, Morton. (1956), *The Loyal and the Disloyal: Social Boundaries of Patriotism and Treason*, Cleveland: Meridian books.
Guido-DiBrito, Florence. (1995), 'Student Affairs Leadership and Loyalty: Organizational Dynamics at Play', *NASPA Journal*, 32, 3, Spring, pp. 223–231.
Guy, Sandy. (2000), 'All For One', *Australian Good Taste*, November, pp. 141–144.

Guyatt, Chris. (1968), 'The anti-conscription movement, 1964–66', in: Roy Forward and Bob Reece (eds.), *Conscription in Australia*, St. Lucia: University of Queensland Press.
Hage, G. (1998), *White Nation: Fantasies of White supremacy in a multicultural society*, Annandale: Pluto Press.
Hamel-Green, Michael. (1983), 'The Resistors: a history of the anti-conscription movement 1964–1972', in: Peter King (ed.) *Australia' Vietnam: Australia in the Second Indo-China War*, North Sydney: George Allen & Unwin.
Hammerton, A. James and Coleborne, Catharine (2001), 'Ten-pound Poms Revisited: Battlers' Tales and British Migration to Australia, 1947–1971', *Journal of Australian Studies*, no 68, pp. 86–8.
Harré, R. (1986), *The Social Construction of Emotion*, London: Blackwell.
Hecht, Jeff. (2002), 'Early Americans used First Writings to Promise Loyalty', *New Scientist*, December 14.
Henderson, Gerard (2002) 'Them and US, a Question of Security', *Sydney Morning Herald*, 15 January 2002.
Hirschman, A. (1970), *Exit, Voice, and Loyalty: Responses to Decline in Firms, Organizations, and States*, Cambridge: Harvard University Press.
Hochschild, Arlie Russell. (1983), *The Managed Heart: Commercialization of Human Feeling*, Berkeley: University of California Press.
Hochschild, Arlie Russell. (1998), 'The Sociology of emotion as a way of seeing', in: Gillian Bendelow and Simon J. Williams (eds.), *Emotions in Social Life: Critical Themes and Contemporary Issues*, London: Routledge, pp. 3–15.
Hoggard, Liz. (2003), 'Is He a Man or a Mouse?', *Guardian Unlimited*, 7 December 2003.
Hollingworth, P. (2003), 'The March-Out Parade Of 22 And 23 Platoon Army Recruit Training Centre, Kapooka', http://www.gg.gov.au/speeches/html/speeches/2003/030314b.html, Accessed 20/8/2004.
Hughson, John. (1998), 'Is the carnival over? Soccer support and hooliganism in Australia', in: Rowe, D. and Lawrence, G. (eds.), *Tourism, Leisure, Sport: Critical Perspectives*, Rydalmere: Hodder, pp. 170–179.
Inglis, K.S. (1968), 'Conscription in peace and war, 1911–45,' in: Roy Forward and Bob Reece (eds.), *Conscription in Australia*, St. Lucia: University of Queensland Press.
Jauncey, Leslie C. (1935), *The Story of Conscription in Australia*, London: George Allen & Unwin LTD.
Jenkins, Richard. (1996), *Social Identity*, London: Routledge.
Jenkins, R. (1997), *Rethinking Ethnicity: Arguments and Explorations*, Sage, London.
Katz, Jack. (1999), *How Emotions Work*, Chicago: The University of Chicago Press.
Katz, Jack and Jackson-Jacobs, Curtis. (2004), 'The Criminologists' Gang', in: C. Sumner (ed.), *Blackwell Companion to Criminology*, London: Blackwell, pp. 91–124.
Kaveney, Roz. (2001), "she saved the world. A lot': An introduction to the themes and structures of *Buffy* and *Angel*' in: R. Kaveney (ed.), *Reading the Vampire Slayer*, London: Tauris.
Kellner, Douglas. (2004), '*Buffy, The Vampire Slayer* as Spectacular Allegory: A Diagnostic Critique', http://www.gseis.ucla.edu/faculty/kellner/, downloaded, 10/9/04.
Kelly, P. (1992), *The End of Certainty*, St. Leonards: Allen & Unwin.
Kemper, Theodore D. (1978), *A Social Interactional Theory of Emotions*, New York: John Wiley & Sons.
Kemper, Theodore D. (1984), 'Power, Status, and Emotions: A Sociological Contribution to a Psychophysiological Domain', in: Klaus Scherer and Paul Ekman (eds.), *Approaches to Emotion*, New Jersey: Lawrence Erlbaum.

Kershler, Ray. (2001), 'The Family that couldn't Live Without South Sydney', *The Daily Telegraph*, 23 November, p. 142.

Korsmeyer, Carolyn. (2003), 'Passion and Action: In and Out of Control', in: James B. South (ed.), *Buffy the Vampire Slayer and Philosophy*, Illinois: Open Court, pp. 160–172.

Kristjánsson, Kristján. (2003), 'On the Very Idea of "Negative Emotions"', *Journal for the Theory of Social Behaviour*, 33, 4, pp. 351–364.

Leathers, Sonya J. (2003), 'Parental Visiting, Conflicting Allegiances, Emotional and Behavioural Problems Among Foster Children', *Family Relations*, 52, 1, pp. 53–64.

Linsay, Norman (1917), This picture is available at http://john.curtin.edu.au/manofpeace/homefrontg.html, and is from the National Library of Australia collection, Aust-Defence-1917 Conscription, Plate no. 8474.

Loose, Cindy. (1996), "Loyal to Her Friends, Family And Country'; McCarthy Era Victim Posthumously Cleared', *The Washington Post*, 8 March 1996.

Lutz, Catherine A. (1996), 'Engendered Emotion: Gender, Power, and the Rhetoric of Emotional Control in American Discourse', in: Rom Harré and W. Gerrod Parrott (eds.), *The Emotions: Social, Cultural and Biological Dimensions*, London: Sage.

Main, J.M. (1970), *Conscription: The Australian Debate, 1901–1970*, North Melbourne: Cassell.

Markus, A and Sims, E. (1993), *Fourteen Lives Paths to a Multicultural Community*, Clayton: Monash Publications in History.

Mascord, Steve and Walter, Brad. (2003), 'Sport – Something to Crow About', *Sydney Morning Herald*, 9 June, p. 25.

Masters, Roy. (1996), "'Loyal' Clubs To Wait On $30m Deal Assurance', *The Age*, 7 October, p. 4.

McKell, Bill. (2004), 'Boilermaker Bill on NRL cultural change', *crikey.com.au*, http://www.crikey.com.au/columnists/2004/05/05–0003.htm, accessed 5/5/04.

McKernan, M. (1980), *The Australian People and the Great War*, West Melbourne: Nelson.

McNeal, Keith E. (1999), 'Affecting experience: Toward a biocultural model of human emotion', in: Alexander Laban Hinton (ed.), *Biocultural approaches to the Emotions*, Cambridge: Cambridge University Press.

Menzies, R. (1939), 'Declaration of War Speech', National Archives of Australia, Series C102, item barcode 859228, Australian Broadcasting Commission sound recording.

Merton, Robert K. (1980), 'The Self-Fulfilling Prophecy', in: Lewis A. Coser (ed.), *The Pleasures of Sociology*, New York: Mentor.

Mewett, Peter G. (1999), 'Fragments of a Composite Identity: Aspects of Australian Nationalism in a Sports Setting', *The Australian Journal of Anthropology*, 10, 3, Pp. 357–376

Mills, C. Wright. (1959), *The Sociological Imagination*, New York: Oxford University Press.

Misztal, Barbara A. (1996) *Trust in Modern Societies*, Cambridge: Polity.

Modleski, Tania. (1990), *Loving with a Vengeance: Mass-produced Fantasies for Women*, US: Routledge.

Moir, A. (2003), 'Axis of Justice . . . The Vigillantes' *Sydney Morning Herald*, 23 April 2003.

Moller, Michael. (2003), 'Grassroots Ethics: The Case of Souths versus News Corporation', in: Lumby, C. and Probyn, E. (eds.), *RemoteControl: New Media, New Ethics*, Cambridge: Cambridge University Press, pp. 216–229.

Morsbach, H. and Tyler, W.J. (1986), 'A Japanese emotion: *Amae*', in: Rom Harré (ed.), *The Social Construction of Emotions*, Oxford: Basil Blackwell.

Mulcair, John. (1996), 'Loyal League Fan Mourns'. Sydney Morning Herald, 2 March, p. 45
Mycak, S. (2003), A Dual Existence in a Seemingly Singular Country. *Mots Pluriels*, 23, http://www.arts.uwa.edu.au/MotsPluriels/MP2303sm.html.
Newcastle Herald. (2000), "'Rabbit' Hopping Mad Over NRL Bunny Chop', 4 November 2000, p. 4.
Newell, Frederick. (2000), *Loyalty.com: Customer Relationship Management in the New Era of internet Marketing*, New York: McGraw-Hill.
Newman, Philip. (1964), '"Wild Man" Behaviour in a New Guinea Highlands Community', *American Anthropologist*, 66, 1–19.
Newton, Tim. (1998), 'The sociogenesis of emotion: A historical Sociology?', in: Gillian Bendelow and Simon J. Williams (eds.), *Emotions in Social Life: Critical Themes and Contemporary Issues*, London: Routledge, pp. 60–80.
Noble, G. and Tabar, P. (2002), 'On being Lebanese-Australian: hybridity, essentialism and strategy among Arabic-speaking youth', in: G. Hage (ed.), *Arab-Australians Today: Citizenship and Belonging*, Carlton South: Melbourne University Press.
Nutting, D. (2002) http://www.teachers.ash.org.au/dnutting/germanaustralia/e/ww1.htm, accessed 21 March 2002.
Oatley, Keith. and Johnson-Laird, P.N. (1987), 'Towards a Cognitive Theory of Emotions', *Cognition and Emotion*, 1, 1, pp. 29–50.
O'Dell, Larry. (1998), 'Trooper's Family Divided Over his Killer's Execution', *Associated Press Newswires*, 16 June 1998, P. 14.
Oldenquist, A. (1991), 'Community and de-alienation', in: A. Oldenquist and M. Rosner (eds.), *Alienation, Community, and Work*, Westport: Greenwood Press, pp. 3–14.
Ong, A. (1996), 'Cultural Citizenship as Subject-making: Immigrants Negotiate Racial and Cultural Boundaries in the United States', *Current Anthropology*, 73, 5, pp. 737–762.
Oxford English Dictionary. (1933), London: Oxford University Press.
Pemberton, G. (1987), *All The Way: Australia's Road to Vietnam*, North Sydney: Allen & Unwin.
Perkins, M. (2004), 'Australian Mixed Race', *European Journal of Cultural Studies*, 7, 2, pp. 177–199.
Planalp, Sally. (1999), *Communicating Emotion: Social, Moral and Cultural Processes*, Cambridge: Cambridge University Press.
Potts, Ken. (1999), 'Family Loyalty shouldn't keep Us from Confronting Problems', *Chicago Daily Herald*, 27 March, D3, p. 4.
Powell, Joy. (1996), 'Tavais Minor Says Gang Loyalty prevented Him From Testifying', *The Omaha World-Herald*, 23 March 1996, p. 1.
Price, C. (1991), 'Conclusion', in: C. Price (ed.), *Australian National Identity*, Canberra: The Academy of the Social Sciences in Australia.
Priesnitz, Horst. (1987) 'Introduction' in Irmhild Beinssen (ed), *Fates and Fortunes: Expriences of German migrants in Australia*, Gunter Narr Verlag: Tübingen.
Rabbitoh Warren. (1999), Image 26.
http://www.rabbitohs.com/burrows/gallery/1999/reclaim-rally/pics/026.shtml, accessed 13/4/04.
Rabbitoh Warren. (2000), Image 30.
http://www.rabbitohs.com/burrows/gallery/2000/savethegame-rally/html/030.html, accessed 13/4/04.
Rabbitoh Warren. (2000), Image 36.
http://www.rabbitohs.com/burrows/gallery/2000/savethegame-rally/html/036.html, accessed 13/4/04.

Rabbitoh Warren. (2000), Image 34. http://www.rabbitohs.com/burrows/gallery/2000/savethegame-rally/html/034.html, accessed 13/4/04.

Ricketts, Steve. (2002), 'Supporters put Dogs scandal behind them', *The Courier-Mail*, 2 September 2002, p. 2.

Riefenstahl, Leni. (1934), Triumph of the Will, Leni Riefenstahl-Produktion

Rosenspan, Alan. (1998), 'Delusions of Loyalty: Where Loyalty Programs Go Wrong', *Direct Marketing*, 60, 10, p. 24.

Rothstein, Jeff. (2001), 'Family Loyalty: Implications for Planners', *Journal of Financial Planning*, 14, 3, pp. 50–54. http://www.fpanet.org/journal/articles/2001_Issues/jfp0301-art7.cfm?renderforprint=1

Rowe, David. and Lawrence, Geoffrey. (1998), 'Framing a Critical Sports Sociology in the Age of Globalisation', in: Rowe, D. and Lawrence, G. (eds.), *Tourism, Leisure, Sport: Critical Perspectives*, Rydalmere: Hodder, pp. 159–169.

Royce, Josiah. (1908), *The Philosophy of Loyalty*, New York: MacMillan.

Royzman, Edward B. and Sabini, John. (2001), 'Something it Takes to be an Emotion: The Interesting Case of Disgust', *Journal for the Theory of Social Behaviour*, 31:1, pp. 29–59.

RSV, Revised Standard Version of the Bible.

Rule, Andrew. (1996), 'Soldiers of Misfortune', *The Age*, 16 June 1996,

Runkle, Gerald. (1958), 'Some Considerations on Family Loyalty', *Ethics*, 68, 2, pp. 131–136.

Sabini, John and Silver, Maury. (1998), 'The Not Altogether Social Construction of Emotions: A critique of Harré and Gillett', *Journal for the Theory of Social Behaviour*, 28, 3, pp. 223–235.

Sartre, Jean-Paul. (2002), *Sketch for a Theory of the Emotions*, Philip Mairet (trans.), London: Routledge.

Scheff, Thomas. (2003), 'Strategies for the Social Science of Emotion', http://www.soc.ucsb.edu/faculty/scheff/31.html, accessed 9/4/05.

Schrecker, Ellen. (1998), *Many are the Crimes: McCarthyism in America*, Boston: Little, Brown and Company.

Schrecker, Ellen. (2002), *The Age of McCarthyism: A brief history with Documents*. 2nd Edition, Boston: Bedford/St. Martin's.

Sennett, Richard. (1997), 'The New Capitalism', *Social Research*, 64, 2, pp. 161–180.

Shain, Yossi. (1989), *The Frontier of Loyalty: Political Exiles in the Age of the Nation-State*, Connecticut: Wesleyan University Press.

Shklar, Judith N. (1993), 'Obligation, Loyalty, Exile', *Political Theory*, 21, 2, pp. 181–197.

Silver, Alan. (1985), '"Trust" in Social and Political Theory', in: Gerald D. Suttles and Mayer N. Zald (eds.), *The Challenge of Social Control: Citizenship and Institution Building in Modern Society*, pp. 52–67, New Jersey: Ablex.

Skrbis, Zlatko. (1999), *Long-distance Nationalism: Diasporas, Homelands and Identities*, Aldershot: Ashgate.

Smith, A. (1991), *National Identity*, London: Penguin.

Smith, P. and Phillips, T. (2001), 'Popular Understandings of 'UnAustralian': An Investigation of the Un-national', *Journal of Sociology*, 27, 4, pp. 323–339.

Smolicz, J. (1991), 'Who is an Australian? Identity, core values and the resilience of culture', in: C. Price (ed.), *Australian National Identity*, Canberra: The Academy of the Social Sciences in Australia.

Sniffen, Michael J. (1996) 'Brother of Unabomber Suspect Agonized Over Tipping FBI', *Associated Press*, 4 April 1996.

Soloman, Robert C. (1981), 'Sartre on Emotions', in: *The Philosophy of Jean-Paul Sartre*, Paul Schilpp (ed.), Illinois: Open Court Publishing.

Solomon, Robert C. (2002), 'Back to Basics: On the Very Idea of "Basic Emotions"', *Journal for the Theory of Social Behaviour*, 32, 2, pp. 115–144.

Solomon, Robert C. and Stone, Lori D. (2002), 'On "Positive" and "Negative" Emotions', *Journal for the Theory of Social Behaviour*, 32, 4, pp. 417–435.

South Sydney Rabbitohs. (2000) Image 157. http://www.southsydneyrabbitohs.bravepages.com/souths157.jpg, accessed 16/4/04.

Spark, Geraldine M. (1977), 'Marriage Is a Family Affair', *The Family Coordinator*, 26, 2, pp. 167–174.

State Library of Victoria, This picture is available at http://john.curtin.edu.au/manofpeace/homefrontf.html, and is from the State Library of Victoria: Riley Collection. Accessed 26/9/2002.

Stearns, Peter N. and Stearns, Carol Z. (1985), 'Emotionology: Clarifying the History of Emotions and Emotional Standards', *The American Historical Review*, 90, 4, pp. 813–836.

Stearns, P.N. and Stearns, C.Z. (1986), *Anger: The Struggle for Emotional Control in America's History*, Chicago: University of Chicago Press.

Stets, Jan E. and Burke, Peter J. (2000), 'Identity Theory and Social Identity Theory', in: *Social Psychology Quarterly*, vol. 63, no. 3, pp. 224–237.

Stryker, Sheldon and Burke, Peter J. (2000), The Past, Present, and Future of an Identity Theory', *Social Psychology Quarterly*, vol. 63, no. 4, pp. 284–297.

Sullivan, Gavin B. and Strongman, Kenneth T. (2003), 'Vacillating and Mixed Emotions: A Conceptual-Discursive Perspective on Contemporary Emotion and Cognitive Appraisal Theories Through Examples of Pride', *Journal for the Theory of Social Behaviour*, 33, 2, pp. 203–226.

The Kennel. (2004), atomic_crimson, 26/2/2004, 10:45 am, http://www.thekennel.com.au/forums

The Kennel. (2004), Christabella, 27/2/2004, 3:24 am, http://www.thekennel.com.au/forums

The Kennel. (2004), club_sweat, 19/4/2004, 3:25pm, http://www.thekennel.com.au/forums

The Kennel. (2004), whippet_hound, 1/3/2004, 1:48am, http://www.thekennel.com.au/forums

The Kennel. (2004), K E, 28/4/2004, 6:39pm, http://www.thekennel.com.au/forums

The Kennel. (2004a), riomhach, 26/2/2004, 11:08 am, http://www.thekennel.com.au/forums

The Kennel. (2004b), riomhach, 1/3/2004, 2:48 am, http://www.thekennel.com.au/forums

The San Francisco Chronicle. (1992), 'Friends or Family More Loyal', 29 December 1992, p. A19.

Tumin, Melvin M. (1970), 'In Dispraise of Loyalty', in: Jack Douglas (ed.), *The Relevance of Sociology*, New York: Meredith.

Turner, Jonathan H. (1999), 'Toward a General Sociological Theory of Emotions', *Journal for the Theory of Social Behaviour*, 29, 2, pp. 133–161.

Turner, Jonathan H. (2000), *On The Origins of Human Emotions: A Sociological Inquiry into the evolution of Human Affect*, Stanford: Stanford University Press.

Vogler, Carolyn. (2000), 'Social Identity and Emotion: The Meeting of Psychoanalysis and Sociology', *The Sociological Review*, pp. 19–42.

Wahlke, John C, (ed). (1952), Loyalty in a Democratic State, Boston: DC Health & Co.

Weir, Peter. (1998), *The Truman Show*, Paramount Pictures.
Wierzbicka, Anna. (1990), 'Introduction', *Australian Journal of Linguistics*, 10, pp. 133–138.
Wierzbicka, Anna. (1995), 'Everyday conceptions of emotion: A semantic perspective', in: J. Russel, J. Fernández-Dols, A. Manstead and J. Wellenkamp (eds.), *Everyday Conceptions of Emotions: An introduction to the Psychology, Anthropology and Linguistics of Emotion*, Dordrecht: Kluwer Academic Publishers.
Williams, Raymond. (1990), *Television: Technology and Cultural form*, 2nd edition, London: Routledge.
Williams, Simon J. (2001), *Emotion and Social Theory: Corporeal Reflections on the (Ir)Rational*, London: Sage.
Willis, Anne-Marie. (1993), *Illusions of Identity: The Art of Nation*, Marrickville: Hale & Iremonger.
Windschuttle, Kieth. (1993), 'Media as a projection of Values and Socialising Agent', in: T. Jagtenberg and P. D'Alton (eds.), *Four Dimensional Social Space*, Sydney: Harper, pp. 174–7.
Winslow, Donna. (1998), 'Misplaced Loyalties: The Role of Military Culture in the Breakdown of Discipline in Peace Operations', *The Canadian review of Sociology and Anthropology*, 35, 3, pp. 345–367.
Withers, Glenn. (1972), *Conscription: Necessity and Justice*, Sydney: Angus and Robertson.
Woelz-Stirling, Nicole., Manderson, Lenore., Kelaher, Margaret. and Benedicto, Anne-Marie. (2001), 'Young Women in Conflict: Filipinas Growing Up in Australia', *Journal of Intercultural Studies*, 22, 3, pp. 295–306.
Wolff, Robert Paul. (1968), *The Poverty of Liberalism*, Boston: Beacon Press.
Wong, J. (2002), 'What's in a Name? An Examination of Social Identities', *Journal for the Theory of Social Behaviour*, 32, 4, pp. 451–463.
Yamine, Evelyn & Williams, Natalie. (2003), 'Obsessions of footy's true fanatics – Supporters are hitting fever pitch', *The Daily Telegraph*, 13 September, p. 12.
Zevallos, Z. (2003), 'That's My Australian Side': The Ethnicity, Gender and Sexuality of Young Australian Women of South and Central American Origin. *Journal of Sociology*, 39, 1, pp. 81–98.
Zdaniuk, Bozena and Levine, John M. (2000), 'Group Loyalty: Impact of Members' Identification and Contributions', *Journal of Experimental Psychology*, 37, pp. 502–509.
Zubrzycki, Jerzy (1991), 'The evolution of multiculturalism', in: Charles A Price (ed.), *Australian National Identity*, Canberra: The Academy of the Social Sciences in Australia.

Episodes of BtVS

Becoming, Part Two, Episode 2/22, Writer: Joss Whedon.
Innocence, Episode 2/14, Writer: Joss Whedon.
The Zeppo, Episode 3/13, Writer: Dan Vebber.
Choices, Episode 3/19, Writer: David Fury.
The Prom, Episode 3/20, Writer: Marti Noxon.
Graduation Day, Part One and *Part Two*, Episodes 3/21 & 3/22, Writer: Josh Whedon.
The Initiative, Episode 4/7, Writer: Douglas Petrie.
A New Man, Episode 4/12, Writer: Jane Espenson.
The I in Team, Episode 4/13, Writer: David Fury.
Goodbye Iowa, Episode 4/14, Writer: Marti Noxon.
This Year's Girl, Episode 4/15, Writer: Douglas Petrie.
The Yoko Factor, Episode 4/20, Writer: Douglas Petrie.
Into the Woods, Episode 5/10, Writer: Marti Noxon.
The Gift, Episode 5/22, Writer: Joss Whedon.
Grave, Episode 6/22, Writer: David Fury.
Conversations With Dead People, Episode 7/7, Writers: Jane Espenson and Drew Goddard
Lies My Parents Told Me, Episode 7/17, Writers: David Fury and Drew Goddard.
Empty Places, Episode 7/19, Writer: Drew Z. Greenberg.
End of Days, Episode 7/21, Writers: Jane Espenson and Douglas Petrie

Index

A

Action and loyalty, 51–53
Actor's identity and loyalty, 49–51
Ambrose's bond of brotherhood, 72
Ang's argument on nation-state, 90
Anger, 17, 43, 54
　Utku Eskimos, among, 46
ANZUS treaty, 83
Armstrong's neurophysiological states
　　of emotions, 25
Australian immigrants and national loyalty
　Australian muslim communities, 96
　empowering nature of dual identity, 94–95
　issue of dual loyalty, 89–91
　long distance nationalism of Ukranian-
　　Australian, 95
　treatment of Germans during
　　World War II, 91–92
　treatment of Japanese decendants during
　　World War II, 93
　un-Australian, use of, 96
Australian nationalism
　and conscription issues, 85–89
　fall out with British, 83–84
　immigrant experiences, 89–97
　response to World War I declarations, 82–83, 85
　during Vietnam conflict, 83, 86
　during War on Terror (2002), 84–85
　during World War II, 84
Australian SAS unit, incidents
　　of loyalty in, 73–74
Australian trade practices act, 105
Averill's emotional behavior, 40–41, 141

B

Baca' familial influence on loyalty, 66
Baines's national identity, 80
Banfield's comments on economic
　　development, 60
Barbalet on loyalty as emotion, 16, 28–29, 32,
　　36, 42, 47–48, 51, 77–78, 133, 135–136
Basham's comment on loyalty, 71
Beaumont's comments, on war around
　　loyalties, 83, 86
Bendicto's arguments, on familial conflict, 68
Benedict's comments, on familial loyalty, 40
Beowulf, 11
Birmingham Post, 64
Birrell's argument of sports, 105, 115
Boszormenyi-Naggy's explanations
　　of family loyalty, 13–14, 60–62, 64–65
Bowden's hierarchies of loyalty, 48
Boyer's comments on national loyalty, 90
Brotz's arguments on bonding, 73
Buffy the Vampire Slayer, case of cultural
　　loyalty, 131
　actor's identity, 122–123
　contested nature, 124–126
　layered emotions, 123–124
　motivation factor, 121–122
　social emotion, 120–121

C

Canadian army, in peace keeping
　　operations, 73–74
Canterbury Bulldogs' crises, 11–115
Carroll's definition of emotion, 36, 136
Catholicism
　and loyalty, 52
　and marriage, 60
Character and Social Structure, 36
Chon's explanations on group dynamics, 53
Civic nationalism, 81
The Civilizing Process, 11

Clarence's argument on national identity, 81
Clark' comments on human connections, 15
Clarke's social constructivist theory, 29–30
Collins's emotional energy approach
    to emotions, 27–28
Complex emotions, concept of, 21
The Concept of our Changing Loyalties, 3
Consciousness, 31
Conscripting loyalty, of Australians
    attack on Archbishop Mannix, 87
    common loyalty theme, 88
    Draft Resistance Movement, 88–89
    issue of imperial benefactor, 89
    opponents of, 86–87
    Vietnam war, during, 86
    World War I, during, 85
    World War II, during, 85–86
Contractual loyalty, 14, 81, 98
Courtney's comments on fan loyalty, 109
Craib's argument on human identities, 51
Crossley's emotion theory, 32
Cultue and emotional expressions, 40
Cultural citizenship, 81
Cultural loyalty, 117–126
Customer relationship marketing, 42

D

Darwin's theory of evolution, 17–18, 27, 31
De Ruyter's comments on social group
    membership, 104
Disappointment, 43
Disloyalty, 23, 43
Dizard's definition on familism, 58–59, 70
Docker's arguments on cultural
    loyalty, 45–46, 126, 119
Doherty's comments on parental
    loyalty, 62, 65–66
Donaldson's comments on gang loyalty, 70–71

E

Edgar's idea of 'tribal loyalist', 109
Edwards's arguments on sport
    commercialization 103–104
Ekman's building block models
    of emotions, 20–21
Elias's explanations on rising of nation state, 42
Embarrassment, 43
Emerson' parliament speech on Bulldog
    scandal, 111
Emotional arousal, argument of, 21–22
Emotional capital, 82
Emotional energies, of individuals, 27
Emotional expressions, 43
    British community, 39
    example of Gururumba tribe, 40
    issue of language, 39
    Lebanese community, 39
    limitations of employing language, 39
    medium for, 39
Emotional incongruity, 23
Emotional plots, 20–21
Emotional reality, 118
Emotional resonance, 118
Emotions; *see also* Loyalty; Family loyalty
    binary/oppositional thinking, 43
    biocultural theories, 18–25
    biological theories, 17–18
    building block models, 20–21
    charecterisation of, 41
    complex, 20–21
    computer analogy model, 19
    definitions of, 134–142
    emotional energy approach to, 27–29
    existentialist theories, 30–33
    of fear, 27
    first-order combinations, 22
    flexible responses of, 139–140
    implications of loyalty, 33–34
    Katz's studies, 37
    in linguistics, 29
    methodologies for sociological
        investigations of, 36–38
    negative, 53
    neuropsychological states of, 25
    Newton's views, 11
    positive and negative states of, 44
    principles of, 26
    range of intensities, 22
    social constructivist model, 25–30
    social definition, 139
    Solomon views, 23–24
    in television, 118–119
    theorising of, 16–17
    use of, 51
    in western society, 41
    in work place, 42
Ethinicity, 80–81
Evans's idea of complex emotions, 39–40
Evening Herald, 101
Exit, Voice and Loyalty, 2
*The Expression of the Emotions
    in Man and Animals,* 17

F

Family loyalty, 2
    creation of conflict within families, 64–65
    definition of familism, 58

definition of family, 58–59
and economic backwardness, 60
for immigrant groups, 68
influence on financial decisions, 67–68
inter generational component of, 66
and marriage, 59–60
and moral responses, 64
negative implications of, 63–64
primacy of parent- child bond, 62
reliability factor, 67
in Sena family, 66
study of abused children, 63
use of familial terminology, 63
Vogler's approach to the formation of attachments, 69
Fear, 17
Fehr's comments on methodological dilemma of theorists, 136
Firth's comments on television viewing, 118
Fisher's explanations on group dynamics, 53
Fleeing, act of, 31
Frijda's concept of emotional expression, 39, 137
The Frontier of Loyalty: Political Exiles in the Age of the Nation-State, 2–3
Fukuyama's comment on organizational culture, 72
Furedi's comments on emotional management, 42, 119, 140

G

Gadlin's definition on familism, 58–59, 70
Gang loyalty, 70–71
Gerth's views on identity/role of actor, 36–37, 49, 53
Gloucestershire Echo, 64
Goffman's phenomenon of unit cohesion and loyalty, 72
Gold Coast Bulletin, 108
Grief, 20
Grodzins's arguments on national loyalty, 78–79
Guardian, 67
Guilt, 23
Gururumba tribe, wild pig behaviour of, 40, 45

H

Hagarty's comments on loyalty, 107
Hage's comments on belongingness, 81
Happiness, 17
Harrè's arguments on emotion, 38, 45, 138
Hirschman's comments on loyalty, 106, 114
Hochschild's emotion management, 32, 42
Hoggard's comments on women attitudes, 67
How Emotions Work, 37

Hughson' findings, 104
Hurt, 43, 57, 92, 107, 112, 124, 126

J

Jackson-Jacobs's comments on gang loyalty, 70
Jealous anger, 21
Jealousy, 20
Jenkins's argument on human identities, 50
Johnson-Laird's explanations on social interactions, 14
Journal of Financial Planning, 68

K

Katz's study on emotions, 37, 46, 70, 91, 105, 144
Kelaher's argument on familial conflict, 68
Kellner's comments on cultural loyalty, 118
Kemper's study of emotions, 17, 25–27
The Kennel, 112–113
Kershler's explanation on marriage, 107
Koubi's views on order of betrayal, 48–49
Koumi, 59
Kristjánsson's views on emotions, 53, 63, 138

L

Language
for emotional expressions, 39
of moral discourse, 44
and notion of loyalty
Lawrence's criticism of the literature on Australian sport, 102–103, 114
Leathers's views on bonds, 65–66
Levine's definition of loyalty, 38
Love, 16
The Loyal and the Disloyal: Social Boundaries of Patriotism and Treason, 3
Loyal fan, 103, 108–109
Loyalty; *see also* Cultural loyalty; Emotions; Family loyalty; National loyalty; Sports and loyalty
and actors identity, 49–51, 132–133
as an explanation/justification for action, 51–53, 133–134
as behaviour, 53–54
Collin's views, 27
common sense usage of, 43
computer analogy model perspective, 19
concept of layering, 5, 47–49, 60, 71, 86–87, 89, 130–133
effects on relationships, 6
as emotion, 33–34, 137–138
enduring aspect of, 109
epilogue, 143–144
feudal concept of, 12

Guido-Dibrito's views, 10
historical reviews of, 11
identification in situations, 45
as identifier, 5
Japanese notion, 40
mass, 12–13
as mechanism of social control, 42–43
methedological issues, 36–38
in middle ages, 11
in modern society, 15
moral aspect, 44
as motivator, 5, 61
and nation- state, 13
and natural relations, 14
of Nazi party, 44–45
oaths, 98
occurence, 4
in patrimonial-feudal era, 27–28
political science perspective, 13–14
popular culture perspective, 45–46
as popular discourse, 2
psychological perspective, 13
Ransom's views, 10
relation with English language, 39–40
of a soldier, 2, 71–74
sources, 81
Stearns, C. Z. views, 10–11
Stearns, P. N. views, 10–11
use of, 12
Wolf's views, 14
Loyalty: An Essay on the Morality of Relationships, 3
Loyalty agreements, 103
'Loyalty Day', of USA, 2
Loyalty in a Democratic State, 3
Loyalty-security program, 97
Lutz's argument of emotion, 41, 140

M

Manderson's argument on familial conflict, 68
Markam' concept of emotional expression, 39
Marriage, 59
Mascord's comments on fan loyalty, 108
Mass loyalty, 12–13
McAuley, 87
McCarthyism, 97–99, 131
McKell's comments on fan loyalty, 112–113
McKernan's views on dual loyalty, 83
McNeal's argument on emotions, 18–19
Mewett's arguments on national identity, 50, 115
Military loyalty, 71–74
Mills's views on identity/role
of actor, 15, 36–37, 49, 53

Moller's views on fan loyalty, 105
Morsbach's views on language in emotion, 39

N

National identity, defined, 80
Nationalisation ceremonies, 14
National loyalty, 14, 136–137
  case of Australian nationalism, *see* Australian nationalism
  case of Braude, Beatrice, 98
  human satisfaction in, 79
  McCarthysm, 97–99
  relation with other loyalties, 79
  rememberances and celebrations, 78
  role of social structure, 79
  and sense of identity, 80
Natural loyalty, 14
Natural relations and loyalty, 14
Nature-*versus*-nature debate, 18–19
  critique of Turner, 24
Negative emotion, 53
Newcastle Herald, 106
Newman's views on cultural loyalty, 40
Noble's report on Australian identity, 94

O

Oately's explanations on social interactions, 14
O' Dell's views on family loyalty, 64
Oldenquist's views on emotional satisfaction, 80
Ong's cultural citizenship, 81

P

Patriotism, 79
Phillips's study of 'un-Australian', 96
The Philosophy of Loyalty, 3
Planalp's views on emotion, 24, 43, 136
Popular culture, 45, 141
Potts's study of abused children, 63
The Poverty of Liberalism, 3
Powel's views on gang loyalty, 70
Price's arguments on national identity, 91

R

Remorse feeling, 21
Renaissance loyalty, through patronage, 21
Ricketts's reports on fan loyalty, 111
Role theory, 132
Rosenspan's comments on loyalty, 15
Rothstein's arguments on loyalty, 62, 68
Rowe's arguments on sport loyalty, 102–103, 114
Royce's theoretical explanations of loyalty, 59

Royzman's definition of emotion, 139
Runkle's views on family loyalty, 59–60
Russell's arguments on methodological dilemma, 136

S

Sabini's definition of emotion, 139–140
Sadness, 17
Sato's concept of emotional expression, 39
Satre's emotion theory, 31–32
'Save Our Sons' movement, 88
Shame, 16, 22–23
Shklar's definition of loyalty, 13–15, 136
Silver's emotion process, 104, 140–141
Sir Gawain and the Green Knight, 11
Smith's study of 'un-Australian', 96
Smolicz's arguments on national loyalty, 96
Sniffen's comments on family loyalty, 63
Social learning
    of fear responses, 18
    in fostering social cohesion, 18
    Gururumba tribe, example of, 18
    as information seeking behaviour, 20
    and social structures, 24
    in terms of computer analogy, 19
    transmission of emotions, 18
Social survival, 17–18
Soldier's loyalty, 71–74
Solomon's theory on loyalty, 37–38, 43, 46, 137–138
South Sydney Rabbitohs and loyalty, 105–110
Spark's arguments on loyalty, 58–59, 60–62, 64–65
Sports and loyalty
    Canterbury Bulldogs' crises, 11–115
    case of Burgess family, 107
    consumption and production factor patterns of sports, 102–105
    South Sydney Rugby league club, 105–110
Startlement-surprise, concept of, 22
Stearns and Stearns' discussion on Utku Eskimos, 46
Stone's comments on the nature of emotion, 37–38, 43, 46

Strongman's studies on emotion, 44
Sullivan's studies on emotion, 44
'Survival of fittest', argument of, 17–18, 27, 31
Sydney Morning Herald, 83, 85

T

Tabar's report on Australian identity, 94
Thomas's perspectives on emotions, 141
Transactional needs, 20
Trevillian's comments on the exit strategy of South Sydney Rugby League club, 106
The Truman Show, (Weir, Peter), 24
'Tribal loyalist', idea of, 109
Trust, 16
Tumin's analysis of moral judgement, 44
Turner's theoretical model of basic emotions, 21–23
Tyler's views on language in emotion, 39

V

Vogler's argument on human identities, 50–51, 69

W

Walter's comments on fan loyalty, 108
Weber's idea of different authority types, 27, 42
Wetzels's comments on social group membership, 104
Wiers's concept of emotional expression, 39
Williams's views on television viewing, 118
Willis's comments on nationality, 79
Wilson's arguments on unit bonding, 73
Winslow's writings on Canadian Army in peacekeeping operations, 72–73
Woelz-Stirling's argument on familial conflict, 68
Wolff's arguments on loyalty, 80–81, 98
Wong's concept of self, 96

Z

Zdaniuk's definition of loyalty, 38
Zevallos's views on aspects of Australian identity, 94

Printed in the United States
94311LV00001B/67-72/A

LOA

DISCARD
J.P. LIBRARY